ecpr
PRESS
monographs

Series Editor: Alan Ware

University of Oxford

the politics of income taxation

a comparative analysis

Steffen Ganghof

ecprPRESS

First published by the ECPR Press in 2006

The ECPR Press is the publishing imprint of the European Consortium for
Political Research (ECPR), an independent, scholarly association, which supports
and encourages the training, research and cross-national cooperation of political
scientists in institutions throughout Europe and beyond. The ECPR's Central
Services are located at the University of Essex, Wivenhoe Park,
Colchester, CO4 3SQ, UK

Typeset in Times 10pt by the ECPR Press
Printed and bound in the UK by the University of Essex Print Centre

British Library Cataloguing in Publication Data
A catalogue record for this book is available from the British Library

ISBN: 0-9547966-8-3
ISBN 13: 978-0-9547966-8-6

ecpr monographs

The ECPR Monographs series is published by the ECPR Press, the publishing imprint of the European Consortium for Political Research (ECPR).

As an independent, scholarly, institution, one of the ECPR's objectives is to facilitate research in political science among European universities. To that end, the ECPR has developed a strong publishing portfolio since the 1970s.

The policy to extend that portfolio by launching its own publishing imprint, the ECPR Press, was discussed by the Executive Committee of the ECPR in 2002/03 and the Press was launched in 2005.

It was decided that the first two series to be published under the imprint should be complementary. The ECPR Classics series facilitates scholarly access to significant works from earlier eras of political science by re-publishing books that have been out of print. The ECPR believes this will enable contemporary students and researchers to develop their own work more effectively.

The ECPR Monographs series publishes major new research in all sub-disciplines of political science including revised versions of manuscripts that were originally submitted as PhD theses, as well as manuscripts from established members of the profession.

Alan Ware
Editor, ECPR Classics and ECPR Monographs
Worcester College, Oxford University, UK

Other titles in this series:

Gender and the Vote in Britain
Rosie Campbell

Paying for Democracy: Political finance and state funding for parties
Kevin Casas-Zamora

Representing Women? Female legislators in West European Parliaments
Mercedes Mateo Diaz

Citizenship: The history of an idea
Paul Magnette

Titles in the ECPR Classics series:

Elite and Specialized Interviewing
Lewis A. Dexter

System and Process in International Politics
Morton A. Kaplan

Individualism
Steven Lukes

Political Elites
Geraint Parry

Parties and Party Systems: A framework for analysis
Giovanni Sartori

acknowledgements

This book originates from my PhD dissertation, completed in November 2002 and accepted at the University of Bremen in early 2003, but also includes material derived from subsequent research. I'd like to (once more) thank all of those involved in the production of the dissertation and in my graduation from the University of Bremen, especially Fritz W. Scharpf and Bernhard Kittel. My thanks also go the directors and the staff of the Max Planck Institute for the Study of Societies in Cologne for providing a wonderfully friendly and professional research environment.

I am also grateful to the following colleagues, tax experts and policymakers who took the time to read and comment on parts of my research, discussed tax policy issues with me or shared data: Simone Burkhart, Johannes Becker, David Carey, Sijbren Cnossen, Joseph Cordes, Richard Eccleston, Clemens Fuest, Rune Ervik, Gert Müller-Gatermann, Philipp Genschel, Bernd Genser, Silvia Giannini, Mark Hallerberg, Thorsten Hüller, Ellen Immergut, Sven Jochem, André Kaiser, Achim Kemmerling, Lane Kenworthy, Carsten Koch, Willi Leibfritz, Matthias L. Maier, Philip Manow, Kathleen McNamara, Lars Mjøset, Jonathan Moses, Ingo Müssener, Patrick Nolan, Joachim Lang, Thomas Plümper, Stefan Profit, Birgitta Rabe, Claudio Radaelli, Fritz W. Scharpf, Dirk Schindler, Peter B. Sørensen, Christoph Spengel, Sven Steinmo, Robert J. Stephens, Hans-Werner Sinn, Kari S. Tikka, Michael Wallerstein, Uwe Wagschal, Alfons Weichenrieder, Hannes Winner, Burkhard Winsemann and Reimut Zohlnhöfer. Jenny Braun, Miro Bogner, Dennys Hill and Thomas Pott helped me with finding and analysing data, producing graphs or revising the manuscript. While they have all contributed to making this a better book, all of the remaining shortcomings are my responsibility.

Last but not least, my thanks go to all of those directly involved in the production of this book, especially Richard Bellamy, Rebecca Knappett, Alan Ware, Deborah Savage, Ildi Clarke and two anonymous referees of ECPR Press.

Parts of Chapters one, three, four and seven draw on *Wer regiert in der Steuerpolitik? Einkommensteuerreform zwischen internationalem Wettbewerb und nationalen Verteilungskonflikten* (Frankfurt/Main: Campus Verlag, 2004). Portions of Chapters three and four draw on 'Globalisation, tax reform ideals and social policy financing', *Global Social Policy*, 5: 77–95 (2005) (Sage

Publications). Chapter five draws partly on 'Globalisation and the dilemmas of income taxation in Australia' (with Richard Eccleston), *Australian Journal of Political Science*, 39: 519–34 (2004) (Routledge). Finally, a part of Chapter eight draws on *Konditionale Konvergenz: Ideen, Institutionen und Standortwettbewerb in der Steuerpolitik von EU- und OECD-Ländern, Zeitschrift für internationale Beziehungen*, 11: 7–40 (2005) (Nomos Verlag). I wish to thank the editors and publishers of these journals for permission to use the relevant material in substantially modified forms here.

contents

chapter one | introduction

In the last 30 years, income tax rates for corporations and persons declined substantially in advanced OECD countries (Figure 1.1). Between 1975 and 2005 the headline tax rate on corporate income of advanced OECD countries fell on average from around 50 to around 30 per cent, the top rate on personal income from almost 70 to well below 50 per cent.[1] The decline in corporate tax rates started in the mid-1980s—after the famous US tax reform of 1986—and shows no signs of abating. The downward movement in top personal rates began in the mid-1970s but became more pronounced for a few years after the US reform.

These downward trends in tax rates have figured prominently in the literature on the domestic effects of economic internationalisation (e.g. Genschel 2005). However, many social scientists have been sceptical as to the causal role of tax competition, partly because the cuts in statutory tax *rates* have not generally led to a fall of income tax *revenues* (OECD 2004c). These authors have instead highlighted the importance of changing ideas, partisan politics and democratic institutions at the domestic level (e.g. Garrett 1998a; Hallerberg and Basinger 1998;

Figure 1.1: Top marginal income tax rates in OECD countries, 1975–2005

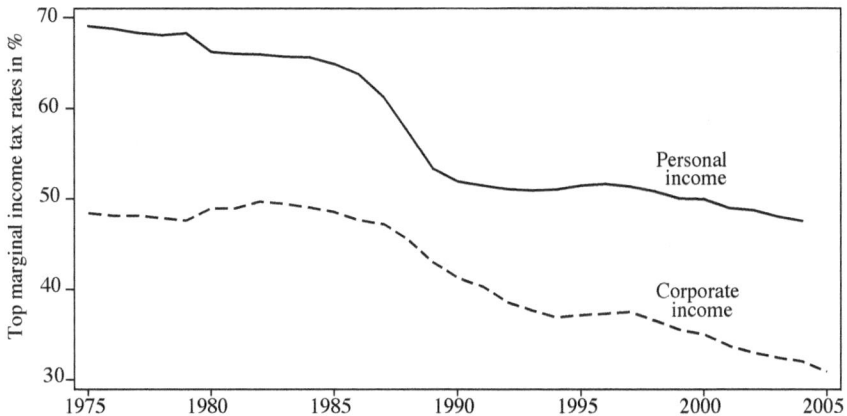

Notes: Unweighted averages. Sources: See appendix

Ottaviani 2002; Swank and Steinmo 2002; Steinmo 2003; Campbell 2004).

The evidence on the effects of domestic factors, though, is far from conclusive. For instance, Wagschal (2001: 154) reports that with respect to recent tax reforms the partisan composition of governments has no explanatory power; and the findings of Hallerberg and Basinger (1998; 1999) seem to contradict conventional wisdom about partisan ideology. For one thing, they claim that in response to the US tax reform of 1986 left-leaning governments in other countries made *deeper* cuts in corporate tax rates than their right-leaning counterparts. For another, they claim that the existence of powerful veto players reduced the magnitude of corporate and personal tax cuts, which, combined with the first result, may suggest that *right-leaning* veto players blocked tax cuts. While ad hoc explanations for such findings abound—e.g. that left-wing governments have to pay a 'risk premium' to international investors in the form of lower corporate tax rates (Hallerberg and Basinger 1998: 345)—there is no *coherent* theoretical account that can explain both the downward trend in tax rates and the international variation in income tax structures.

This study seeks to contribute to such an account. Its analytical focus is rather specific. As to the dependent variables, it mainly focuses on the statutory features of tax systems, such as top marginal rates on different types of incomes. This focus has two related rationales. First, for reasons that will become clearer in the development of the argument, I am strongly interested in the basic structure of income taxation, e.g. whether capital and labour income are taxed jointly or separately; statutory tax rates are a crucial part of this structure. Second, I shall argue that one main 'function' of the income tax has been to bring an element of progressivity into the tax system at large. Marginal rates are important in this respect because they are reasonable, albeit rough, indicators of progressivity. The two arguments are related: for while effective progressivity also depends on the breadth of the tax base (tax credits, deductions, allowances etc.), I shall argue that this breadth does itself follow to a large extent from the basic structure adopted. Many loopholes in capital income taxation were (and still are) the result of policymakers' efforts to tax labour and capital income under a *joint* tax schedule. Once this effort is abandoned, loopholes can be closed without requiring large cuts in the marginal tax rates *on labour*. In sum, then, statutory tax rates are useful indicators if we distinguish systematically between different types of incomes.

As to the independent variables, my focus is on the interaction of party ideology, veto institutions and socio-economic constraints (i.e. economic, administrative and political constraints). Such a focus is hardly an innovation. In practice, however, political science analyses often take insufficient account of economic constraints. The main reason, I contend, lies in the ambiguity of the term 'policy preference' (cf. Ganghof 2003). Actor-centred approaches such as veto player theory (Tsebelis 2002) rightly focus on how the interaction of actors' policy preferences (which are taken to be temporarily fixed) and legislative rules produces legislative outputs. Yet policy preferences are not ends in themselves. Rather, they are means for achieving certain policy *outcomes*. It would be more accurate therefore to speak of policy *strategies*. These strategies derive from parties' ideologies as well as from more specific beliefs about the mapping of policies on to outcomes, given constraints and trade-offs. The problem with policy preferences is that they change (in line with changing beliefs about the mapping of policies on to outcomes) and, partly as a result, are difficult to measure. Empirical studies often ignore this problem by assuming that indicators of 'party positions' based on expert surveys or party manifestos can be regarded as proxies for policy preferences. This can be misleading, though, because such party positions are often at best proxies of outcome preferences. If this is true, we have to include socio-economic constraints explicitly in our theoretical and empirical models in order to avoid misleading inferences. To explain when, how and to what extent party ideology shapes legislative outcomes, we have to understand how domestic and international constraints shape parties' *policy strategies* and how legislative institutions shape their *legislative strategies*.

THE MAIN ARGUMENTS

I argue that the common sense view of partisan income tax policy is basically correct, even if applied to the tax reforms of the 1980s and 1990s: leftist (rightist) parties continue to prefer higher (lower) income taxes, more (less) progressive taxation, and higher (lower) taxes on the capital income of well-off taxpayers. Yet to understand the interaction of party ideology and veto institutions we have to develop a more accurate understanding of socio-economic constraints in income taxation. At the most general level, I argue that these constraints are more severe than has been acknowledged in the political science literature. Hence my account is intended to both qualify and specify argument about ideational changes and policy learning. More specifically, my explanation can be summarised in terms of four core arguments. First, tax competition has been a crucial contributing cause of cuts in statutory corporate tax rates (the tax competition argument). Second, tax competition has had an indirect pull-down effect on tax rates on higher personal incomes (the spill-over argument). Third, this pull-down effect has been counteracted by domestic pressures to maintain a certain degree of progressivity in the income tax system (the domestic constraints argument). Fourth, the importance of party ideology and veto institutions is conditional upon the tightness of structural constraints: in corporate taxation, where international constraints are tight, it is low; in personal taxation (of wages), where domestic constraints are less tight, it is greater. I shall elaborate on the four arguments in turn.

The tax competition and spill-over arguments
The first argument is that tax competition was an important contributing cause of cuts in statutory corporate tax rates, despite the fact that corporate tax bases were broadened and corporate tax revenues did not generally fall. The theoretical reason is that there are various mechanisms through which tax competition puts pressure

on *statutory* tax rates. One of these mechanisms is the profit-shifting behaviour of multinational firms, which is to a large extent driven by statutory rates. Another has to do with competition for *profitable* investment. Roughly speaking, the more profitable an investment project, the more important is the statutory corporate tax compared to tax allowances. As a result of these types of mechanisms, policymakers had a strong incentive to cut statutory corporate tax rates even if this had to be paid for by reducing tax allowances.

The most important type of evidence supporting this argument is the *correlation between tax rates and country size*. The economic theory of tax competition predicts that if two countries of unequal size compete with each other for mobile tax bases, the smaller country will in equilibrium have a lower tax rate. In a small country with a small existing capital stock, a tax cut does not lead to large revenue losses. At the same time, relatively high revenue can be expected due to the inflow of foreign capital. Hence, if tax competition has played a role in the setting of corporate tax rates, we would expect an increasingly positive association between corporate tax rates and country size. I shall show that this is exactly what we see. There has in fact been a strong convergence of corporate tax rates in advanced OECD countries, but it has been *conditional* convergence (Sala-i-Martin 1996; Ganghof 2005c).

But does tax competition also limit the *outcomes* national policymakers can achieve in corporate taxation? Or can policymakers still achieve the same outcomes as before, only with a different mix of policies? I believe tax competition constrains corporate tax outcomes in at least one sense. It has long been argued in political science and economics that a system that taxed very profitable investment significantly higher than less profitable investment *increases* tax efficiency and mitigates the trade-off between economic efficiency and redistribution (e.g. Przeworski and Wallerstein 1988; Frank 1999, 2000; Layard 2005). To the extent that this view is true, tax competition tends to make the structure of corporate taxation *less* efficient, at least with respect to the investment incentives of domestic and less profitable firms. For if reforms have to be revenue-neutral, effective tax reductions for profitable foreign direct investment have to be paid for by higher taxes on less profitable and domestic firms. Hence tax competition on statutory corporate tax rate is a serious constraint, especially for parties—typically left parties—that would prefer taxing enterprises with fairly high marginal tax rates but an investment-friendly tax base.

Note that this argument is *not* challenged by explanations that highlight domestic policy learning and the international diffusion of neo-liberal ideas (e.g. Garrett 1998b; Swank 1998; Swank and Steinmo 2002). These explanations rightly highlight the fact that policymakers cut tax rates and broadened tax bases in order to 'level the playing field' and make capital income taxation more 'market-conforming'. As I shall explain in more detail in Chapter three, however, this argument refers to a different analytical dimension of income tax policy. The question how equally policymakers want to treat different types of taxable income or different types of economic activities is logically independent of the question of how 'investment-friendly' a tax base they want to have. In other words, cutting statutory corporate tax rates was by no means a necessary condition of a level playing field. There was, in principle, a choice to make about the level of 'investment-friendliness' at which the playing field was to be levelled—and this choice was constrained by tax competition.

There is a second reason why corporate tax competition tends to constrain tax policy outcomes, which is related to the second main argument of this book. Corporate taxes function as a *safeguard* for the personal income tax, and this function is generally best fulfilled if the corporate tax rate is equal to the top personal tax rate. If it is much below the top personal rate, high-income taxpayers have large incentives to use the corporate legal form in order to shield some of their income from progressive taxation. A large 'tax rate gap' (between corporate and personal taxation) thus reduces the administrative efficiency of income taxation at large and provides policymakers with incentives to reduce marginal income tax rates for high-income taxpayers. Hence, tax competition on statutory corporate tax rates makes it more costly for policymakers to maintain high marginal income tax rates on high personal incomes and tends to lead to a flattening of income tax schedules. In fact, I will show that this spill-over effect has at least *contributed* to the downward trend in top personal income tax rates after the US tax reform in the mid-1980s. This is the spill-over argument.

The domestic constraints argument
The third argument qualifies the second: if there were no domestic goals other than 'market-conformity' and administrative efficiency, one could expect policymakers in all countries to reduce the personal rate to the level of the top corporate rate (Stotsky 1995: 282; Tanzi and Zee 2000: 130). Figure 1.1 shows that this has not happened. Between 1975 and 1989 the average gap between the two top rates was almost cut in half, from around 20 to around 10 percentage points. As I will show in the case studies that follow, this reduction was no coincidence but reflected policymakers' deliberate attempts to close the tax rate gap; Germany, Australia and New Zealand actually managed to close it completely in 1977, 1988 and 1989, respectively. After 1989, however, when more and more countries implemented their responses to the US reform of 1986, the average tax rate gap widened again (to more than 15 per cent in 2004), with corporate tax rates being cut more heavily than top personal rates. The reason, I contend, is that there are domestic constraints in personal income taxation that are absent in corporate taxation.

The most important constraint is the given level of total taxation in a country. Much of the total tax burden falls on wages—in the form of income taxes, social security contributions and indirect consumption taxes—and one function of the income tax has traditionally been to introduce an element of progressivity into wage taxation at large. For this reason, the higher the total tax burden, the more difficult it becomes for policymakers to reduce marginal tax rates on high incomes. This is the *domestic constraints* argument.

This summary of the argument is of course simplified. The constraint implied by large total tax burdens plays out in two different ways depending on the how much of the overall tax burden on wages takes the form of direct taxes on income. This point is best explained by way of examples:

- In a country such as *Denmark*, where a high total tax burden (around 49 per cent of Gross Domestic Product (GDP) goes together with a very high income tax burden (almost 30 per cent of GDP), it seems impossible to lower the top personal tax rate of more than 60 per cent down to the corporate rate, currently 30 per cent, without significant reductions in progressivity and revenue (*cf.* Ganghof 2005b).

- In a country such as *Austria*—where a high total tax burden (around 43 per cent of GDP) goes together with a rather moderate income tax burden (roughly 13 per cent of GDP)—bringing down the top personal rate of 50 per cent to the corporate rate of 25 per cent would be rather easy, but only because a large part of labour 'taxation' takes the form of social security contributions and general consumption taxes. Since this additional labour taxation is proportional and in part regressive, the progressive income tax tends to assume a 'progressivity adjustment' function within the overall system of wage taxation.

Figure 1.2 visualises the argument. It shows, for the year 2004, the correlations between total tax burdens on the one hand and top marginal tax rates on corporations and persons on the other. For corporate tax rates the figure only shows the regression line. This line is almost identical to a flat line at the average level of corporate tax rates (32 per cent) because there is no systematic relationship between total tax burdens and corporate tax rates. In contrast, top personal income taxes do tend to increase with total tax burdens. High-tax countries such as Denmark and Sweden also tend to have relatively high top personal rates, whereas

Figure 1.2: Top marginal tax rates and total tax levels in OECD countries, 2004

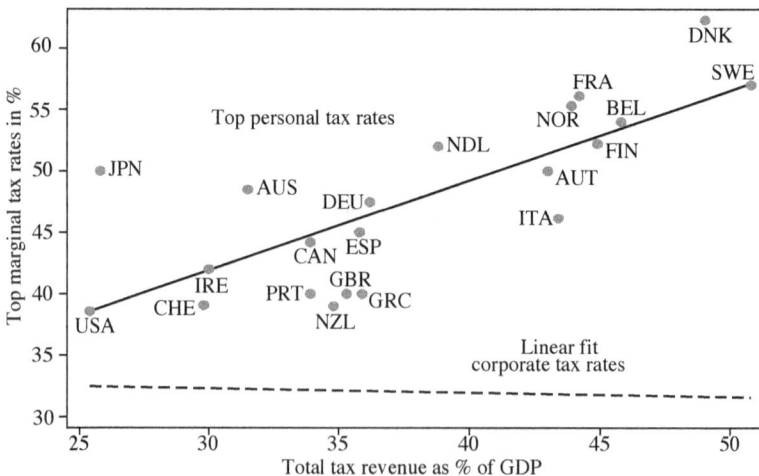

Notes and sources: See appendix

low-tax countries such as Ireland or the USA also tend to have relatively low top personal rates.

Figure 1.2 also helps us to connect the three arguments discussed so far. We have seen that in a perfect 'market-conforming' income tax, the corporate tax rate would be equal to the top personal rate. In the absence of tax competition, governments would have been able to achieve this equality by letting the corporate rate follow the top personal rate. In Figure 1.2, the 'corporate' regression line would then be roughly equal to the 'personal' line. Yet due to tax competition, corporate tax rates had to fall (the tax competition argument), which had two effects. On the one hand, many countries also cut their top personal rate (more than they would have done otherwise) in order to keep the tax rate gap moderate. Hence corporate tax competition has contributed to a downward shift of the 'personal' regression line (the spill-over argument). On the other hand, high tax burdens on wages constrained policymakers' willingness and ability to cut top personal income tax rates, so that the tax rate gap also increased again after the late 1980s, especially in high-tax countries. As a result, the regression line for top personal tax rates in Figure 1.2 has a pronounced upward slope (the domestic constraint argument).

One follow-up question raised by Figure 1.2 is this: if the combination of tax competition and domestic constraints led to a sizeable tax rate gap in most advanced OECD countries, what happened to the goal of 'market-conforming' income taxation emphasised in the political science literature? I shall explore this question and point out a 'trilemma' for policymakers. The traditional normative ideal on which most OECD countries' income tax systems had officially been built was that of 'comprehensive' or 'uniform' income taxation (e.g. Goode 1976). An ideal uniform income tax puts all annual income—both capital income and wages—of a taxpayer into a basket and subjects it jointly to a common, often progressive, tax rate schedule. 'Market-conformity' had been a crucial element of this ideal. For if all types of income are taxed jointly and hence subjected to the same marginal tax rates, the playing field is levelled. In addition, joint taxation of all income was also seen as a precondition for taxation according to taxpayers' 'ability to pay', because all types of income contributed equally to this ability. Now, the problem was that the ideal was nowhere put in practice and that the income taxes actually implemented were in many ways pathological. This fact, together with competitive pressure on corporate tax rates, forced policymakers to make a clearer choice between three stylised options:

- *Flat income tax*: This option was a comprehensive income tax with radically reduced marginal tax rates. The rationale of this option is that very low marginal tax rates enable policymakers to clean up the income tax base and to align the top personal tax rate with a *competitive* corporate tax rate. Its Achilles heel is reduced progressivity and/or revenue-raising potential in the taxation of wages.
- *Differentiated income tax*: The logic of this option is to maintain a comprehensive income tax system with higher marginal tax rates, but allow lower rates on capital income wherever the costs of taxation would otherwise become

too large, e.g. in the taxation of corporate profits retained in the company. The Achilles heel of this model is that these kinds of 'targeted' tax rate cuts for very sensitive capital income render capital income taxation less market-conforming and more arbitrage-prone.

- *Dual income tax*: This option abandons the ideal of comprehensive income taxation (as it is usually understood) and *separates* the income taxation of labour and capital. Whereas wages are taxed progressively, all types of capital income are subject to a uniform proportional tax rate. The Achilles heel of this model is that it implies a very systematic and visible tax discrimination of wages as well as complicated rules for splitting the income of small businesses into its capital and labour components.

As this list shows, maximising the goal of 'market-conforming' capital income taxation is costly. It involves either a reduction in the progressivity and/or revenue-raising potential of the income tax (the flat tax option) or an administratively costly and *prima facie* inequitable separation of labour and capital taxation within the income tax (the dual income tax option). Not surprisingly, therefore, no advanced OECD country has implemented a truly market-conforming income tax system.

The conditional importance of politics argument

In 2004, two of the countries with the smallest gap between the top tax rates on corporate and personal incomes were the USA and New Zealand. The USA comes closest to an equality of the two rates if we take average tax rates at the state level into account; the marginal tax rates on corporate and personal income both stood at around 40 per cent in 2004. This is not surprising from the perspective adopted here, because the US economy is both large and characterised by a relatively low tax burden. The case of New Zealand is more puzzling. Although New Zealand is very small, the tax rate gap was only 6 percentage points in 2004 (39 per cent minus 33 per cent); and all through the 1990s New Zealand actually maintained a strict equality of the two at a level of 33 per cent. Between 1989 and 1999 New Zealand would have been a clear outlier in Figure 1.2. One main reason for this is the fact that New Zealand was governed by a one-party 'Labour' majority government that was dominated by 'neo-liberal' politicians and faced no veto point in addition to the parliamentary majority.[2] This leads us to discuss the final main argument of this study.

This argument is one about the conditional importance of party ideology and veto institutions. It has been argued that party ideology and veto institutions were important in shaping income tax rates (Hallerberg and Basinger 1998; Wagschal 1999a; Tsebelis 2002: 203–4). But these arguments suffer from a lack of analytical differentiation. First, they do not distinguish sufficiently between outcome and policy preferences. If socio-economic constraints are very strong, differences in party ideology are unlikely to translate into differences in policy preferences. And if policy preferences do converge, the partisan composition of government and the number of veto points or players are unlikely to affect policy outputs systematically.

The second lack of analytical differentiation follows from the first: existing hypotheses about veto players and tax rates have not been formulated as being conditional upon the 'tightness' of socio-economic constraints. Based on the arguments presented above, such a formulation becomes possible. As to the setting of corporate tax rates, theory and evidence suggest that competitive pressures are quite significant, so that the partisan composition of government cannot be expected to be very important. I shall present qualitative and quantitative evidence supporting this expectation—and thus indirectly also the tax competition argument.

In contrast, the setting of top personal income tax rates (on labour) income is less constrained. The reason is that, whereas governments cannot unilaterally increase their size or reduce the intensity of corporate tax competition, they can unilaterally choose to reduce the level of taxation and the degree of wage tax progressivity. As a result, party ideology and veto institutions can be expected to be more important. The case of New Zealand provides an example for this importance. I shall provide qualitative and quantitative evidence that this example can be generalised. Right-leaning parties tend to use their power in government or parliament to reduce and flatten income taxes, while left-leaning parties tend to defend progressivity and revenue-raising capacity of personal income taxes (on labour incomes).

METHODOLOGICAL APPROACH AND CASE SELECTION

While there is much conceptual and theoretical debate in the social sciences about methodology, I believe that most inferences, in the social sciences and elsewhere, can usefully be described by a very general 'model' of inductive inference called *Inference to the Best Explanation* (Bird 1998; Lipton 2004). We are interested in a certain phenomenon P and think of possible explanations of P. If putative explanation E is the best available explanation of P, we infer that E is the actual explanation of P. To make a list of putative explanations, we rely heavily on existing background knowledge, and to determine the 'best' of these potential explanations we rely on certain desiderata. For example, good explanations should supply *mechanisms* that can account for correlations between different kinds of events. Good explanations should also have *power* in the sense that they can explain several distinct and disparate facts and are able to integrate or combine with other explanations. A third good-making feature is *simplicity*.

Some further remarks about important desiderata seem useful at this point. One important desideratum is the integration of one explanation with others. I believe that the more recent political science literature on taxation suffers from a lack of integration with previous findings as well as with well-established knowledge in economics. For instance, in their seminal work on the political economy of taxation, Przeworski and Wallerstein (1988) argued that systems with fairly high rates but an investment-friendly tax base mitigate the trade-off between efficiency and redistribution and should therefore be attractive for policymakers, especially those on the left (see also Garrett and Lange 1991). More recently, it was emphasised that low tax rates and broad bases are efficient and that base-broadening allowed high-tax countries to defend their revenue levels despite tax rate cuts (Garrett 1998b; Swank 1998; Swank and Steinmo 2002). But this 'revisionist' argument is itself in need of explaining: if the old Przeworski-Wallerstein argument is now believed to be wrong, we need an explanation of why this is the case. If it is believed to still hold, we need an explanation of why countries *nevertheless* cut tax rates and broadened the tax base (Wallerstein and Przeworski 1995). In the analysis that follows, I try to answer these kinds of questions.

This goal of integrating new explanations with existing ones should not be confused with a search for *complete* explanations. As noted above, my analytical focus is rather specific. For example, I have no systematic interest in the role of interest groups in the politics of income taxation. Part of the reason why incompleteness is less of a problem than often thought has to do with the 'pragmatic' aspects of explanation (Scriven 1966; Van Fraasen 1980; Garfinkel 1981; Hausman 2001; Tucker 2004). That is, explanations are first and foremost answers to Why-questions, and the kind of explanation one develops therefore greatly depends on the precise structure of the questions one asks. Different choices of explanatory variables follow to a large extent from different choices of questions and hence different explanatory *interests*. For instance, if one asks why two countries that are very similar with respect to socio-economic constraints and partisan-institutional configurations have implemented very different tax reforms, interest groups may be an important part of the answer. However, my interest is in Why-questions for which party ideology, legislative power and socio-economic constraints may provide important parts of the answers. Different choices of explanatory variables simply amount to different ways of carving up the social world into possible alternatives, and the goal of this book is merely to show that a focus on the interaction of party ideology, legislative power, and socio-economic constraints can help to answer a number of Why-questions that do or ought to figure prominently in the political science literature.

Another important desideratum of 'Inference to the Best Explanation' is that explanations explain *diverse* evidence and that they explain *in detail*. It follows that historical, case-specific evidence and more precise quantitative evidence should, if possible, be combined. Most of the evidence used in this book is qualitative. One reason is that much of the analysis is more descriptive and exploratory than confirmatory. Because there is not much in the political science literature on the politics of income tax *structure*, I want to understand in some detail how policymakers perceived the relevant trade-offs, e.g. the trade-offs associated with the choice between dual and differentiated income taxation. Developing this understanding requires detailed case analysis.

Another reason for relying strongly on case studies is that the interaction of party ideology, veto institutions and socio-economic constraints is often too complex to be modelled in regression analyses with a very small number of cases. For the same reason, the regression evidence I do provide as a complement to the qualitative analysis is based on rather simple models. In the helpful terminology of Clarke (forthcoming), I try to follow the 'logic of research design' rather than the 'logic of control'. That is, rather than adding—in the (often dubious) hope of reducing omitted variable bias—ever more variables and interaction terms to the regression equation, I try to build simple models that are focused on *discriminating between competing explanations* (see also Achen, forthcoming). I acknowledge the fact that regression results are first and foremost certain kinds of multivariate *observations*. As such they don't provide explanations but can help in discriminating between them (Hoover 1994, 2002; see also Freedman 1991; Berk 2004).

This perspective also implies that the quality of measurement is of the utmost importance. As Atkinson (2004: 178) rightly notes (and demonstrates with an example from the political science literature), it is often wrongly suggested by quantitative scholars that 'data quality is of footnote importance, and that empirical findings are robust to the choice of data'. In fact, many existing regression analyses of top marginal income tax rates are based on inconsistent data sets, containing *general government* tax rates for some countries and *central government* tax rates for others. I have assembled a tax rate data set that consistently measures general government tax rates, taking into account the often complex ways in which tax rates and tax bases at different government levels are linked (see appendix).

The qualitative evidence is based on case studies of tax reforms in seven countries: Australia, Denmark, Finland, Germany, New Zealand, Norway and Sweden. The time period under consideration is the period from the mid-1980s to the early 2000s. My original research extended until 2001 but for this publication I have updated the qualitative and quantitative evidence as much as possible. The seven countries were selected to maximise similarity in some respects and dissimilarity in others, and to allow some degree of 'nesting' individual case studies in case comparisons as well as narrow case comparisons in broader ones.

The seven countries are dissimilar with respect to their *levels of total taxation* (Figure 1.2).[3] As argued above, these levels constitute part of the domestic economic constraints policymakers face. Hence, by letting these levels vary between countries, the risk of 'selection bias' is reduced (King *et al.* 1994). Second, while all seven countries are parliamentary systems with fairly disciplined parties, they are very dissimilar with respect to the *relevant constellations of veto players and other influential actors*. As I will explain in more detail in Chapter two, the seven countries cover many of the partisan-institutional configurations that can exist in parliamentary democracies.

As to similarities, there are two sub-groups of countries the members of which adopted very similar approaches to income taxation, either before the US tax reform of 1986 or afterwards. One group is the four Nordic countries, which all tried to implement the model of dual income taxation. The other group is the Oceanic countries and Germany which, before the US reform, were the only countries that had implemented a very ambitious form of uniform income taxation by aligning the corporate tax rate with the top rate on personal incomes.

Of course, while the two Oceanic countries, like the Nordic countries, are also geographically close to one another and similar on many important background variables, Germany differs from Australia and New Zealand in many important aspects. In addition, the German case is unique in various ways, e.g. due to the presence of a powerful constitutional court as an additional veto player. For this reason, the case study on Germany will be somewhat more detailed than those on the other countries. The German case study is nested in a comparison with Australia and New Zealand, and this three-country comparison is part of the broader seven-country comparison.

THE STRUCTURE OF THE BOOK

Chapter two discusses a number of conceptual and methodological problems in the comparative analysis of legislative politics and outlines the approach adopted in this study. A central aspect of this approach is the *inference to* (rather than 'measurement' of) partisan policy preferences based on an in-depth analysis of the trade-offs and constraints parties face. The next two chapters provide this analysis: Chapter three focuses on the explanation of intertemporal policy change, Chapter four on the explanation of international policy differences. Chapters five through seven contain the seven case studies. Chapter eight summarises the case evidence and complements it with quantitative evidence on the interaction of party ideology, socio-economic constraints and veto institutions. Chapter nine draws conclusions on the tax policy options available to OECD countries both at the national and international level.

NOTES

1   Unless otherwise noted, all averages reported in this book are unweighted and refer to 21 advanced OECD (Organisation for Economic Cooperation and Development) countries. See the appendix for the set of countries, country abbreviations used as well as variable definitions and data sources.

2   The third country with a tax rate gap of 6 percentage points or lower in 2004 is Greece, another country characterised by one-party majority governments and the absence of strong legislative veto points. In addition to the case study on New Zealand in Chapter five, I shall discuss the cases of the United States and Greece in more detail in Chapter eight.

3   Of course, taxation levels *before* the mid-1980s are more important for the purpose of case selection, but these were very similar to those shown in Figure 1.1.

chapter two | conceptual and methodological issues in empirical veto player analysis

This study can be seen as an instance of empirical veto player analysis (Tsebelis 2002). This kind of analysis raises a number of conceptual and methodological issues (Ganghof 2003). The first goal of this chapter is to discuss some of these issues. On this basis the second goal is to give a systematic overview of the partisan-institutional configurations that characterise the seven countries selected for in-depth case analysis. The next section discusses some of the general problems of intentional actor explanation, of which veto player explanation is a variant. The second section discusses more specific problems of veto player analysis having to do with the identification of veto players and their preferences. The final section characterises the seven cases.

INFERENCE TO THE BEST PREFERENCE ATTRIBUTIONS

Contemporary political science is deeply divided over the pros and cons of rational choice theory (e.g. Friedman 1996). Yet to a large extent rational choice theory is merely an idealised and formalised version of core features of what philosophers call 'folk psychology'. Folk psychology is the theory we use in everyday life to make sense of people's behaviour—a psychology that interprets behaviour in terms of people's desires and beliefs. The most basic version of folk psychology states that if an agent A aims at goal G and believes that M is a means to attain G under the circumstances, then A does M. A core assumption of folk psychology is thus that an agent's beliefs and desires have an underlying structure that is independent of a particular choice situation. By using folk psychology, we distinguish an agent's *actions* from her mere *behaviour*.

Much of the recurrent criticism of rational choice theory as being either false or vacuous and untestable may be traced to the employment of folk psychology. The intentional concepts of folk psychology are not natural kinds or descriptions of brain states. Intentional notions are irreducible to non-intentional notions. It is *subjective* human preferences and beliefs, not just the *objective* realities about which people have preferences and beliefs, that are crucial to understanding human behaviour, but unfortunately there is no 'cerebroscopic' device to simply measure people's preferences and beliefs. As a result, theories in the social sciences are difficult to improve in the way that the laws of physics improve with advances in measurement and conceptualisation (Rosenberg 1995: Chapters two and three).

Many social scientists and psychologists have unsuccessfully tried to avoid the problems of folk psychology by avoiding intentional notions altogether. One example, which continues to play an important role in economics and political science, is 'revealed preference theory' (Samuelson 1938). For instance, the well-known 'Analytic Narratives Group' (Bates *et al.* 1998) rejected one of Elster's (2000) criticisms of their work by insisting that '[b]ecause it is so difficult to judge intentions, rational choice theorists tend to rely instead on revealed preferences and behaviour. Indeed, even in instances in which Elster claims we considered intentions directly, we did not do so' (Bates *et al.* 1998). But this distinction between considering intentions 'directly' and letting them be 'revealed' by behaviour is unconvincing. For in fact neither of the two options is available. We *cannot* consider intentions directly because they are unobservable, and behaviour cannot simply reveal preferences to us because there are in principle an infinite number of combinations of preferences and beliefs that can explain the same observable behaviour.[1] This is the problem of the 'underdetermination' of theory by data. So the question remains: how can we, in historical analyses, approximate actors' beliefs and preferences?

The answer, in my view, is found in the application of the general perspective on inductive inference sketched in the introduction. Unobservable beliefs and preferences have to be *inferred* from observable behaviour through a process of 'Inference to the Best Explanation' (e.g. Bartelborth and Scholz 2002; Tucker 2004; *cf.* Mackie 2003: 41–2). That is, we try to attribute those beliefs and preferences to causes that jointly explain the entire set of observable behaviour (i.e. qualitative and quantitative data) better than the relevant alternatives. In what follows I want to make a few remarks about how such inferences to preferences and beliefs do work or should work.

The first point concerns the importance of the rationality assumption and deductive consistency. In inferring beliefs and preferences we generally *must* presume a degree of rationality among the actors. We have to apply what is often called a 'principle of charity' (e.g. Johnson 1991: 117). Otherwise the number of potential explanations of behaviour would become far too large. This principle of charity typically implies two distinct assumptions: that actors have a degree of true belief about the world (as it is seen by the researcher) and that their preference profiles fulfil certain standards of rationality (Bartelborth and Scholz 2002). Due to the second assumption, rational choice theories such as Tsebelis' veto player theory can be important tools. The formalisation of common sense notions of rationality can increase deductive rigor and hence help us to think through the implications of particular assumptions.

In actual historical analyses, though, putting too much emphasis on logical consistency can be misleading. One much-discussed reason is that we must not assume too much rationality ('hyper-rationality') on the part of the actors (Elster 2000). Another reason is that the consistency assumption may not be a very good guide to approximating actors' 'true' preferences. What seems more important in this respect is the assumption of *coherence*. In order to make sense of actors and to distinguish 'good' from 'bad' preference attributions, we should try to attribute to actors a coherent view of the world—one in which their explanatory schemes, beliefs, and preferences fit together and support one another. This may be called the 'inner coherence' of preference profiles (Bartelborth and Scholz 2002).

However, aiming at inner coherence can usually not reduce the set of plausible belief-preference combinations sufficiently. Therefore, social scientists should also be able to *explain*, at least in principle, how an actor's beliefs and preferences *developed*, given her basic interests and needs, her sources of information, and her cognitive capabilities. This can be called a demand for 'outer coherence' (Bartelborth and Scholz 2002). Our preference attributions ought to cohere with our knowledge of the conditions under which the agents act. This includes both our more general knowledge about the effects of norms and institutions—as highlighted by the various institutionalisms in the social sciences—as well as more specific knowledge about the type of actors in question (*cf.* Mackie 2003: 41–2). In the explanation of economic policy outcomes, it also includes knowledge of the relevant economic constraints, trade-offs and policy options (Scharpf 1997; 2000a).

Of course, the set of data that 'best' explanations have to accommodate is not fixed. On the contrary, data is always short in supply in comparative social science. Hence, to maximise leverage on competing hypotheses, we have to search actively for data on actors' behaviour as well as for theoretical and empirical knowledge on the world which these actors populate (*cf.* Lipton 2004: Chapter five). This is the main reason why I put much emphasis on coming to grips with economic tax theory, on combining historical and comparative analysis and on combining qualitative and quantitative evidence.

METHODOLOGICAL ISSUES IN EMPIRICAL VETO PLAYER ANALYSIS

Elsewhere, I have identified three basic problems of empirical veto player and veto point analyses (Ganghof 2003):
- the problem of *identifying* veto players, both 'vertically' (aggregating individuals or groups of individuals into collective players) and 'horizontally' (distinguishing veto players from merely influential players);
- the problem of *measuring* veto players' policy preferences; and
- the problem of establishing the *equivalence* between different veto players.

In what follows, I shall focus on the first two issues. The problem of equivalence concerns, first and foremost, the question of whether some types of veto players have a greater average effect on policy stability than others because *electoral* considerations induce them to veto policy change even when their *substan-*

tive policy preferences would induce them to welcome this change (Ganghof and Bräuninger 2006). This kind of explanation has been advanced with respect to income taxation in Germany, for instance (see, especially, Zohlnhöfer 2001; 2003: 150). I have argued against this perspective elsewhere on the grounds that it does not provide a better explanation of data than a perspective that focuses on the substantive policy differences between parties (Ganghof 2004; see also Bräuninger and Ganghof 2005). I believe the same is true for the other six countries analysed in more detail in the present study. Therefore, and for the sake of simplicity, the empirical analysis of this book is based on the *assumption* of equivalence between different (potential) veto parties.

I shall discuss the other two problems of veto player analysis in three steps. I shall start with the vertical problem of identification, move on to the problem of preferences measurement and finally deal with the horizontal problem of identification.

Vertical identification

The previously discussed problems of intentional explanations increase once we have to deal with collective rather than individual actors. The distinction between veto point and veto player approaches is in part based on different treatments of the resulting problems. Proponents of veto point approaches tend to take *executive* decisions as an analytical starting point and focus on institutional veto points (e.g., parliaments, referenda) as points of strategic uncertainty where these decisions can be overturned. They are hesitant to associate a particular veto point with specific behavioural regularities or particular policy preferences (e.g. Immergut 1992; Kaiser 1997). In contrast, veto player theory is committed to replacing, whenever possible, institutional veto points with the individual or collective actors and to ascribe particular policy preferences to them (Tsebelis 2002).

Hence one important difference between the two approaches is the typical assumptions they make about collective actors' internal unity. Following Carey (2002), among others, the concept of 'unity' is here meant to be more general than the concepts of 'cohesion' or 'discipline'. The former refers to the degree to which members of a group share similar preferences, the latter to the degree to which group leaders are able to elicit unified action (voting) on the part of the group regardless of member's preferences. Because both 'cohesion' and 'discipline' refer to unobservable situations and processes, it is difficult to distinguish between them empirically.

Because the focus of the present study is on the interaction between party ideology, economic constraints, and institutional veto power, I have selected for my comparative case studies parliamentary systems that generally display high levels of party unity. There are exceptions, though. Party unity in the German upper house is not always high, and in some countries independent legislators may at times play a role. In these situations, it is necessary to relax the assumption of unified collective actors and move to a more fine-grained analysis.

Preference 'measurement'

If we can generally assume party unity to be high, the crucial task is to identify parties' collective policy preferences. In doing this, we have to be mindful of the distinction between outcome and policy preferences discussed in Chapter one. The translation of basic preferences over outcomes into legislative output (policies) can be understood as a two-step procedure. First, political actors translate their outcome preferences into policy preferences, based on their beliefs about the behaviour of societal/economic actors (e.g., firms); then they translate these policy preferences into a legislative strategy, based on the allocation of veto and agenda-setting power as well as their beliefs about other veto players' preferences.

Rational choice analyses often ignore or downplay the distinction between policy and outcome preferences. One consequence is the conflation of the two concepts in empirical applications. What many empirical veto player analyses actually measure is not policy preferences but outcome preferences or party ideology (e.g. Hallerberg and Basinger 1998). For even if quantitative indicators go beyond a simple left-right distinction and estimate parties' positions on particular issue dimensions, they generally do not measure the 'final' policy preferences that figure in the theoretical models. For instance, one important indicator of 'party positions' is the scores on 'increasing services versus cutting taxes' derived from the expert surveys of Michael Laver and colleagues (Laver and Hunt 1992; Benoit and Laver 2006). Yet this indicator as such tells us nothing about parties' policy preferences on, say, the level of the corporate tax rate. Moreover, even if the dependent variable in an empirical analysis was the overall level of taxation or spending, the indicator does not necessarily measure *short-term* policy preferences. For instance, if a small country with an already high tax burden and macroeconomic difficulties has to deal with large budget deficits, the short-term fiscal policy preferences of parties are likely to converge strongly, basic ideological differences notwithstanding.

Another consequence of downplaying the distinction between outcome and policy preferences is inattention to *changes* in policy preferences. Political actors learn, they update their beliefs about constraints and trade-offs — about the mapping of policies on to outcomes — so that their policy preferences (or rather: policy *strategies*) change even when outcome preferences remain stable. The resulting problem of controlling for preference change is often ignored in rational choice analyses. For instance, Stewart (1991) analyses US tax policy using the tools of rational choice institutionalism (veto players, agenda control, etc), but in contrast to the conclusions of other in-depth analyses (Conlan *et al.* 1990) he dismisses changes in economic beliefs out of hand. At the same time he acknowledges that his analytical construction of a two-dimensional policy space and his attribution of policy preferences to the actors are merely illustrative. It is difficult to see, therefore, why his story should count as explanatory at all (Bradford 1991).

To deal with these problems, I adopt two strategies. In the *case studies*, I use the expert survey results for the 'taxes versus spending' dimension as a rough proxy of *outcome* preferences. Using this data, rather than simply relying on parties' names, helps to control for changes in outcome preferences. For example, based on the survey, I treat New Zealand's Labour Party as a right-leaning party in the 1980s but as a left-leaning party in the second half of the 1990s. To infer policy preferences, I also rely on theoretical and empirical analysis of economic trade-offs and constraints as well as the available qualitative information. In the *quantitative analyses*, I eschew the measurement of preferences altogether and rely exclusively on theoretical assumptions. In other words, my approach in the regression analyses will be similar to quantitative veto point approaches (Huber *et al.* 1993) but I shall try to be more explicit about the underlying assumptions about policy preferences.

Horizontal identification

To establish whether some actor is a veto player or not, at least two questions have to be answered (Tsebelis 2002; Ganghof 2003): Does this actor actually have *veto* power or is it only an *influential* actor? How likely is this actor's ideal point to be located in the Pareto Set (Unanimity Core) of other, already identified VPS, in which case this actor could be ignored?[2] There are three types of actors for which at least one of these questions is not so easy to answer: courts engaged in judicial review, member parties of oversized coalitions, and opposition parties under minority governments. I discuss all three cases in turn.

Tsebelis (2002) argues that courts reviewing legislation can usually be disregarded as veto players. The reason is that when judges are appointed by partisan veto players, parties will select them for their competence and '(known) policy position' (Tsebelis 2002: 227). But this argument ignores the distinction between outcome and policy preferences made above. For it is likely that judges are often selected mainly for their *outcome* preferences. This type of selection is cognitively less demanding because many of the judges' policy preferences on *future* issues are not known and cannot so easily be anticipated. Yet even if judges' outcome preferences are in the respective Pareto Set (Unanimity Core) of the partisan veto players, their policy preferences may frequently be outside of the respective set. One main reason is, once more, that politicians and judges face very different *constraints* in translating outcome into policy preferences. For example, whereas parties have to trade-off various norms and principles of tax equity against budgetary, electoral, and efficiency goals, constitutional courts may choose to disregard many of these other goals. Hence policy preferences of judges and parties can diverge strongly, and constitutional courts can become crucial veto players in the area of taxation.

Consider next oversized coalitions and minority governments. As to the former, Tsebelis (2002: 95–6) argues that all member parties of these types of coalitions have veto power, but other authors, most notably Strøm (2000: 280), object that particular parties can be outvoted. As to minority governments, Tsebelis (2002: 98) argues that opposition parties can generally be neglected as veto players if a number of conditions hold. Most notably, the government must be centrally located in the policy space, it must have agenda-setting power and opposition parties must behave as policy-seekers. Other authors have noted that these assumptions are frequently not fulfilled (e.g. Schnapp 2004: 157; Rasch 2005; Ganghof and Bräuninger 2006).

These objections to Tsebelis' arguments point to a more general problem of his theory. This theory focuses on the composition of *governments* while the actual *legislative decision rules* tend to recede into the background. Yet these rules are crucial. Whether or not members of oversized coalitions can be outvoted depends on the underlying decision rule. If there is a legislative supermajority requirement such that all member parties of an 'oversized' coalition are needed to change the legislative status quo, they clearly are veto players according the logic of Tsebelis' theory. In contrast, if an absolute majority is sufficient the argument advanced by Strøm has greater force. In a similar vein, since a minority of legislative seats is generally not sufficient to pass policy, opposition parties can certainly become quite influential. In fact, the dividing line between majority and minority government can be rather fuzzy. This is highlighted by the recent development of so-called 'contract parliamentarism' in Sweden, where the management of the cooperation between the governing Social Democrats and the left support parties—in terms of detailed written agreements and monitoring—comes rather close to a coalition government (Bale and Bergman, forthcoming).

This discussion highlights the more general fact that in the case of simple majority rule in a unicameral parliament, there is really only one institutional veto point: the parliamentary majority. Even a minimum-winning coalition can, in principle, dissolve at any time if one party or several parties within the existing coalition think they can make a better deal by forming a different majority coalition (McGann 2005). Hence even in the case of minimum-winning coalitions *no party is a veto player in a strict sense*. Only a one-party majority government can unambiguously be identified as a veto player.

While this is a rather fundamental problem for veto player theory, it can be treated pragmatically in empirical analysis. Veto player theory, as well as the veto point literature on which it builds, provides us with a useful framework for approaching empirical analyses, but it does not always allow a sharp distinction between veto players and merely influential players and it should not distract us from the underlying distribution of formal decision-making resources. In *quantitative analyses*, therefore, it can be useful to focus on formal *veto points* and make theoretical assumptions about preferences rather than to work with rather arbitrary definitions of veto player and measurements of these players' preferences. As already noted, this is the approach I shall take in Chapter eight. In the *case studies*, making a strict distinction between veto players and merely influential players is also often less important than one might think, given the problem of preference measurement discussed above. For how we *name* particular actors is less important than how well we understand their policy preferences and their coalition-building options, given the underlying decision problem and decision rules. For example, a minority government that can flexibly choose between different support parties is likely to be more powerful vis-à-vis opposition parties than one that has to rely on the support of one particular party in order to pass important bills. We can take account of this difference without having to decide which of relevant players qualify as true veto players. Similarly, if an ideologically diverse oversized coalition can easily agree on policy change, this is itself evidence of a convergence of operative preferences. What is more difficult to decide is the extent to which the preference change of a particular player is the result of this player's changed *policy preferences* (due to changed beliefs about socio-economic constraints) as opposed to the threat of being excluded from the coalition. However, we often will not want or need to answer this question; and if we do, the answer will, once more, crucially depend on what policy preferences we could *expect* the relevant players to develop, given socio-economic constraints.

PARTISAN-INSTITUTIONAL CONFIGURATIONS
IN THE SELECTED CASES

This section gives an overview of the partisan-institutional configurations that characterise the seven countries selected for in-depth study in the period under consideration (mid-1980s to mid-2000s). The goal is to give the reader an idea of the relevant variation across the cases.

I want to start, though, by noting two related commonalities of the seven countries. First, all countries are *parliamentary systems*. This claim may be contested with respect to Finland, which has often been described as a 'semi-presidential' system. For three main reasons we can neglect the Finnish president as a potential veto player in this study. First, the president's *formal* power had always been restricted to foreign policy as well as cabinet formation and dissolution (Shugart and Carey 1992: 61–3, 155). Second, already in 1987 David Arter (1987: 151–2) wrote that actual 'presidential incursions into the domestic-policy process have been limited and exceptional'. Finally, after 1987, the role of the president was formally weakened by a series of constitutional reforms. 'The result is a Finnish president that now has more-or-less the same, rather weak, powers as those found elsewhere in Western Europe' (Gallagher *et al.* 2005: 30). The second important commonality, partly resulting from the first, is that all seven countries reveal *high levels of party unity*, allowing us generally to treat parties as unitary actors.

As noted above, veto point approaches focus on institutional structures while veto player theory also pays attention to government types. Table 2.1 provides information on both dimensions (*cf.* Woldendorp *et al.* 2000). As to government types, majority coalitions are treated as the standard case and therefore not mentioned. *One-party majority governments* existed in Australia and New Zealand. Until 1993 New Zealand's electoral system was single-member plurality ('first-past-the-post'), which manufactured one-party majority governments. In 1993 a successful referendum led to the switch to a mixed-member proportional representation system, which was first used in the 1996 elections. The electoral system in Australia is a majoritarian system (alternative vote). *One-party minority governments* existed in Norway and Sweden, two countries with proportional

Table 2.1: Partisan-institutional configuration in the seven cases

	AUS	DNK	DEU	FIN	NOR	NZL	SWE
Special government types							
One-party majority governments	√					√	
One-party minority governments					√		√
Minority coalitions		√			√	√	√
Oversized coalitions				√			
Veto points important in this study							
Sub-national governments and strong second chambers	√		√				
Strong judicial review			√				
Veto points less important in this study							
Supermajority rules in parliament		.		(√)			
Minority referendum		(√)					
European Union/European Court of Justice		(√)	(√)	(√)			(√)

Notes: For country abbreviations, see appendix. Sources: See text.

representation systems. Both countries were also governed by *minority coalitions*, as were Denmark and post-1993 New Zealand. Finally, Finland, another country with a proportional representation system, also experienced oversized coalition government.

As to veto points, Table 2.1 distinguishes between veto points that figure prominently in the seven countries and those that don't. The important veto points are sub-national governments and second chambers on the one hand and judicial review of legislation on the other. I discuss them in turn.

Sub-national governments and/or strong second chambers matter only in Australia and Germany. But let us nevertheless start by briefly discussing the other countries. New Zealand is a very small, centralized and unicameral country; sub-national income taxes are lacking completely (OECD 1999: 52–6). The four Nordic countries are also small, non-federal countries with either unicameralism or weak bicameralism. In Denmark the upper house was abolished in 1953, in Sweden in 1970. The Norwegian Storting divides into two chambers (on non-financial bills), but this has 'virtually no consequence for legislation' (Strøm and Narud 2003: 524). In Finland a large parliamentary committee is sometimes seen as a quasi-second chamber but as in Norway the legislative system is essentially unicameral (Lijphart 1999: 212).

The taxation systems of the Nordic countries are more decentralised. In all four countries, local governments levy income taxes and sometimes have some discretion in setting local tax rates. Nevertheless, in all four countries the *legislative* powers of central governments vis-à-vis local governments are so strong that the latter can be disregarded as veto players (Blom-Hansen 1999: 54; OECD 1999: 31–6, 57–60, 70–1). That is, one can generally assume that central governments have the legislative power to deal with any problems of local governments' discretion in setting tax rates. This powerful position of central governments is partly reinforced by the relative weakness of judicial review (see below). For example, when the Swedish government was concerned about municipal tax increases in the early 1990s, it passed a provision making any local government that increased its tax rate face an almost matching cut in government subsidies—despite the fact that the constitutionality of this measure was 'doubtful, to say the least' (Andersson and Mutén 1998: 344).

Although Australia is a federal country, the states play hardly any role in the politics of income taxation. The federal government has taken over income taxation entirely (Eccleston 2004). However, Australia does have a strong second chamber: the Senate. It has been claimed that the Australian Senate does have veto power in all types of legislation except money bills (Tsebelis and Money 1997: 624; Hallerberg and Basinger 1998), but this is incorrect. While the Senate can neither initiate nor amend money bills, it can veto them. Disputes between the two houses are eventually settled by a joint session, in which the House majority has greater weight, but this joint session is preceded by double-dissolution and re-election of both houses (Evans 2001). The Australian Senate is directly elected with a proportional representation system (single transferable vote). One consequence is that governments typically have secure majorities in the House but not in the Senate. Hence the Australian Senate is an important veto point or institutional veto player. Another consequence is that the politics in Australia's second chamber—which is more a 'partisan' than 'federal' chamber—is rather similar to the politics in minority governments in unicameral systems, e.g. in Denmark, Norway, New Zealand or Sweden: the government has to seek support of at least one of the opposition parties or independent legislators (Ganghof and Bräuninger 2006).

Germany is also a federal country but its federalism is different from the Australian. On a notional continuum ranging from 'dual' to 'joint' federalism, Germany clearly is at the joint federalism end; the actions of the federal government and the states (the *Länder*) are highly interdependent rather than separated (Schmidt 2003: 56–65; Thorlakson 2003). Taxation, too, is a joint enterprise of the federation and the states. Tax *legislation* is mainly a federal matter and tax *administration* mainly a state matter. The revenues from most of the major taxes, including the income tax, are allocated to the federal government, the states, and local government according to rules specified mostly in the constitution. The states participate in federal legislation through the 'Bundesrat' (Council of States), which is not a second chamber of parliament in a technical sense but nevertheless Germany's de facto second chamber. The Bundesrat consists of the prime ministers and certain other members of the state governments (or their appointed substitutes). The Bundesrat has a veto over legislation that affects the power of the states (so-called 'mandatory legislation'), which includes most tax legislation. Hence the Bundesrat is typically an institutional veto player. The government needs an absolute Bundesrat majority for a tax law to become effective. Finally, there is an important income tax on businesses levied by the German municipalities (*Gewerbeertragsteuer*). Local governments cannot veto the reform or abolition of this tax but their taxing rights are guarded by the Federal Constitutional Court (see below). Changes of the constitution require two-thirds majorities in both Bundesrat and Bundestag.

Consider next judicial review. In New Zealand and the four Nordic countries it is either weak or absent (Alivizatos 1995; Lijphart 1999: 226). In Australia judicial review is stronger and has also been important on tax matters. Nevertheless, with respect to the kind of tax issues discussed in the present study, the Australian High Court can be neglected as a veto player. There is no legal basis for ruling on issues such as the differentiation of tax rates on different types of income (Saunders 2002). In contrast, judicial review is generally very strong in Germany (Kommers 1994). It has also strongly constrained tax policy. Part of the reason is that there is a powerful constitutional court, which has adopted what may be called a 'comprehensive' or 'holistic' conception of constitutional rights (Alexy 2003: 131). That is, in Germany, norms conferring constitutional rights do not simply protect certain abstractly described positions of the citizen against the state. Rather, the Constitutional Court has interpreted constitutional rights as embodying a system of values or principles which affects the entire legal system. In this way, constitutional rights tend to become ubiquitous. And because such rights tend to collide, it often becomes the job of the court, rather than democratic politics, to balance colliding principles.

Another reason for the constraining effect of the Court is that judicial activism in the area of taxation increased in the 1980s and 1990s. This was partly the result of some judges' dissatisfaction with the state of tax law and the results of the democratic process. As the former judge Paul Kirchhof (2003: 50), the main protagonist of the Court's activism on tax matters, states in the English abstract of a recent article: 'The democratic hope that the parliamentary process...will guarantee a moderate and consistent tax law, has not been fulfilled. For this reason, the fundamental rights of taxpayers in Germany are increasingly becoming the primary measure of legislation'. As a result of the court's activism, 'German theory and practice on matters of the tax constitution seems to be the strictest in the whole world' (Lang 2001: 54).[3] Virtually every important issue of tax policy is discussed as a constitutional issue and democratic legislators usually try to anticipate the Court's likely position on it. In short, the Federal Constitutional Court is a veto player, albeit a rather special one.

Finally, there are number of veto points that are of minor importance in this study but have to be discussed briefly. The first is *supermajoritarian legislative rules* in Finland. Such rules, which are equivalent to a minority veto, are the most direct way of reducing the power of the parliamentary majority. The Finnish parliament had such rules until the early 1990s: one-third of all members or parliament could postpone the adoption of an ordinary law by two to four years (Nousiainen 2000: 269).[4] In addition, there also existed special rules for tax law, as emphasised by Powell (2000: 39, 56): a law introducing a new state tax and lasting for more than one year, also had to be passed with a two-thirds majority

(Jungar 2000: 284; Nousiainen 2000: 269). On closer inspection, though, *the special tax rules actually provided governments with a way around the general qualified majority requirements*. Governments were able to implement tax reforms in the form of yearly tax laws—an option they used frequently (e.g. Tikka 1989).

Another form of 'protecting' the minority in a unicameral parliament is to give this *minority the right to initiate a referendum on a bill*. This kind of minority veto exists in Denmark (Qvortrup 2000). When a bill has been passed by parliament, one-third of the members of parliament may request the submission to a referendum. Nevertheless, for a variety of reasons the resulting minority protection is not particularly strong. More importantly here, certain types of bills are excluded from the procedure, including finance and taxation bills (Qvortrup 2002: 131).

Finally, the legislative and judicial institutions of the European Union could in principle be considered veto points from the perspective of domestic policy-makers in Denmark, Finland, Germany and Sweden (*cf.* Wagschal 1999a). In practice, however, we can neglect the European level, for two main reasons. First, EU legislation in the area of income taxation has not come very far. Second, the European Court of Justice clearly influenced domestic tax reforms in some countries, especially with respect to the integration of corporate and personal taxation but, as I shall explain in more detail in the empirical chapters, this influence has been marginal and has mainly reinforced the policy trends induced by corporate tax competition and the resulting convergence of veto player preferences. Therefore, one can argue that the Court was 'absorbed' by the domestic veto players and that there is no need systematically to discuss the effect of the EU level in these four countries.

CONCLUSION

This chapter has discussed a number of conceptual and methodological problems in the comparative analysis of legislative politics and explained the approach adopted in this study. A central aspect of this approach is the inference to (rather than 'measurement' of) partisan policy preferences based on an in-depth analysis of the trade-offs and constraints parties face. The next chapter begins this analysis.

NOTES

1   For an excellent analysis and critique of revealed preference theory, see Hausman (2000). For a defence, which does not, however, focus on historical analysis, see Dowding (forthcoming).
2   In the language of veto player theory, the actor would be 'absorbed' by the other veto players.
3   Here and elsewhere I translate German sources without explicit mention.
4   The rules were already weakened in 1987. See Jungar (2000: 107) for a more detailed discussion.

chapter three | policy ideal types, policy change and the constraint of tax competition

The previous chapter explained the importance of understanding the structural constraints and trade-offs that policymakers face. This understanding is a prerequisite of making adequate inferences about parties' *policy* preferences and hence to understand the interaction between party ideology, socio-economic constraints and legislative institutions. This chapter starts the analysis of constraints and trade-offs in the area of income taxation.[1] It begins by explaining the differences between two basic types of income taxes and the trade-offs and constraints policymakers face in choosing between them. This trade-off analysis partly follows up on the seminal analysis of Przeworski and Wallerstein (1988). It provides the basis for a stylised and selective summary of the historical development of income taxation in the OECD world, which differs in important ways from that given by other authors (Ottaviani 2002; Swank and Steinmo 2002; Steinmo 2003; Campbell 2004: Chapter five). The summary highlights the importance of distinguishing two Why-questions about the post-1970s tax reforms: (1) why policymakers tried to 'clean up' their income tax systems *rather than maintaining the status quo*, and (2) why policymakers cleaned up their income tax systems in *some rather than other ways*? I shall argue that existing explanations can answer question (1) but not question (2) and that corporate tax competition is part of an adequate answer of both.

IDEAL TYPES AND TRADE-OFFS

In this section I intend to show that there are two basic types of income taxes—or two basic types of income tax *bases*—and that, given the socio-economic constraints, policymakers had good reasons to try to find a compromise between these two types. While the material is somewhat technical, it is crucial for understanding some of the pathologies of OECD countries' income tax systems as well as the options for responding to these pathologies.

The most basic choice policymakers can make about income tax concerns the type of tax they want, or, in other words, the tax *base*. To understand this choice we have to distinguish two different uses of the term 'income tax'. In the political science literature the terms 'income tax' and 'consumption tax' are typically understood in an *institutional* sense, following the usage in, say, the Revenue Statistics of the OECD (2004c). An income tax in this sense is a direct and often progressive tax on corporations and individuals, whereas a consumption tax is an indirect and often proportional tax such as a European-style value-added tax. Yet there is also an *analytical* distinction between income taxes and expenditure taxes (also known as consumption taxes), which is based on economic theory and unrelated to the method of implementation. To avoid confusion of these two different meanings, I shall hereafter use capital letters whenever I use the terms 'income taxes' and 'consumption taxes' in an analytical sense (Income Taxes and Expenditures Taxes).

To understand this analytical distinction, we first need to understand a related distinction between two analytical types of what we typically call 'capital income' (on the following: Slemrod and Bakija 2004: 203–4). The *normal return* to capital is the return to deferring consumption, the (risk-free) return to wealth. For instance, if I buy a machine, I want this investment to generate at least the return I would have received from buying (risk-free) government bonds. This is the normal return—the return that can be earned on a marginal investment in capital, which is competed down to a fairly low level. *Above-normal returns* go beyond that level. They include various things, e.g., returns to innovation, returns to establishing a monopoly in some market or returns to entrepreneurial skill. Bill Gates' income, which comes mainly from his share of profits from Microsoft, would typically be labelled 'capital income', but only a small portion of that income represents a reward for postponing consumption. Mostly, it consists of above-normal returns. Based on the distinction between normal and above-normal capital income—and ignoring gifts and bequests for simplicity—we can characterise two analytical types of 'income' taxes: an *Expenditure Tax* (or Consumption Tax) taxes wages and above-normal returns but exempts normal returns, whereas an *Income Tax* taxes all three types of income.[2]

As already noted, the distinction between normal and above-normal returns is analytical. These two types of returns do not 'naturally' appear on businesses' balance sheets. Therefore, if policymakers want to completely exempt normal returns, they typically change the definition of the tax *base*. There are essentially two ways to do this, which we shall look at in more detail below. One approach taxes savings and investments but exempts the normal return on capital; the other approach exempts savings and investments but taxes the return. In both approaches, the resulting tax base is largely identical to that of a European-style value-added tax.

The distinction between Income and Expenditure Taxes is important because standard closed-economy models of taxation suggest that taxing normal returns reduces savings and investment, while taxing above-normal returns does not. Hence the taxation of above-normal returns promises to obtain revenue in a completely 'neutral' or 'non-distorting' manner (Boadway and Bruce 1984: 231; *cf.* Przeworski and Wallerstein 1988). Expenditure Taxes ideally allow policymakers to 'regulate investment and income distribution independently' within certain limits (Przeworski and Wallerstein 1986: 250).[3] But the exemption of normal returns is not like a free lunch. For one thing, in the *real world* high taxation of above-normal returns might be problematic and thus limited. For another, given a certain revenue requirement, the exemption of normal returns also requires higher taxes on wages, everything else being equal, which also has efficiency costs (e.g. Gaube and Schwager 2004; Slemrod and Bakija 2004: 207). Obviously, then, the choice between Income and Expenditure taxation involves trade-offs, some of which have to be analysed in some detail in order to understand policy change.

The following trade-off analysis is based on two main assumptions. The first assumption is that the taxation of normal capital income is severely constrained. In other words, it is assumed that taxing normal capital income highly and progressively is very *costly* for policymakers and that policymakers are aware of this fact. The relevant costs can be economic, political and administrative. For example, high tax rates on investment in business equipment may be associated with high economic costs (De Long and Summers 1991), high tax rates on the 'imputed' rent of owners of owner-occupied housing tend to give rise to high political (electoral) costs (e.g. Sørensen 1998), and high and progressive tax rates on capital gains and other types of capital income tend to imply high administrative costs (e.g. Slemrod 1990a). The assumption of tight constraints in taxing normal capital income is in line with much economic theory as well as empirical evidence (Summers *et al.* 1993; Lindert 2004; Ganghof, 2006).

The second assumption is that politics is centrist, i.e. oriented towards the preferences of the median voter (e.g. McDonald *et al.* 2004). At this point in the analysis I am interested in understanding the basic trade-offs faced by a 'typical' centrist OECD government, which aims at a balance between efficiency and redistribution.

To better understand the trade-offs resulting from these assumptions, it is useful to relate the two basic dimensions of income tax policy — tax base and tax rates — to one another (Figure 3.1) The horizontal axis of Figure 3.1 captures the tax base dimension: the tax rate on normal capital income can range between a minimum of zero (Expenditure Tax) and a maximum defined by the top tax rate on wages and above-normal capital income (Income Tax). The vertical axis captures the tax rate dimension: a rough distinction is made between a low top tax rate and a progressive tax rate schedule with fairly high marginal rates.

The conceptualisation in Figure 3.1 leads to four rather pure types of income taxes, two of which are fairly radical and therefore difficult to sell to the median voter. (The fifth, hybrid system represented by the question mark will be discussed further below.) A *flat Expenditure Tax* with a low rate is the prototypical right-wing proposal. Ex-Republican presidential candidate and billionaire Steve Forbes proposed such a tax, with a rate of 20 per cent, for the United States. This tax conforms to the structural constraints in capital income taxation by exempting normal returns; but it also imposes a strong constraint on the progressivity and revenue-raising potential of the income tax. It tends to 'overemphasise' efficiency.

Figure 3.1: Ideal-type income taxes

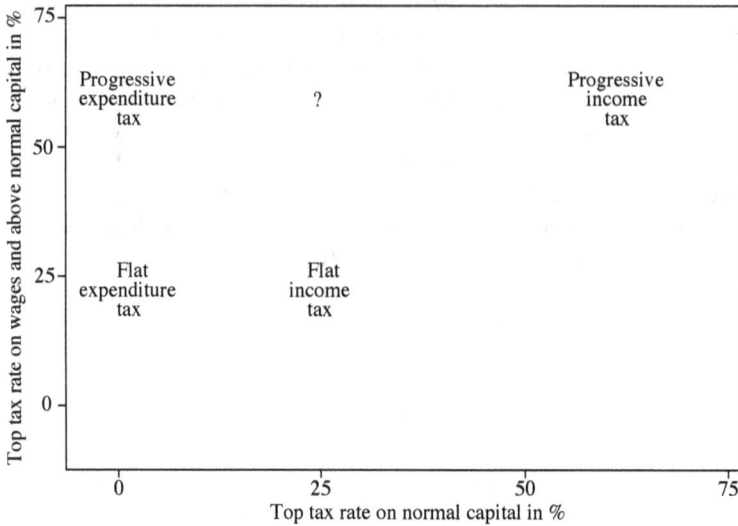

Notes: The actual levels of marginal tax rates chosen in the four types of taxes are merely exemplary.

A *progressive Income Tax* is the prototypical left-wing proposal. Many activists of trade unions and social movements like ATTAC (Association pour une Taxation des Transactions financières pour l'Aide aux Citoyens et Citoyennes) tend to be in favour of such a tax. It can achieve significant progressivity and high revenues but does not take account of the structural constraints of taxing capital income. It tends to 'overemphasise' redistribution.

The other two types of income tax systems are more centrist, but in different ways. They emphasise different aspects or notions of tax justice and tax efficiency. I begin with a *progressive Expenditure Tax*. As to tax efficiency, proponents of this type of income tax highlight the efficiency advantages of exempting normal capital income. One advantage already noted is that an Expenditure Tax does not distort taxpayers' choice between savings and consumption; it is neutral in this respect (e.g. Przeworski and Wallerstein 1988). In addition, it has been argued that an Expenditure Tax is simpler and for that reason imposes lower administrative costs (Bradford 1986: 313–15). There are also efficiency arguments for progressive taxation of wages and above-normal returns. For one thing, wage tax progressivity seems be desirable because the adverse effect of labour taxes on unemployment may on average be more severe for low-wage than for high-wage workers (e.g. Scharpf 2000b; Røed and Strøm 2002; Kemmerling 2005). For another, progressive wage taxation may reduce the negative externalities of status-seeking work and consumption behaviour (Frank 1999; Layard 2005). A preference for progressive wage taxation also reinforces the efficiency case for a tax on above-normal returns, because such a tax fulfils a *safeguarding function* for the taxation of wages. As Slemrod and Bakija (2004: 204) explain: 'Under a wage tax, relabeling your labour compensation as capital income would be an easy avenue to escape taxation altogether. The difficulty of distinguishing what is labour income and what is capital income is an important reason that a pure wage tax would end up being highly inequitable and costly to enforce.' Ideally, there-fore, above-normal returns and wages should be taxed jointly and equally.

As to tax justice, the main argument in favour of progressive Expenditure Taxes is ultimately that the adequate measure of 'ability to pay' is lifetime rather than periodical income. The foundations of this kind of argument (or lack thereof) are complex and need not concern us here (Murphy and Nagel 2002: Chapter five). One important idea, though, is that Income Taxation would result in over-taxation of individuals with relatively high savings propensities, because the normal return is a reward for the saver's willingness to postpone consumption. In contrast, above-normal returns are seen as often representing windfall gains that ought to bear a high tax rate. An important practical argument is that direct expenditure taxes can achieve exactly the same overall degree of progressivity as income taxes if tax rates are adequately progressive (e.g. Bradford 1986: 162; Weisbach and Bankman 2005). Hence for proponents of direct Consumption Taxes, the exemption of normal capital income is a *precondition* for progressive tax rate schedules in efficiency terms; and this progressivity in turn *justifies* the exemption of normal returns in justice terms.

Proponents of *flat Income Taxes* have a different view on the issues of tax efficiency and equity. As to tax efficiency, they agree that the tax burden on nor-mal capital income should be moderate but are opposed to shifting the income tax burden onto above-normal returns and wages. This is because they emphasise the efficiency losses associated with high and differentiated tax rates. One argument is that differentiation of tax rates, even if supposedly efficient, leads to ineffi-cient tax arbitrage of taxpayers (BMF 1999c: 78). Another is that the efficiency costs of taxation tend to increase exponentially with the marginal tax rate (*cf.* Auerbach 1997; Becker and Mulligan 2003). More specifically, a high tax rate on above-normal returns can be problematic for two main reasons. First, it may have adverse effects on investors' expectations, because they fear that the reach of the tax will at some point be extended again to include normal returns (Summers 1987: 15). Second, from a more Schumpeterian economic perspective high taxes on the returns to entrepreneurial skills and good ideas may reduce entrepreneurial efforts. Expenditure Taxes tend to punish the innovative entrepreneur and favour the lazy heir. Similarly, high taxes on wages are seen as inefficient because they distort the choice between leisure and work and therefore reduce labour supply (e.g. Gustafsson 1996: 822).

As to tax justice, proponents of flat income taxes tend to see periodical rather than lifetime income as the adequate measure of 'ability to pay'. Again, the foundations of this kind of argument are beyond the scope of this book. One important idea, though, is that wealth is an independent source of welfare, apart from the fact that some of it may be consumed later. For example, it contributes to people's security, their social standing and their political power (Simons 1938: 97; e.g. Avi-Yonah 2004). A more practical and important consideration is also that the regressivity of Expenditure Taxes is not so easily avoided *in practice*. The graduation of tax rates necessary to achieve a particular revenue target and match the overall progressivity of an income tax might not be achievable (Murphy and Nagel 2002: 113).

In sum, then, proponents of Income and Expenditure Taxes adopt very different perspectives on equity and efficiency in income taxation. The type of efficiency important for proponents of Expenditure Taxation has to do with the right type of *differentiation* of tax burdens (between normal and above-normal returns), whereas for proponents of Income Taxation efficiency is largely a matter of *non-differentiation*. Similarly, proponents of Expenditure Taxes highlight what one may call *'intra-labour equity'*, i.e. tax progressivity in (and revenue-raising through) the taxation of wages, whereas proponents of Income Taxes highlight *'capital-labour equity'*, i.e. equal treatment of wages and all capital income.[4]

The problem of our representative centrist government is now clearer: both flat Income Taxes and progressive Expenditure Taxes have a certain appeal but the empirical and normative issues involved seem too complex as to allow a clear-cut decision for the 'better' system. More recent work in economics and philosophy has reinforced this impression (e.g. Deaton 1987; Murphy and Nagel 2002): whether a certain aspect of a tax system is efficient or just essentially depends on so many other relevant parameters—of the tax system and the socio-economic system more generally—that a principled choice for one or the other type of taxation is virtually impossible. In such a situation, policymakers will try to turn the seemingly discrete decision problem into a more continuous one. That is, they will try to treat the choice between Income and Consumption Taxes as a matter of degree. Figure 3.1 already suggests such a perspective. In principle, the level and progressivity of taxation of normal capital income on the one hand and above-normal capital income and wages on the other might be treated as independent parameters than can be set so as to balance the pros and cons of Income and Expenditure Taxes.

In what follows, I want to suggest that this is, at least in part, what policymakers have tried to do. I interpret income tax policy between the end of World War II and the late 1970s as an effort to find a functioning *compromise* between Income and Expenditure Taxation (Aaron *et al.* 1988). I argue that the well-known pathologies of income taxation—I shall give examples shortly—that led to the reforms of the 1980s and 1990s partly resulted from this effort. I do not intend to suggest that these pathologies were only the result of such compromise-seeking. Other aspects certainly played a role, many of which have been highlighted in the political science literature. In fact, the selective perspective offered here is explicitly intended to complement and partly to qualify the 'standard' interpretation in the political science literature. I shall first give a rough summary of this interpretation and then develop an alternative perspective.

THE STANDARD INTERPRETATION OF POLICY CHANGE

The standard political science explanation highlights policy learning and idea-tional change. The main argument, as I understand it, is that before the late 1970s policymakers deliberately tried to influence the *structure* of capital income taxa-tion, trying to steer savings and investments into certain 'sectors' of the economy. Investment and saving incentives were tools for the 'micro-management' of the supply-side (Steinmo 2003). However, these management efforts turned out to create a 'horrible mess' (Steinmo 2003: 227). As a result, the 1980s witnessed a 'paradigm shift' (Swank and Steinmo 2002: 645). The manipulations of the struc-ture of capital taxation, so the argument goes, were found to be inefficient (Garrett 1998b). The new goal was not to steer savings and investments into particular sectors but to achieve 'neutrality' between sectors. This goal of 'inter-sectoral neutrality' was also known as the 'level playing field' and 'market-conforming' taxation (Swank 1998). The way to achieve this goal was to cut marginal tax rates and broaden tax bases by removing many incentives from the tax code. As Swank and Steinmo (2002: 643) summarise:

> After World War II, tax policy became a central instrument for achieving social and economic policy goals. Indeed, the regime of high marginal tax rates—combined with generous tax incentives for investment and controls of regulating capital export—was a centerpiece of the post-war compromise between capital and labor in all industrialized democracies and contributed to the joint pursuit of equity and growth in the Keynesian welfare state... From the early 1980s, national policy makers significantly altered the character of tax policies. The transition in tax policy constituted a shift in policy paradigm: the relative weight accorded the goals of equity and growth, the use of tax policy instruments (e.g., the extent of investment incentives), and the setting of the instruments (e.g., the level of rates) were all notably changed by post-1970s tax reforms.

While I believe there is much truth to an analysis that highlights policy learn-ing and a shift to 'market-conforming' taxation, I also believe that it is subject to two types of problems: (1) it tends to exaggerate the shift to market-conformity and (2) it tends to paint a somewhat biased picture of what market-conformity implied in terms of marginal tax rates. I discuss both points in turn.

The policy learning-explanation exaggerates the paradigm shift to 'market-conforming' or 'uniform' income taxation because it gives relatively little atten-tion to the administrative, economic and political constraints and trade-offs faced by policymakers. That policymakers intervened into the structure of savings and investments was not only a result of their eagerness to 'micro-manage' the economy but also a reaction to tight constraints and multiple trade-offs. As these constraints and trade-offs persists, so does differentiated income taxation.

We have already seen above that efficiency in economic tax theory is not only understood as non-differentiation but also as some form of 'optimal' differentiation. While we have so far discussed this point with respect to the distinction between the normal and above-normal return on capital, it applies much more generally. Real world policymakers have many good reasons to subject different types of capital income to different tax rates.

One set of reasons is purely economic. In the real world the case for uniform taxation of capital income is much less clear than in theory, for two main reasons. The first is that *real world markets are not perfect*, implying that the social returns to different types of savings and investments are unlikely to be equalised. One important example is positive externalities. Certain types of investments—e.g. in business equipment, research and development or in home ownership—may yield significant positive externalities, so that preferential taxation may increase overall economic efficiency (De Long and Summers 1991; Gravelle 1994: 63). The second reason why uniform capital income taxation would not necessarily be efficient, even if private market were efficient, is that *other taxes or public policies may cause distortions* (Slemrod 1990a; Gravelle 1994: 61).[5] To offset other deviations from optimality, policymakers may have good economic reasons to differentiate the tax burden (Auerbach 1989; Feldstein 1990).

The second set of reasons for differentiated capital income taxation has to do with the administrative and political (electoral) costs of taxing certain types of capital income. These costs may be so high as to suggest preferential taxation. One example is the *taxation of capital gains*. Capital gains are capital income that results from changes in the value of assets. Ideal-type income taxation of capital gains would require the taxation of all capital gains, those 'realised' by selling assets as well as those existing only on paper. Such a tax treatment is called accrual-based taxation. Due to onerous problems of measurement, though, virtually all income tax systems only include gains in the value of assets when they are sold—realisation-based taxation. This treatment creates a deferral of tax with various attendant distortions such as favouring some assets over others or discouraging taxpayers from selling assets (lock-in effect).

Another example for the importance of political and administrative constraints is the *treatment of taxpayers' interest payments* (Gravelle 1994: 70–1). An ideal-type Income Tax would treat all durable consumption goods as investments. That is, it would allow financing costs (interest payments) to be deducted from the tax base while at the same time including the implicit income earned by the consumer item into the tax base. Automobiles or household furnishings are in theory candidates for Income Taxation. However, measuring and reporting the flow of such income would be *administratively* very difficult, so that in practice only the most significant type of imputed income is considered to be taxable income: the rental value of owner-occupied housing. Yet for *political* reasons, no OECD country has ever succeeded in fully taxing this type of income. As Sørensen (2001: 4) notes: 'Politically it is close to impossible to sell the idea that owner-occupied housing actually yields a return in the form of the value of the housing service and that this return ought to be taxed along with other forms of capital income.' Hence, as a result of tight administrative and political constraints, policymakers tend to privilege owner-occupied housing by taxing the return to owner-occupied housing lowly or not at all. If they try to reduce these privileges, they typically do so by adopting an offsetting deviation from the income tax ideal: they disallow or restrict the deductibility of mortgage interest (Messere 1993: 137–8, 234–36, 274, Table 10.8). In this case it is mainly households without mortgages that receive preferential tax treatment. Those renting have to pay rent out of after-tax income, while those with mortgages have to meet interest costs out of after-tax income.

Recognising economic, political and administrative constraints is important because it makes us wary of exaggerating any 'ideational' shift towards the goal of uniform or 'market-conforming' taxation. For if the absence of such taxation had been rooted in structural constraints, its realisation cannot simply be a matter of changing ideas. If the same constraints continue to exist, any citation of the idea of uniform taxation as a cause of policy change is question-begging. In fact, in all OECD countries important tax experts and policymakers remained sceptical towards the ideal of uniform (capital) income taxation. A good example is Lawrence Summers, the US Finance Minister under President Bill Clinton. He has vigorously criticised the rhetoric of 'levelling the playing field' that accompanied the US tax reform of 1986, focusing on the issue of positive externalities:

> The level playing field principle focuses attention on the question of the differential taxation of different types of capital income. It diverts attention from the issue of the overall level of the taxation of capital income...The available evidence suggests that...intertemporal distortions...are far more important than any intersectoral distortions that taxes may cause...This suggests the importance for economic efficiency of reducing the tax rate on equipment investment, even though this would raise the wedge between its tax rate and the tax rate on certain other classes of business investment. (Summers 1987: 15–16)[6]

Of course, such views may have become less common than they used to be. It is plausible that negative experiences with differential taxation have pushed policymakers *towards more* uniform taxation. But we are then talking about matters of degree; and the *degree* to which market-conforming taxation has been implemented in OECD countries is an empirical issue that has hardly been addressed in the political science literature.

Summers' statement also points us towards the second problem of the standard political science interpretation of tax reform trends. This interpretation seems to assume that cutting tax rates and broadening tax bases was a *necessary* condition of 'market-conformity'. Yet it is important to separate two analytical dimensions of income tax policy. The question how equal policymakers want to treat different types of taxable income or different types of economic activities is logically independent of the question how 'investment-friendly' a tax base they want to have. If this distinction is made, it becomes clear that cutting statutory corporate tax rates was by no means a necessary condition of a level playing field. There was, in principle, a choice to be made about the level of 'investment-friendliness' at which the playing field was to be levelled (Bond 2000). This choice, I shall argue, was severely constrained by corporate tax competition.

AN ALTERNATIVE PERSPECTIVE ON POLICY CHANGE

The standard interpretation underestimates the extent to which the 'horrible mess' in OECD countries' tax systems was the result of efforts to increase the *level* of savings and investments. Inter-sectoral distortions were to a certain extent negative side-effects of policymakers' efforts to combine the advantages of (flat) Expenditure Taxes and (progressive) Income Taxes. As explained above, this effort was only understandable given the trade-offs between competing equity and efficiency goals. Policymakers tried to get the best of both worlds.

The problem was that the *particular way* in which policymakers tried to combine the two ideal-type income taxes turned out to be very problematic. Rather than relying on a well-developed hybrid Income-Expenditure Tax—a blueprint for which did not exist at the time—they selectively combined elements of Income and Expenditure Taxation. Norrman and McLure (1997) aptly call this the *Chinese menu approach* to tax policy: policymakers chose 'some provisions from the income tax column and some from the consumption tax column' (Norrman and McLure 1997: 117), assuming that the resulting meal would still be digestible. But it wasn't. The results were distortions of economic choices, widespread tax avoidance, inequitable income taxation, the public perception that the system was unfair, and administrative complexity, as efforts were made to prevent abuse. Policymakers got the worst rather than the best of both worlds.

Two examples may clarify the problem (*cf.* Fullerton 1994: 195; McLure and Zodrow 1994): One type of direct Expenditure Tax (a so-called cash-flow tax) allows investment outlays of businesses to be deducted immediately, thereby exempting the normal return on capital. If this 'expensing' of investment outlays is combined with the income tax-feature of interest deductibility, however, as done in the past by some OECD countries, the tax rate on the normal return to debt-financed investment becomes *negative* and opens up a large 'tax loophole'. The situation is similar if the depreciation of investment is greatly accelerated (relative to actual economic depreciation), as it used to be in many advanced OECD countries. A similar problem existed in the taxation of owner-occupied housing, especially in the Nordic countries: if interest payments are deductible (a feature of a pure Income Tax) but the resulting implicit rent earned by owner-occupiers is taxed lowly or not at all (an Expenditure Tax-feature), such housing investment is greatly subsidised and opens up a loophole (Sørensen 1998).

As these examples show, many tax distortions can be interpreted, at least in part, as resulting from inadequate attempts to find a compromise between Income and Expenditure Taxes. Such an interpretation leads to a perspective on policy change that differs in important ways from that offered by Swank and Steinmo (2002), among others. By applying Peter Hall's (1993) concept, adapted from Kuhn (1962), of a policy paradigm shift to income taxation, Swank and Steinmo suggest the following: (1) there were two more-or-less incommensurable (i.e. incomparable and/or non-combinable) policy paradigms, (2) policy change involved a more-or-less discrete shift from one paradigm to another, (3) this shift implied a new weighting of basic goals (equity and growth) and (4) there was no alternative direction of policy change. Based on the interpretation offered here, all four suggestions seem problematic.

First, the important 'paradigms'—or, in the terminology proposed here, ideal types—in income taxation were Income Taxation and Expenditure Taxation, and these ideal types were *not* incommensurable. Second, the two ideal types are based more on different *notions* of equity and efficiency rather than on a different weighting of these goals. Hence it is rather unclear what it means to say that policy change involved a new weighting of basic goals. In fact, there is broad consensus among economists that tax reforms like those pursued in the United States were intended to increase both efficiency and equity (e.g. Fullerton 1994; Walker 1994). As Weiss (1996: 450) argues, it 'hard to overemphasise the degree to which horizontal equity was the driving force behind the Tax Reform Act of 1986'. Third, there was at best a *movement towards* purer Income Taxation rather than a clear shift from one ideal type to the other. In fact, income tax systems in most OECD countries continue to be hybrid Income-Expenditure taxes. Fourth, there clearly existed alternatives to the policy of tax-cut-cum-base-broadening. Rather than moving to toward flat Income Taxes, policymakers had the option of implementing consistent progressive Expenditure Taxes or modernised Income-Expenditure taxes that would provide a level playing field for economic actors. This insight raises important questions largely ignored by the existing literature. (1) To what extent did policymakers pursue these alternative paths of policy change? (2) If they did not pursue them, why not? In what follows, I provide a partial answer to these questions. I argue that OECD governments did in fact pursue alternative reform models and that their implementation was severely constrained by corporate tax competition.

In developing this argument, I shall focus on the second option of making hybrid Income-Expenditure taxes more market-conforming. This focus is not due to the fact that full-fledged Expenditure Taxes weren't seriously considered by policymakers in OECD countries. To the contrary: 'Between 1975 and 1985, the view of most tax policymakers was that the PIT (personal income taxes) should be replaced rather than reformed. During this period, proposals emerged from a number of public finance economists as well as tax reform commissions in Ireland, Sweden, the United Kingdom, and the United States to replace or supplement the income tax by a progressive expenditure tax…' (Messere *et al.* 2003: 68). The reason for focusing on hybrid Income-Expenditure Taxes is rather that—as explained above—they were generally more acceptable for centrist OECD governments and that the argument about the tax competition constraint applies even more strongly to pure Expenditure Taxes. I shall first sketch what a modernised hybrid Income-Expenditure Tax could (have) look(ed) like and then explain the effects of tax competition.

What could a modernised hybrid approach (have) look(ed) like?
This question is less hypothetical than it sounds because important elements of a modernised compromise between flat Income Taxes and progressive Expenditure Taxes were and still are implemented in OECD countries. But before we discuss these, we have to clarify some technical basics about the implementation of direct Expenditure Taxes.

As noted above, there are two main ways of implementation, which, under simplifying assumptions and ignoring transition problems, are equivalent. Here I want to characterise these two ways in more detail.

- *Classical Expenditure Tax*: Saving is deductible, so that someone earning EUR 30,000 and saving EUR 5,000 is taxed on EUR 25,000. The return on the saving is taxed. This general approach is also labelled cash-flow taxation with respect to business taxation and abbreviated as EET with respect to pension taxation (contributions Exempt, fund income Exempt, payments Taxed).
- *Pre-paid Expenditure Tax*: Savings are included in the tax base but the return on it is deductible. Someone earning EUR 27,500, of which EUR 2,500 is interest income, is taxed on EUR 25,000. This approach is labelled Allowance for Corporate Equity with respect to business taxation and TEE with respect to pension taxation (contributions Taxed, fund income Exempt, payments Exempt).

I shall focus on the latter because, under this approach, the modernisation of a hybrid Income-Expenditure tax is most straightforward. In a pure pre-paid Expenditure Tax individuals' capital income is tax-exempt. Businesses determine profits according to the same rules as under a conventional Income Tax but can deduct fictitious interest income up to some administratively determined 'standard' interest rate on their equity. This standard rate is determined by the government. In Croatia, for instance, which operated a pre-paid Expenditure Tax between 1994 and 2000, the standard rate was 5 per cent—11.2 per cent after accounting for inflation (Keen and King 2003: 325).

Now, our assumption has been that the typical government in an advanced OECD country is unlikely to follow Croatia in implementing a *pure* Expenditure Tax.[7] So the question is: how does the pre-paid approach have to be modified in order to lead to a hybrid Income-Expenditure tax? The answer is simple: because the approach implies the administrative determination of the 'normal return' on capital, all that is needed is to tax this normal return at a moderate positive tax rate rather than at a tax rate of zero. In other words, once the 'normal return' is determined, policymakers actually can determine the tax rates for the two dimensions of Figure 3.1 independently. More specifically, they can choose a separate proportional tax rate for normal returns, as they would under a flat Income Tax, while subjecting above-normal returns and wages to a progressive tax rate schedule, as they would under a progressive Expenditure Tax. This type of tax is represented by the question mark in Figure 3.1 above.

The choice between the two ideal types thus becomes a matter of degree: if the tax rate on normal returns is very low, the income tax approaches a pure Expenditure Tax, if it is equal to the top rate on wages and above-normal return, it approaches a pure Income Tax. Note also that the level of taxing normal returns has no effect whatsoever on the 'inter-sectoral neutrality' discussed above. As long as all tax rates are uniformly applied to all sectors of the economy, there will be a level playing field. Hence policymakers have to make two distinct choices: (1) how level the playing field ought to be and (2) at what level of taxing normal capital income the playing field is to be levelled.

To see that the kind of hybrid Income-Expenditure Tax just sketched is not merely a theoretical possibility, consider the so-called 'dual income tax' existing in Italy between 1998 and 2004 (Bordignon *et al.* 2001). Firms' normal return on (new) equity was taxed at a rate of 19 per cent, whereas above-normal returns were either subjected to the corporate tax rate of 37 per cent or, in case of unincorporated businesses, to the top personal tax rate 46 per cent, which of course also applied to wages. Hence, the Italian-style 'dual income tax' contained the most important building blocks of a modernised hybrid income tax that is investment-friendly without distorting the structure of investments.

This discussion makes clear that cuts in headline top marginal tax rates weren't a necessary condition of a shift towards more 'market-conforming' income taxation. Therefore, the standard 'policy learning' explanation of income tax reforms offered in the political science literature is not fully convincing. More concretely, this explanation can only answer the question why policymakers *preferred reform over the status quo*? It cannot answer the more interesting question of why policymakers adopted a certain reform approach *rather than another* (*cf.* Wallerstein and Przeworski 1995)? Why did they cut corporate tax rates and flatten personal income taxes? While an adequate answer to these questions is surely complex, I believe that corporate tax competition must be an important component. But to understand the importance of this competition, we first have to understand the general role of the corporation tax for the personal income tax.

Tax competition and the safeguarding function of the corporation tax

Corporate income taxes are for legal persons what personal income taxes are for natural persons. But ultimately, of course, all taxes are paid by natural persons. So why are there corporate taxes at all?

One crucial reason is that the corporation tax fulfils a safeguarding function for the personal income tax (Mintz 1995). The main reason is that the administrative costs of taxing certain types of capital income—most notably, capital gains that have not yet been 'realized' through selling—at the level of the shareholder are rather high. If the corporation tax did not exist, the corporate legal form would become a major loophole in the income tax base at large. Capital owners could shelter their income from taxation by letting tax-free corporations hold their assets. This is not only a problem for personal capital taxation but also for personal wage taxation, because many high-wage taxpayers can find ways to 'reclassify' their wages as capital income (e.g. Gordon and Slemrod 2000). Of course, this argument about the absence of a corporate tax also applies to a corporate tax whose tax rate is much below the (top) tax rate on personal capital income and/or wages. Ideally, therefore, the corporate rate should be equal to the top rate on personal income (Stotsky 1995: 282; Tanzi and Zee 2000: 310).

The recommendation of equal top rates on corporate and personal income applies to Income and Expenditure Taxes alike. As to Income Taxes, the 'integration' of corporate and personal taxation is a perennial topic, because actual income taxes have had graduated tax rates (direct progressivity), which greatly complicates integration. For in a world of graduated personal tax rates, reconciliation between corporate taxes already paid and the eventual individual tax liability must be done at the individual level, in order to achieve a graduated taxation of corporate income. Given administrative constraints, the most practical approach to a quasi-integration of corporate and personal taxation was developed by the Canadian 'Carter Commission' in the 1960s (Royal Commission on Taxation 1966), and a strict equality of corporate and top personal income tax rates was one of its crucial aspects. Another was to give shareholders a tax credit—the so-called 'imputation tax credit'—for the income tax already paid at the corporate level. In combination, these two measures were aimed at making corporate taxation quasi-progressive. In addition, they were to increase the overall 'market-conformity' of capital income taxation. The imputation tax credit was to prevent the double taxation of dividends and hence the discrimination against *distributing* profits. And the equality of (top) tax rates was to induce corporations to 'voluntarily' allocate all profits to shareholders on an annual basis: 'Since the top personal tax rate is set equal to the corporate tax rate, a full voluntary allocation of corporate net income could generally be expected; lower-bracket shareholders would stand to gain while top-bracket shareholders should be indifferent' (Head 1997: 80). The resulting 'bias' towards profit distributions did not reduce market-conformity because shareholders were free to directly reinvest their dividends into the corporation. The underlying view was that capital allocation through the market is always better than 'locking in' capital in a corporation.

But the equality of corporate and top personal income tax rates is also important for Expenditure Taxes. In one respect it is even more important. For we have seen above that Expenditure Taxes need a more progressive tax rate schedule to achieve a similar overall degree of progressivity as an Income Tax. As a result, if the (above-normal) profits of corporations are taxed at a rather low rate, the arbitrage incentives for high-wage earners will tend to be higher under an Expenditure Tax than under an Income Tax.

This leads us to the problems of corporate tax competition. Much of the political science literature on corporate tax competition—and the political debate for that matter—has argued along the following lines: Because cuts in statutory tax rates did not generally lead to losses in corporate tax revenue (as per cent of GDP), we can infer these cuts were not generally motivated by tax competition and/ or that they are unproblematic in terms of achieving domestic policy outcomes. Based on the analytical perspective developed above, such an inference seems simplistic. For we have to analytically distinguish between at least three types of tax competition: competition on (1) tax rates on normal profits, (2) tax rates on above-normal profits and (3) statutory tax rates. If only or mainly competition on tax rates on normal profits mattered empirically, the situation would be rather similar to that of a closed economy. This point was emphasised by Wallerstein and Przeworski, who summarise:

> Increased international integration of financial markets increases the social costs of distortionary taxes on income from capital. What cannot be explained by the increased capital mobility is why most OECD countries responded by lowering the rate at which profits are taxed. Tax neutrality can be attained with either a zero tax on profits, or 100 per cent deductibility of investment.
>
> (Wallerstein and Przeworski 1995: 441)

The question that Wallerstein and Przeworski raise here is an important and much neglected one, but they do not give an adequate answer because they do not consider the possibility that tax competition also—or even predominantly—concerns tax rates on above-normal returns as well as statutory tax rates.[8] Yet this is seems to be the case (Bond 2000; Haufler and Schjelderup 2000; Devereux et al. 2002). For one thing, enterprises' choices about where to locate new investment are to a significant extent based on the tax rates on above-normal returns, and this argument holds particularly for very profitable enterprises (Richter et al. 1996; Chennells and Griffith 1997; Devereux and Griffith 1998; Bond 2000). For another, there is also competitive pressure (broadly understood) on statutory corporate tax rates. One reason is that statutory tax rates play a crucial role in the strategies of international tax avoidance used by multinational enterprises (e.g. Slemrod 1990b; Hines Jr. 1999). Such enterprises can to some extent shift profits from high-tax into low tax jurisdictions, and incentives for this kind of profit-shifting are often increased by high statutory tax rates. In this case, the competition on statutory tax rates is a competition for the tax bases of multinational enterprises rather than their investment.

In addition, there are also rather complicated mechanisms through which statutory tax rates may have an effect on the location of new investment. To understand one of these mechanisms, we have to grasp an important feature of international taxation: In many OECD countries, a parent company can claim a foreign tax credit for repatriated profits of a foreign subsidiary in order to avoid double taxation of foreign income. However, such countries invariably do not pay refunds when their taxpayers pay a foreign income tax at a rate that is higher than the domestic rate (OECD 1996b: Article 23B). In addition, the tax code of some countries, most notably the US, attempts to redefine the base on which foreign taxes are levied to bring them in line with US definitions (Arnold et al. 1996; Chennells and Griffith 1997: 172, n. 50). In such countries, therefore, it is the statutory rate that defines the credit limitation. For example, a US parent pays the US rate on foreign profits as long as the foreign statutory rate is lower than in the US; if the foreign rate is higher, though, the firm ends up paying the foreign tax. Therefore, US multinationals have an incentive to locate subsidiaries in countries with a tax rate lower than or equal to the US domestic rate. In turn, governments have an incentive to keep their rate in line with other countries. As the 'Ralph Committee' in Australia noted:

> By providing a competitive corporate tax rate, non-portfolio foreign inves-
> tors in Australian companies can benefit because they will be better placed to
> utilize foreign tax credits available in their home jurisdictions — reducing the
> possibility of foreign tax credits being lost because the Australian tax rate is
> higher than their home country rates.
>
> (Review of Business Taxation 1999: 425)

The link between statutory corporate tax rates and foreign tax credits gained special importance after the US tax reform in 1986. The reason was not only that US foreign direct investment is especially important for many countries, but also that 1986 reform included a number of technical details that made US-based multinational corporations more sensitive to tax rate differentials (e.g. Bossons 1988; Lyon 1996). This was immediately recognised by the bureaucrats in the national Ministries of Finance. For example, an official of the German Ministry of Finance explained (drawing on the Ministry's internal analysis of the US tax reform made in the mid-1980s):

> [T]he 1986 reform did not really change competitiveness between the Federal
> Republic of Germany and the United States of America; it had, however,
> competitive effects between Germany, and for example, Great Britain or
> the Netherlands; indeed it reactivated European tax differentials which had
> been neutralized for American groups operating in Europe by intricacies of
> the United States tax credit system; the lowering of the US corporate income
> tax rate made American investment in Europe quite sensitive to these intra-
> European tax differentials. This is a strange paradox indeed, but it has been
> confirmed by those who are responsible for the decision-making process of
> multinational enterprises.
>
> (McLure et al. 1990: 45)

In sum, in open economies the advantages of a corporate tax that completely exempts normal profits seem to vanish: '[T]he corporate tax rate can no longer be a non-distortionary instrument in the presence of FDI and transfer pricing opportunities' (Haufler and Schjelderup 2000: 319). By cutting the statutory corporate tax rate and broadening the tax base while maintaining a given revenue level, policymakers tend to *increase* the tax rate on normal profits and hence the so-called 'cost of capital'. However, the negative 'effect of a higher cost of capital on domestic investment will tend to be mitigated by the effect of a lower statutory tax rate on inward investment' (Bond 2000: 173).

This logic helps to explain the downward trend in corporate tax rates after the US tax reform of 1986. What is more, it probably also helps to explain the similar trend in top personal income tax rates, because, due to the safeguarding function of corporate taxation, lower corporate tax rates can be expected to exert downward pressure on marginal tax rates on high personal incomes. In fact, the arguments about corporate and personal taxation are inexorably linked. On the one hand, the safeguarding function that the corporation tax fulfils for the personal income tax is part of the reason why, in the absence of tax competition, policymakers would have had good reason to stick to fairly high corporate tax rates on above-normal returns; it is part of the reason why tax competition was a significant constraint for policymakers. On the other hand, it is the *combination* of competitive pressures and the safeguarding function that helps to explain why personal income tax rates came down as well.

CONCLUSION

In this chapter I have developed an analytical perspective on *policy change* in the income tax system of OECD countries which complements and qualifies the dominant perspective in the political science literature. My argument can be summarised as follows. Due to the basic trade-offs in income taxation, the 'typical' centrist OECD government has had good reason to experiment with hybrids between pure Income Taxes and pure Expenditure Taxes. The 'horrible mess' (Steinmo) that characterised OECD income tax systems in the late 1970s was partly the result of this experimentation. Nevertheless, moving towards purer Income Taxes by cutting tax rates and broadening the tax base was not the only option available in response to the mess. The other two options were to move toward purer Expenditure Taxes or to develop a more systematic hybrid approach. The deep cuts in marginal rates are therefore not self-explanatory; they need a special and systematic explanation. I have argued that corporate tax competition is an important part of that explanation. Corporate tax competition (broadly understood) has created significant pressure on statutory tax rates as well as tax rates on above-normal returns and thereby pushed countries towards an Income Tax approach in corporate taxation. What this implies for income taxation at large as well as for the role of party ideology and veto institutions in explaining *international differences* is analysed in the next chapter.

NOTES

1 For more general analyses of countervailing pressures in taxation policy, see Ganghof (2000), Genschel (2002) as well as Swank and Steinmo (2002).

2 I use the terms 'Consumption Tax' and 'Expenditure Tax' interchangeably. Note also that the summary of analytical types of income just given ignores compensation for inflation and returns to risk-taking, both of which need not be taxed under either income or consumption taxes.

3 Przeworski and Wallerstein (1986: 250) believed these limits to be 'relatively broad' (see also: Wallerstein and Przeworski 1995). However, this belief wasn't only—and perhaps not even mainly—based on the efficiency advantages of taxing above-normal instead of normal returns (so-called 'static efficiency'). It was also based on the 'dynamic efficiency' associated with a *switch* from Income to Consumption Taxes. This efficiency results from an implicit lump-sum levy on existing wealth (cf. Gaube and Schwager 2004). Przeworski and Meseguer Yebra's (2005: Fn. 1) scepticism about Expenditure Taxes seems to be based on the presumed inability of policymakers to tax existing capital highly in the absence of capital controls. Here and throughout this book, I focus on issues of static efficiency.

4 Note that capital-labour equity is distinct from the established public finance criterion of 'horizontal equity'. For example, violating labour-capital equity by privileging capital income also violates 'vertical equity' because richer taxpayers tend to receive a larger share of their overall income as capital income. For a useful discussion and critique of traditional equity standards see Murphy and Nagel (2002). On the notion of wage tax progressivity see also OECD (2001d: 19).

5 A classical result in optimal tax theory, the so-called *production efficiency theorem*, suggests that uniform income taxation is efficient if there is a set of efficient commodity taxes (Diamond and Mirrlees 1971). Such *Ramsey taxes* will in general differ by commodity, so that more inelastically demanded goods, e.g., food and medicine, are taxed at higher tax rates. However, Ramsey taxes don't exist in the real world, partly because, to the extent that they can be approximated at all, they would be regressive and give rise to high administrative costs (Gravelle 1994: 61–2).

6 Summers' claims about the efficiency advantages of privileging equipment investment have not gone uncontested (Abel 1992; Auerbach *et al.* 1994). It is in part this kind of disagreement and hence uncertainty on which the case against differential taxation is based.

7 As discussed below, the Expenditure Tax experimented in Croatia was discontinued in 2001.

8 For a summary of the relevant institutional background of international taxation and further references, see Ganghof (2000: 603–10).

chapter four | domestic constraints and international policy differences

The previous chapter has focused on the constraints and trade-offs faced by a 'typical' centrist OECD government in order to better understand the common policy *trend* towards lower marginal tax rates. I argued that the centrist government has had good reasons to adopt a 'hybrid' approach to income taxation—one that balances the pros and cons of Income and Expenditure Taxes but does so in a systematic and 'market-conforming' way. By putting pressure on statutory corporate tax rates, tax competition has increased the costs of such an approach (the *tax competition* argument). Tax competition has thus also increased the costs of maintaining a relatively high corporate tax rate as a safeguard for the progressive personal income tax. It has thereby spilled over into personal taxation and contributed to the downward trend in marginal tax rates on high incomes (the *spill-over argument*).

The present chapter shifts the focus on to explaining policy *differences* and hence on to explanatory factors that vary across countries. Two factors are of special importance. One is party ideology. I shall investigate the areas of income tax policy in which we can, and cannot, expect parties to make a systematic difference (the *conditional importance of politics argument*). The other factor is the overall tax burden, most of which falls on labour incomes. While tax competition has increased policymakers' incentives to flatten personal income taxes, their willingness and ability to do so partly depends on the level of taxation (the *domestic constraint argument*).

The second goal of this chapter is to explore the trade-offs resulting from tax competition on the one hand and domestic constraints on the other. I shall start with a discussion of how tax competition has stacked the deck in favour of flat income taxes and explain in more detail why advanced OECD countries have found it difficult to actually implement full-fledged flat Income Taxes (hereafter: flat taxes). Then I shall explain the main alternatives to flat taxes and their respective pros and cons. What emerges, as we shall see, is a 'trilemma' situation in which governments have to sacrifice one of three desirable policy goals. The final section of the paper reviews my selection of cases for comparative case analysis and explains how this analysis will proceed.

MARKET-CONFORMITY VERSUS INTRA-LABOUR EQUITY

In the presence of downward pressures on the level of the statutory corporate tax rate, the flat tax approach is the best way to make an income tax truly market-conforming and to minimise incentives for tax avoidance. This follows from the discussion in the previous chapter. If the top tax rate on personal income is equal to the corporate tax rate, high-income taxpayers have little incentive to shift income into the corporate sector in order to avoid taxes. A flat income tax takes the equal treatment of different types of incomes and activities to its logical extreme. Of course, I have emphasised that a full-fledged Expenditure Tax or a systematic hybrid such as an Italian-style dual income tax can also achieve a level playing field, but only if all above-normal returns to capital are taxed at the same (top) tax rate as wages. Therefore, by constraining the taxation of above-normal profits at the level of the corporation, tax competition increases the relative attractiveness of flat income taxes.

Why has no advanced OECD country moved to a flat income tax?

Despite the attractiveness of flat income taxes, we have already seen in Chapter one that no advanced OECD country has ever implemented such a tax. The reason is that policymakers continue to pursue other goals than the 'equal treatment' of different types of incomes. I believe the most important and closely related goals are revenue-raising through–and progressivity in–the taxation of wages. The basic argument is simple: a flat income tax embodies a 'lowest common denominator' approach to income taxation. A sensitive type of capital income, such as retained profits of corporations, defines the top tax rate for *all* types of income and *thereby constrains the revenue-raising potential and/or progressivity of the income tax.* In what follows I shall elaborate this argument and explain the close connections between the goals of revenue-raising and progressivity, which are components of what I call 'intra-labour equity'.

Let me first explain why, in discussing the goals of revenue-raising and progressivity, I focus on the taxation of wages. The main reason is that advanced OECD democracies simply raise most of their total tax revenues by taxing wages (*cf.* Ganghof 2000: 631). For example, Summers *et al.* (1993: 108–9) estimated ratios of labour tax revenues to total tax revenues (for the period 1980–4) of between 70 per cent in Japan and 95 per cent in Sweden. Of course, not all of this wage taxation takes the form of income taxation but this leads us to the second important observation: apart from income taxes, the other two important ways of taxing wages are (1) social security contributions and payroll taxes as well as (2) indirect consumption taxes, e.g. European-style value-added taxes.[1] These ways of taxing wages, though, are typically not progressive. Indirect consumption taxes are generally levied at a flat rate, so that the implicit wage taxation is proportional. Social security contributions are often regressive because they do not have basic tax allowances, which reduce the relative tax burden on low-income earners, but do have ceilings on contributions, which reduce the relative tax burden on high-income earners.

Given these observations, it is clear that the goals of revenue-raising through income taxation and wage tax progressivity are closely connected. For example, a flat income tax with a rate of 30 per cent can achieve substantial progressivity—by way of a large basic allowance—if the revenue target is 15 per cent of GDP, while it cannot aim at any progressivity if the revenue target is close to 30 per cent of GDP. Hence policymakers confronted with pressure to cut marginal income tax rate can defend progressivity *within the income tax* by reducing income tax revenue; if the *overall* revenue target remains unchanged, however, other taxes, which tend to be proportional or regressive taxes on wages, have to be increased in compensation. In short, the overall progressivity of wage taxation depends not only on the progressivity of wage taxation within the income tax but also on the share of labour tax *revenues* generated by the personal income tax.

Figure 4.1 helps to make the discussion more concrete. It shows the correlation between total taxation as a percentage of GDP and income taxation (corporate and personal) as a percentage of GDP for the latest year available (2002 or 2003). The figure suggests that there are only very few countries for which a revenue-neutral shift to an indirectly progressive flat tax is *impossible*. The prime example is Denmark, which has an exceptionally large income tax burden of almost 30 per cent of GDP (*cf.* Ganghof 2005b). Because Denmark has a corporate tax rate of only 28 per cent (from 2005), the situation is actually similar to the made-up example sketched above: if policymakers tried to implement a flat tax at rate of 28 per cent, they would have to give up progressivity entirely; and, because

Figure 4.1: Total tax burdens and income tax burdens in OECD countries, 2002/03

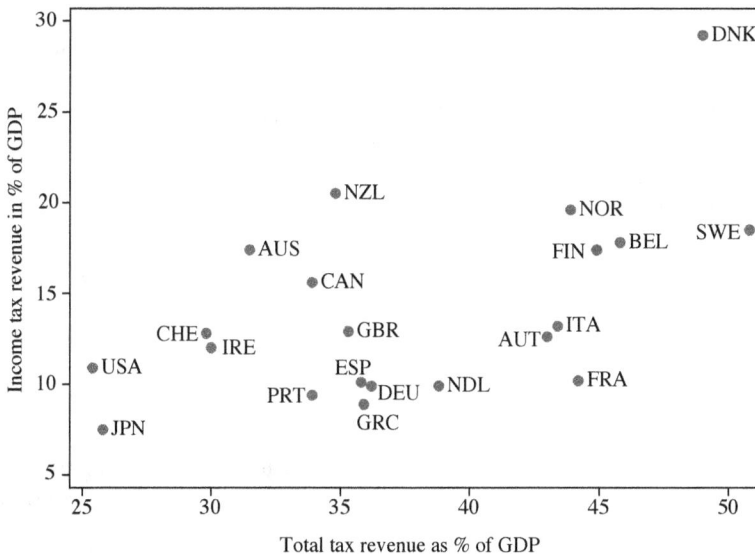

Notes: Income tax revenue includes personal and corporate taxes. Sources: OECD (2004)

tax enforcement is far from perfect, they would probably still have to accept substantial revenue losses compared to the status quo. The second exception is Ireland. While Denmark has an exceptionally large income tax burden as a percentage of GDP, Ireland has an exceptionally low corporate tax rate of only 12.5 per cent. The result is the same: like their Danish counterparts, Irish policymakers could not adopt a flat income tax at the current level of the corporate tax rate without abolishing progressivity and significantly reducing the revenue level of currently 13–14 per cent of GDP.

As emphasised, though, Denmark and Ireland are exceptions. Most countries could achieve strict equality between the corporate tax rate and the top rate on personal income without losing revenue if policymakers were willing to reduce progressivity *within the income tax*, especially in the upper half of the income scale. As Figure 4.1 shows, more than half of the countries have an income tax ratio of 15 per cent or lower and, with the exception of Ireland and Switzerland, none of these countries has a corporate tax rate below 25 per cent (see Chapter eight, Figure 8.2). Hence it is rather clear that these countries could move to an indirectly progressive flat tax of 25–30 per cent without losing revenue. Progressivity within the income tax would, of course, be reduced but, *if one focuses on the income tax in isolation*, this loss of progressivity may well seem worth accepting in return for significant gains in administrative efficiency and market-conformity. Yet policymakers *should not* focus on the income tax in isolation if they care about overall wage tax progressivity. Especially in countries with relatively high total tax burdens, such as Austria, France, Germany or the Netherlands, relatively low income tax burdens are made possible by a large tax burden on wages *outside* of the income tax (social security contributions and indirect consumption taxes). In these kinds of countries, therefore, the progressive income tax tends to assume a 'progressivity adjustment' function, and this function helps to explain why policymakers have not yet moved to flat income taxes.

The analysis of this section therefore suggests that the main domestic constraint faced by policymakers is not so much the given level of income taxation but rather the level of *total* taxation. The reason is that the difference between low-tax countries and high-tax countries is mainly accounted for by taxes on wages. If a large share of wage taxation takes the form of income taxes, the constraint is of a rather direct nature, as exemplified by the Danish case. That is, it may become impossible for policymakers to adopt a flat tax with a rate equal to that of the corporate tax rate without abolishing progressivity completely and/or losing significant amounts of revenue. In contrast, if a large share of wage taxation takes the form of social security contributions or indirect consumption taxes, the constraint arising from a high *total* tax burden is more indirect: indirectly progressive flat taxes would be rather easy to achieve but the resulting loss in progressivity would undermine the progressivity adjustment function that income taxes fulfil in such countries.

By implication, it is a considerable advantage of my selection of countries for case comparisons that these countries not only represent a large variation in income tax ratios but also in total tax ratios. As Figure 4.1 shows, the income tax ratios of these countries range from around 10 per cent in Germany to around 30 per cent in Denmark and the total tax ratios from around 30 per cent in Australia to around 50 per cent in Denmark and Sweden. This variation in tax ratios helps to avoid biased causal inferences. Of course, Figure 4.1 presents only a snapshot for the end of the period under consideration; we will see in the following chapters that income tax revenues remained remarkably stable.

The conditional relevance of party ideology and veto institutions

The previous section has completed my summary of countervailing pressures that policymakers in advanced OECD countries faced after the mid-1980s. On the one hand, there were strong competitive pressures on statutory corporate tax rates (the *tax competition argument*), which also put indirect pressure on personal income tax rates in higher incomes (the *spill-over argument*). On the other hand, the goal of 'intra-labour equity', i.e. revenue-raising from income taxation and overall wage tax progressivity, creates a countervailing pressure to keep marginal tax rates on high incomes relatively high. The combination of these pressures helps to explain why most OECD countries made drastic cuts in their corporate tax rates as well as the marginal tax rate on high personal incomes but stopped short of introducing full-fledged flat taxes.

As readers will have noticed, though, the two countervailing constraints are of a very different nature. Corporate tax competition is a constraint in a rather strict sense. Countries cannot unilaterally reduce the force of competitive pressures. In contrast, the constraint resulting from a large total tax burden (on labour incomes) is under the control of policymakers, at least in the medium term. Hence, right-wing parties may embrace the ideal-type of a flat income tax as part of a more general strategy of reducing the overall level of taxation and spending.

This difference between the two types of constraints has direct consequences for the importance of parties and veto institutions in shaping policy outputs. As explained in Chapter two, the tightness of socio-economic constraints affects the extent to which differences in party ideology or *outcomes preferences* translate into differences in *policy preferences*; and the extent of differences in policy preferences in turn determines whether veto institutions matter. More concretely, I expect partisan-institutional configurations to play very different roles in the setting of corporate tax rates and in the setting of marginal income tax rates on high wages. As to corporate tax rates, I do not follow authors like Hallerberg and Basinger (1998; Basinger and Hallerberg 2004) and Wagschal (1999a; 1999b), who expect a high number of veto players or a large ideological range between veto players to negatively affect the size of corporate tax cuts. I believe that competitive pressures were strong enough to render party ideology largely irrelevant in the setting of corporate tax rates; as a consequence, veto institutions should not generally be expected to make much of a difference.

The situation is quite different in the setting of marginal tax rates on personal income, for the reasons explained above. Here we can expect that differences in party ideology do translate into differences in policy preferences. Right parties are more likely to flatten the income tax schedule and to embrace the ideal-type of a flat income tax. Left parties are more likely to defend the progressivity and revenue-raising potential of the income tax, even if this defence comes at the cost of greater administrative complexity and less market-conformity. By extension, veto institutions are bound to play a greater role in the setting of income tax rates. Whether a higher number of veto points leads to greater or lesser cuts in top personal income tax rates depends on the details of the allocation of veto and agenda-setting power as well as the linkage between different issues. But in general we can expect—broadly in line with the hypotheses of the aforementioned authors—that a higher number of, or greater ideological distance between, veto players *reduces* the size of cuts in marginal tax rates. The reason is that a higher number of veto players, or a greater ideological range, between veto players increases the likelihood that a player who opposes tax rate cuts—most likely a left party—actually has veto power.

Before we move on, a caveat has to be noted. Some theoretical accounts suggest a relationship between party ideology and policy preferences that is directly opposed to the one just sketched. These accounts focus on the interrelationship between tax *structures* and tax *levels* and suggest that parties may choose tax structures mainly with an eye towards the resulting effect on tax levels. More concretely, they suggest that right parties have a systematic incentive to choose *less efficient* tax structures than left parties in order thereby to constrain the overall level of taxation. Hence, authors that consider Expenditure Taxes to be more efficient than Income Taxes have suggested that this efficiency difference should make *the latter* attractive for proponents of low taxation, because it implies a lower level of social transfers (Krusell *et al.* 1996). Similarly, authors who believe that flat tax rates are crucial to tax efficiency have warned advocates of a low-tax economy of embracing flat taxes, precisely because this rise in efficiency may lead to higher levels of taxation (Becker and Mulligan 1998).

While I agree that the mutual relationship between tax structure and tax levels is important (Ganghof, forthcoming), I believe that these arguments are too far detached from the real world. The reasons are manifold. For one thing, the models underlying these arguments make very restrictive assumptions. For instance, if right parties believe that there are other ways to entrench a low tax levels, the need to adopt inefficient tax structures is reduced. For another thing, I suggested in Chapter three that the relative efficiency of Income and Expenditure Taxes is subject to considerable controversy, which is unlikely to be resolved in the near future. Essentially the same is true for the efficiency of flat and progressive wage taxation (e.g. Røed and Strøm 2002). Given this uncertainty (or rather, indeterminacy) it is likely that parties adopt beliefs about efficiency that fit into their overall ideology. For example, left parties are likely to continue to embrace progressive income taxes on wages unless there is *conclusive* evidence that the equity benefits of progressivity are outweighed by their efficiency costs.

DUAL VERSUS DIFFERENTIATED INCOME TAXATION

So far I have focused on the pros and cons of radically flattened income taxes with equal (top) tax rates on corporations and personal incomes. Now I want to discuss the pros and cons of the two main alternatives to flat taxes. What these alternatives are is clear if we focus on the goal of 'market-conforming' capital income taxation.

As Figure 4.2 shows in a stylised way, policymakers have three options, depending on the extent to which they want to treat different types of income equally. If they want to treat *all* incomes equally, they will ultimately have to a choose something like a flat tax, as discussed above. That is, the marginal tax rate on wages and less sensitive capital income will be levelled down to the 'lowest common denominator' defined by the acceptable tax rate for sensitive (i.e. costly-to-tax) capital income. Alternatively, policymakers can try to make at least the taxation of *capital* income as market-conforming as possible by subjecting all of this income to a uniform, low and proportional tax rate while taxing wages more progressively and with a significantly higher top marginal tax rate. I shall refer to this model as *'Nordic-style' dual income tax*. One reason, obviously, is that it orig-inated in the Nordic countries and has been most influential there. Another reason is that I want to distinguish it from the Italian-style dual income tax discussed in

Figure 4.2: Three 'stylised' income tax systems

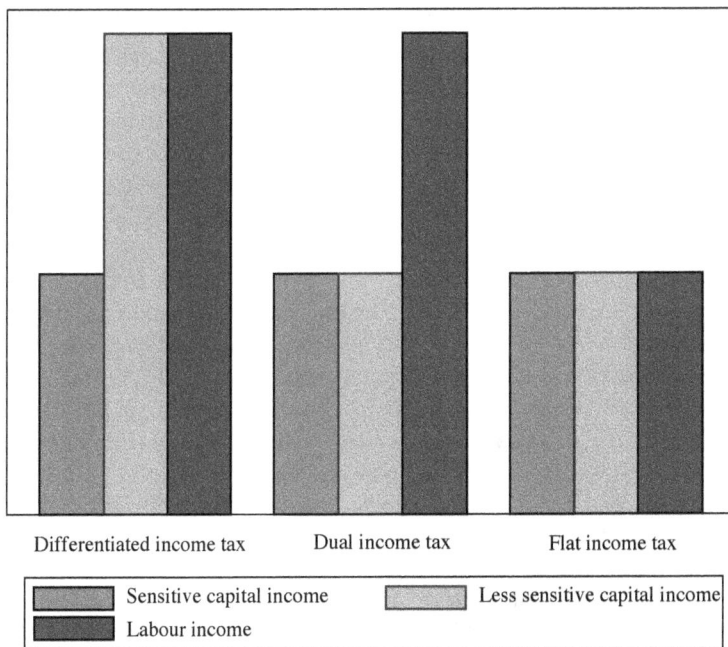

Differentiated income tax   Dual income tax   Flat income tax

Sensitive capital income   Less sensitive capital income
Labour income

Notes: See text.

Chapter three. The final option is a *differentiated income tax*. It resembles a dual income tax in that policymakers have to draw a line between a sphere of low, proportional taxation and higher, progressive taxation. However, the differentiated income tax draws this line *within* the capital income tax rather than between capital income and wages. This implies that less sensitive capital is taxed jointly with wages, and hence progressively but also that the goal of market-conformity has to be compromised. I shall discuss both alternatives to the flat tax in turn.

'Nordic-style' dual income taxation

The Nordic model of a dual income tax is characterised by a low, proportional and uniform tax rate applied to all capital income and a separate, progressive taxation of wages.[2] Dual income taxation creates administrative problems whenever capital and labour incomes accrue jointly, i.e. in unincorporated businesses (partnerships and proprietorships) and in so-called 'closely held corporations', i.e. corporations in which a large part of the shares are held by shareholders actively involved in running the business. In both cases, if the owners were allowed to determine their ratio of wage and capital income they could transform highly taxed wages into lowly taxed capital income. To counteract this type of tax arbitrage, policymakers have to implement special rules for splitting businesses' profits into labour and capital components. The standard way of doing this has already been outlined in the discussion of a modernised Income-Expenditure tax in Chapter three. Some 'normal return' on business assets is administratively determined, for example, with reference to the interest rate on long-term government bonds. This imputed return is taxed as capital income while the residual is taxed as labour income. As a result, unincorporated businesses' *above-normal* profits can be taxed together with labour, at a higher top rate than normal profits.[3] In contrast to the Italian-style dual income tax discussed in Chapter three, the splitting of profits into normal and above-normal returns is *not* applied to corporations. Instead, there is one proportional corporate tax rate for all profits, which, ideally, is identical to the proportional tax rate on personal capital income.

This tax rate equality, in combination with the abolition of graduated tax rates in capital income taxation, significantly simplifies the 'integration' of corporate and personal taxation. As discussed in Chapter three, in a world of graduated personal tax rates, reconciliation between corporate taxes already paid and the eventual individual tax liability must be done at the personal level and is subject to severe administrative constraints. In contrast, when all personal marginal tax rates on capital income are equal to one another and to the corporate rate, a form of integration between corporate and personal taxes can be accomplished by simply exempting dividends.[4] Hence, under a dual income tax, policymakers can avoid going 'through the rigmarole of taxing the dividend income with full credit for underlying corporate tax (imputation system) to achieve the same result, i.e. typically no tax on the shareholder' (Mutén 1996: 15, n. 15). Capital income taxation is greatly simplified by the flat and uniform tax rate because much of the complicated issues of measuring income can be handled at the most efficient point: the firm. The corporate tax rate becomes the 'linchpin' of capital income taxation (Cnossen 1999: 22).

Of course, everything just said about the simplification advantages of a dual income tax also applies to a flat tax (e.g. Slemrod 1997). After all, the dual income tax is a flat tax when it comes to capital income taxation. However, it tries to combine the resulting strength of simplification and market-conformity in capital taxation with the goal of revenue-raising and tax progressivity in wage taxation (intra-labour equity). That combination sets it apart from the flat income tax.[5]

What sets the dual income tax apart from a differentiated income tax is the rejection of graduated tax rates (direct progressivity) in capital income taxation. While proponents of the two alternatives to flat taxes agree that the case for flat taxation of *wages* is unconvincing or at least inconclusive, advocates of dual income taxation see a strong case for flat taxation of capital income. One reason is the great administrative simplification associated with flat tax rates, discussed above. Another, closely related, one is that progressive and high marginal tax rates on capital make it much more difficult to actually include many types of capital income into the progressive income tax. As a consequence, incentives and opportunities for tax avoidance may be greatly increased, as taxpayers try to channel more savings into lowly taxed assets (Sørensen 2001: 12; Agell *et al.* 1994). In the extreme, the effort to tax at least some capital income together with wages only generates administrative costs but not additional revenue.

Dual income taxes also have obvious drawbacks. First, they create administrative complications of their own due to the income splitting required for unincorporated businesses and closely held corporations. Second, the ability of 'Nordic-style' dual income taxes to reduce tax avoidance through income shifting is reduced by the fact that the above-normal profits of corporations are generally taxed at the same rate as normal profits.[6] Third, because the 'discrimination' against wages within the income tax becomes a matter of principle (rather than untransparent practice), the dual income tax may be difficult to sell to the electorate. Even if the reasons for giving up strict labour-capital equity are good, they may be too complex to be effective politically. Acknowledging painful trade-offs and sacrifices in public is seldom rewarded (Tetlock 2000: 242–5). Finally, if one believes that progressive taxation of some types of capital income is possible at tolerable levels of administrative costs, the dual income tax generates less revenue from capital income than a differentiated income tax, everything else being equal.

Differentiated income taxation

All of these drawbacks may lead policymakers to adopt a *differentiated income tax*, i.e. a system in which some types of capital income are taxed jointly with wages and hence progressively while other, very sensitive, types of capital income are taxed at low and proportional tax rates.

We should note at the outset that *all* real-world income taxes are, strictly speaking, differentiated income taxes. Some types of especially sensitive (i.e. costly-to-tax) capital income will always be *too* costly to be taxed as part of the general income tax system, regardless of whether this system is modelled after a flat tax or a dual income tax. In addition, because differentiation hardly qualifies as 'systematic' in public discussion, policymakers will typically try to *justify* income tax reforms as following the models of uniform or dual income taxation. It is nevertheless useful to treat differentiated income taxation as a 'model' of its own, for two reasons.

The first reason is that the models of flat or dual income taxation imply a strong emphasis on 'market-conformity' and hence uniform capital income taxation. The underlying logic is one expressed by the influential British Meade Report of the 1970s: 'There will, of course, inevitably be some special exceptions and exemptions; but it is desirable to start from some simple, reasonable, clearly understood general set of rules, from which only a limited number of very special exceptions are permitted' (Institute for Fiscal Studies 1978: 44). In contrast, proponents of differentiated income taxation adopt a more pragmatic stance, exemplified by Lawrence Summers' scepticism about the 'level playing field' rhetoric cited in Chapter three. For these proponents, the goal of equal taxation or market-conformity is just one among many others, rather than the overarching principle that should guide tax policy. If knowledge is available that certain forms of differential taxation are beneficial, proponents of differentiated income taxation want to act on that knowledge (*cf.* Murphy and Nagel 2002: Chapter eight).

The second reason why the differentiated income tax can be treated as a model of its own has to do with the important linkage between corporate and personal taxation. I have emphasised that the corporate tax rate can be seen as the 'linchpin' of capital income taxation and that under *any* income system—flat or progressive, uniform or dual—it seems highly desirable to set the corporate tax rate equal to the top rate on personal (capital) income. Therefore, differentiated income taxation as understood in this book implies first and foremost that this goal of tax rate equality is sacrificed. It implies that the corporate tax rate is well below the top rate on personal capital income and thus that some complications and/or distortions in capital income taxation are inevitable.

There are different forms of differentiated income taxes, depending on *where exactly* the line is drawn between a sphere of low and proportional taxation of capital income on the one hand and a sphere of higher and progressive taxation on the other. Certain parts of the overall playing field can still be levelled. With respect to the corporate-personal linkage, two variants are of special importance. One variant simply reduces the corporate tax rate on retained profits, while, in principle, taxing all other forms of capital income jointly with wages. Another variant tries to avoid unequal treatment of different organisational/legal forms of doing business. That is, the preferential tax rate for retained profits is also, in one way or another, granted to *unincorporated* businesses. For the sake of brevity and simplicity, I shall refer to the equal treatment of different types of businesses as *organisational neutrality* (Gordon and MacKie-Mason 1994; MacKie-Mason and Gordon 1997; Goolsbee 1998).

The reasons for choosing a differentiated income tax are rather straightforward, and the most important ones have already been discussed. Proponents of this kind of taxation are obviously unwilling to compromise the goal of 'intra-labour' equity too much. In addition, they are more willing to compromise the goal of 'market-conformity' in return for taxing at least some types of capital income progressively and jointly with wages ('capital-labour equity'). This will probably make it easier to justify differentiated taxation to the public, and it might also raise additional revenue which can be used to limit the tax burden on wages.

The trilemma of income taxation

It is rather obvious that the choice between flat, dual and differentiated income taxation constitutes a 'trilemma' in which one of three goals has to be sacrificed or at least seriously compromised (Figure 4.3).

- The ideal *flat income tax* achieves market-conformity and equal treatment of capital income and wages at the cost of reducing intra-labour equity;
- the ideal *dual income tax* reconciles market-conformity and intra-labour equity but has to give up the equal treatment of capital income and wages (capital-labour equity);
- the *differentiated income tax* reconciles intra-labour equity with a higher degree of capital-labour equity by compromising market-conformity in capital income taxation.

Three issues have to be discussed with respect this trilemma. First, it is useful to briefly review the relation between the analysis of the trilemma and the discussion of Income and Expenditure Taxation in Chapter three. One the one hand, both discussions deal with the same set of goals and hence the same basic trade-offs. The goals relate to two different notions of efficiency (efficient *differentiation* and efficient *non-differentiation*) and two different notions of equity (*intra-labour* equity and *capital-labour* equity). On the other hand, in exploring the resulting trade-offs, the two discussions have assumed different constraints. In Chapter three I have started by ignoring the constraints of tax competition and focused mainly on market-conforming types of income taxation. As a result, the option of

Figure 4.3: The trilemma of income taxation

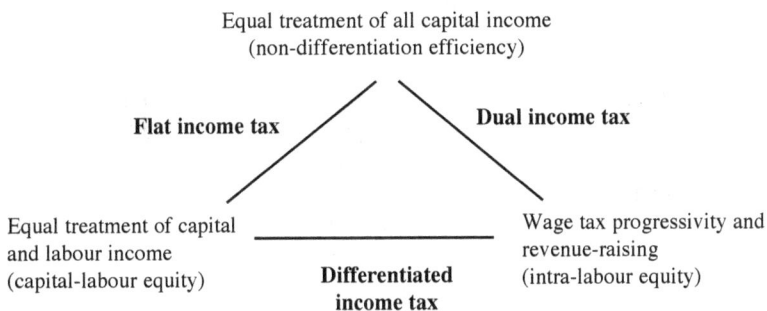

Notes: See text

differentiated income tax was not discussed as a separate 'model'. In contrast, the present discussion is based on the premise of strong competitive pressures on corporate tax rates. It has therefore ignored the theoretical option of Progressive Expenditure Taxes, which has become less attractive due to tax competition. For the same reason, the dual income tax as a systematic 'hybrid' between Income and Expenditure Taxes has only been discussed in its 'Nordic' rather than 'Italian' version, i.e. without higher taxation of above-normal profits at the corporate level. Tax competition tends to favour the Nordic version, thereby also compromising the corporation tax's safeguarding function for progressive wage taxation. As a result, under a Nordic dual income tax, high-income taxpayers tend to have higher incentives for shifting income into the corporate sector. This adds to the problems of this model and thereby increases the relative attractiveness of either flat or differentiated income taxes.

The second important issue concerns the *generality* of the trilemma. Since my discussion has focused on the policy trends in the OECD world and the role of corporate tax competition, my explication of the trilemma has also highlighted the linkage between corporate and personal income taxes. That is, the kind of 'sensitive' (costly-to-tax) income I have focused on is *retained* corporate profits, and I have treated the corporate tax rate as the lowest common denominator to which the top rate on personal (capital) income would have to fall in a flat or dual income tax. As the next chapters will show, this focus is a very useful one, because competitive pressures on corporate tax rates played a crucial role in the tax reform debates of advanced OECD countries. Yet the trilemma structure just sketched is of a much more general nature and importance. As discussed in Chapter three, there are many important types of sensitive capital income, most notably retirement savings, the returns to owner-occupied housing and capital gains. The taxation of these and other types of capital income is associated with high economic and/or administrative and/or political costs. Policymakers often perceive these types of incomes as even *more* sensitive than retained corporate profits, in the sense that a uniform (capital) income tax rate that could realistically applied to these incomes would have to even lower than a corporate tax rate that is viable in international tax competition.

Consider the example of retirement savings. Hardly any advanced OECD country treats retirement savings as they would be treated under a pure Income Tax. Instead, they are often treated as they would be under an Expenditure Tax or even more favourably, regardless of the 'official' approach to income taxation. The reasons for this extreme privileging of pension savings include the usual mixture of economic, political and administrative considerations (e.g. OECD 2001d: 40–1). Preferential taxation may increase the overall *level* of savings, influence the *structure* of savings in favour or long-term saving by households (to ensure that households are less prone to moral hazard), reduce *administrative* costs, and increase the *electorate's acceptance* of (partially) funded pension systems. However, some economists argue strongly against the preferential taxation of retirement savings:

A frequent motivation for the extreme tax privileges granted to pension saving is that policy makers wish to stimulate private saving. But if this is the basic goal, it would seem to call for a generous tax treatment of the return to all forms of private saving rather than a special privilege for a particular type of saving which mainly affects the composition rather than the overall level of saving.

(Sørensen 2001: 3)

This example underlines the general importance of the income tax trilemma. For if a uniform capital taxation that includes retirement savings must not lead to excessive economic, administrative and political costs, the uniform tax rate will likely have to be extremely low. However, this would imply drastically reduced intra-labour equity under the flat tax approach and a large 'tax rate gap' under the dual income tax approach. It is perhaps not surprising, therefore, that virtually all OECD countries opt for a differentiated income tax for pension savings. In short, the benefits of true 'market-conformity' may not be worth the costs.

The third and final issue that has to be discussed in relation to the trilemma concerns the *role of political parties*. At the end of the previous section I developed general hypotheses about the conditional role of political parties. I argued that party ideology cannot be expected to systematically influence the setting corporate tax rate—which is heavily constrained by tax competition—but that it can be expected to systematically influence the setting of top personal income tax rates, which is related to the goal of 'intra-labour equity'. Naturally, the question arises whether it is possible to formulate similarly general hypotheses about partisan effects on the choice between dual and differentiated income taxation. In my view, it isn't. Many factors influence that choice and none is strong enough to allow broad generalisations. Therefore, as far as the choice between dual and differentiated income taxation is concerned, the case evidence presented in the following three chapters is more explorative than confirmatory.

CASE SELECTION

To explore the politics of the income tax trilemma empirically, I have deliberately selected countries for which the goal of market-conformity was very important, especially in the area of business taxation. As explained in this chapter and the last, perhaps the best indicator for the importance of this goal is whether there is strict equality between the tax rate on retained corporate earnings and the (top) tax rate on personal capital income. This equality tends to be crucial for market-conformity regardless of the general approach (uniform versus dual taxation), the degree of progressivity (flat versus progressive) or the definition of the tax base (Income versus Expenditure). Selecting countries in which market-conformity was considered an important policy goal provides good conditions for getting insights into policy-maker's views of and reasoning about the income tax trilemma.

Table 4.1: Corporate-personal rate equality in selected OECD countries

	Basic model	
Tax rate equality introduced...	Uniform income taxation	Dual income taxation
... prior to increased corporate tax competition	Germany New Zealand Australia	Denmark
... as part of adjustment to tax competition		Sweden Norway Finland

Sources: See Chapters 5 through 7.

Table 4.1 provides an overview of the cases. The rows distinguish the periods in which the selected countries introduced a strict equality between (top) corporate and personal capital income tax rates: either prior to increased tax competition or as part of the country's adjustment to this competition. The columns distinguish the general approach to income taxation under which tax rate equality was achieved: uniform or dual income taxation. Based on the table, we can distinguish two sub-groups of countries:

- *'Uniform income tax' countries*: Australia, Germany and New Zealand tried to make income taxation more market-conforming before the period of increased tax competition, and as part of this effort they introduced the system of corporate-personal integration proposed by the Canadian Carter Commission (see Chapter three). They levelled out the corporate tax rate and the top personal rate and gave shareholders a full 'imputation tax credit' for the tax already paid at the corporate level. When corporate tax competition heated up, these countries faced the choice between flattening their income taxes in order to maintain tax rate equality at lower corporate tax rates (the flat tax option) and switching to dual or differentiated income taxes.

- *Dual income tax countries*: Danish policymakers introduced the rate alignment prior to the period of increased tax competition as part of a dual income tax approach. The other three Nordic countries later adopted the dual income tax approach as part of their efforts to adjust to tax competition. All four countries had to decide whether this approach was sustainable in the face of tax competition and public concerns about tax rate gap between capital and labour taxation.

CONCLUSION

This chapter has investigated basic trade-offs in income taxation as they present themselves to policymakers *given strong competitive pressures on the statutory corporate tax rates*. One goal has been to develop hypotheses about the factors that explain the setting of corporate and personal income tax rates in international comparison. The main hypotheses are as follows.

- Parties and veto institutions cannot be expected to make a difference in the setting of corporate tax rates because strong tax competition leads to a convergence of veto parties' *policy* preferences.
- Left parties can be expected to prefer higher marginal tax rates on *personal* income than right parties, including top marginal rates. By extension, the allocation of veto and agenda-setting power can also be expected to systematically affect the setting of such rates. Left parties are likely to use their institutional power to push for higher marginal tax rates on high personal incomes or at least maintain the status quo, whereas right parties are more likely to push for a flattening of personal income taxes.
- A country's total tax level (as per cent of GDP) can be expected to have a positive effect on the top personal income tax rate, either via the revenue-raising function of the income tax (larger income taxes require higher tax rates, *ceteris paribus*) or via its progressivity adjustment function (smaller income taxes in high-tax countries require greater progressivity, *ceteris paribus*).

The second goal of this chapter was to explore in more details the policy options OECD governments have had, given corporate tax competition. Three basic options were described: flat, dual and differentiated income taxation. It was shown that these three options constitute a 'trilemma' structure, in which at least one of three goals has to be sacrificed or seriously compromised. These three goals are: (1) market-conforming capital income taxation (non-differentiation efficiency); (2) equal treatment of capital and labour incomes (capital-labour equity); and (3) revenue-raising and wage tax progressivity (intra-labour equity).

The purpose of the following four chapters is to explore how policymakers dealt with this trilemma structure as well as to provide tests of the three hypotheses. The next chapter compares the tax reforms in Australia and New Zealand. Chapter six then analyses the reforms in the four Nordic countries. Chapter seven provides an in-depth analysis of tax reform in Germany. Chapter eight will then complement the qualitative comparative analysis with focused quantitative tests.

NOTES

1   Recall from Chapter three that the latter, while also taxing above-normal returns to capital, fall heavily on wages.

2   How systematically wage taxation is really *separated* from the taxation of capital income differs across the Nordic countries. See Chapter six.

3   The actual practices in dual income tax countries are diverse. We will see in Chapter six that residual income is not always and entirely taxed as 'labour income'.

4   Capital gains on corporate shares are taxed as personal capital income, with appropriate adjustments of the tax base. See Chapter six.

5   As we will see in Chapter six, dual income taxes have also been justified as *more uniform* income taxes, i.e., income taxes that treat *all* incomes equally. The argument is that *traditional* income taxes discriminate against certain types of capital income in the definition of

the tax base, most notably by making no full adjustments for inflation or by favouring human capital investments, and that the dual structure of tax rates compensates for this discrimination (Sørensen 1994; Nielsen and Sørensen 1997). While this reasoning is of some *theoretical* importance, its credibility as an actual political justification tends to be undermined by the details of how dual income taxes were implemented in the Nordic countries as well as policymakers' responses to reduced inflation rates.

6   As discussed in Chapter six, there have recently been proposals for changing the model of dual income taxation by taxing above-normal profits at the level of the shareholder.

chapter five | income tax reform in australia and new zealand

This chapter analyses the first two of the seven countries in my sample: Australia and New Zealand. These two countries provide an excellent opportunity for comparing the effects of party ideology and veto power on tax policy choices, because they are very similar with respect to important control variables. First, both countries are small and were subject to very similar competitive pressures (Schwartz 2000). Second, both had very similar tax systems. Most notably, both countries did not have broad-based value-added taxes in the mid-1980s, so that the politics of income taxation was closely intertwined with the issue of shifting the tax burden on to indirect taxes. Third, due to their common language and neighbourhood both countries were subject to the same tax policy ideas (Sandford 1993: Chapters four and five). Fourth, tax reform in both countries had a parallel sequence—a sequence that provides an excellent opportunity for isolating the effect of partisanship and veto power on income tax structure. In the mid-1980s, parallel to but unaffected by the 1986 US tax reform, both countries decided to *increase* their corporate tax rates in order to align them with their top personal rates. Yet by the time these reforms were fully implemented, they had already become obsolete; corporate tax rates had to be reduced, which forced policymakers to make a clear choice between uniform and differentiated income taxation.

NEW ZEALAND

Introducing the actors and the status quo ante
As shown in Chapter two, there existed no relevant institutional veto points in New Zealand in addition to the parliamentary majority. Before 1993 there were essentially two parties in New Zealand's parliament: Labour and National. After 1993 a number of additional parties gained seats. The names of those parties that mattered as potential members of government or legislative coalitions are displayed in Table 5.1. The table also displays for each party, where available, the average tax-vs-spend scores derived from the expert surveys of Michael Laver and his colleagues conducted in late 1980s and early 2000s (Laver and Hunt 1992; Benoit and Laver 2006).

Table 5.1: Important parliamentary parties in New Zealand, 1984–2005

Name	Abbreviation	Tax-vs-spend late 1980s	Tax-vs-spend early 2000s
Alliance (NewLabour etc.)	Allc	na	3.1
Greens	GPA	na	5.3
Progressive Coalition	PC	na	6.0
Labour	NZLP	13.8	8.6
New Zealand First	NZFP	na	11.3
United Future	UF	na	13.0
National Party	NP	11.2	14.7
ACT	ACT	na	18.1

Notes: na = non-available. Tax-v-spend scores refer to party leadership and range from 1 to 20. The Greens were part of the Alliance in 1996. 'United' renamed 'United Future' in 2000 following merger of United and Future NZ. Sources: Laver and Hunt (1992), Benoit and Laver (2006).

The most important message of Table 5.1 is that during the period when core tax policy choices were made—1987 to 1990—the Labour Party was, *de facto*, a centre-*right* party. Its tax-vs-spend score was more rightist than that of National. This picture is consistent with qualitative accounts noting that the Labour Party was captured by a small 'cabinet coterie of market-liberal reformers' (Denemark 2001: 81) that had policy preferences fundamentally 'inconsistent with its previous traditions' (Vowles 1995: 100; see also Wallis 1997). This interpretation is consistent with the fact that some leading figures of this 'coterie' later left the party and founded the Association of Consumers and Taxpayers, which developed into a right-wing political party, ACT, comparable to the anti-tax parties in Scandinavia. After 1995, the Labour Party returned to its centre-left stance on economic issues. The other parties that became important players after 1995 are the 'Alliance', the Greens (part of the Alliance in 1996) as well as the Progressives on the left, and New Zealand First as well as United Future on the right (*cf.* Miller 2005).

Table 5.2 displays New Zealand's governments in the period under consideration. Between 1984 and 1993 New Zealand was governed by stable one-party majority governments, first by the Labour Party, then, from the end of 1990 to the end of 1993, by the National Party under Prime Minister Bolger. The 1993 elections, which were held at the same time as the referendum about the reform of the electoral system, ended the era of stable one-party majority governments. Party fragmentation increased in anticipation of the new electoral system (e.g. Boston *et al.* 1996). As a result, the years of the second Bolger government, 1993–6, were characterised by political and governmental turmoil. Fortunately, because this government was happy with the basic shape of income taxation, we do not have to deal with the complications of policymaking during the 1993–6 parliamentary term in any detail. After the elections in October 1996, National continued to govern in a minimum-winning coalition with New Zealand First (NZF), first under Prime Minister Bolger, then, after a leadership coup, under Shipley. Due to a split

Table 5.2: Governments in New Zealand, 1984–2005

Begin	Prime Minister (Party)	Type	Parties	Government seats	Total seats
07.1984	Lange I (NZLP)	majority	NZLP	56	95
08.1987	Lange II (NZLP)	majority	NZLP	58	95
08.1989	Palmer (NZLP)	majority	NZLP	58	97
09.1990	Moore (NZLP)	majority	NZLP	58	97
11.1990	Bolger I (NP)	majority	NP	58	97
11.1993	Bolger II (NP)	various	NP, various	various	99
12.1996	Bolger III (NP)	majority	NP, NZFP	63	120
12.1997	Shipley I	majority	NP, NZFP	63	120
08.1998	Shipley II	minority	NP, Independents	53	120
12.1999	Clark I (NZLP)	minority	NZLP, Allc	59	120
08.2002	Clark II (NZLP)	minority	NZLP, PC	54	120

Sources: Woldendorp *et al.* (2000), Kaiser (2002), Vowles (2003).

of NZF, the Shipley government had to continue as a minority government after August 1998, with support from the ACT and United parties (Vowles 1999: 476). After the 1999 elections a centre-left minority coalition of Labour and Alliance took office, supported by the Greens (7 seats). After the 2002 elections Labour continued to govern in a coalition with the newly formed Progressives (2 seats)— led by the Alliance's former party-leader Jim Anderton—and with the parliamentary support of the centre-right United Future (8 seats) (Miller 2005: 222).

During the 1970s and early 1980s New Zealand's income tax system was exceptional in that it accounted for a large share of total taxation. In the mid-1980s corporate and personal income taxes jointly amounted to more than 70 per cent of the total tax level. The resulting income tax revenue/GDP ratio of around 23 per cent was only topped by that of Denmark (Chapter six). One main reason for the peculiar tax mix was that New Zealand does not have separate social security contributions. New Zealand had a narrowly based wholesale sales tax that generated comparatively small revenue. Partly as a result of the weak revenue-raising potential of the tax system, public deficits were very high (around 9 per cent in fiscal year 1983–4).

New Zealand's income tax system was typical for the OECD world in that it had fairly high tax rates (Figure 5.1) and a narrow tax base. In 1983, the top personal income tax rate was 66 per cent. The corporate tax rate, which had become a flat rate only in 1978, stood at 45 per cent all through the 1970s and early 1980s (Sandford 1993: 63). Widespread usage of tax expenditures had narrowed the income tax base; important types of capital incomes, e.g., the return to owner-occupied housing or capital gains, were not taxed at all; and the so-called 'classical' system of corporate taxation implied a double-taxation of dividends. Effective tax rates for companies in different sectors varied from minus 50 per cent to plus 39 per cent (Stephens 1993).

Figure 5.1: Top income tax rates and income tax revenue in New Zealand, 1980–2005

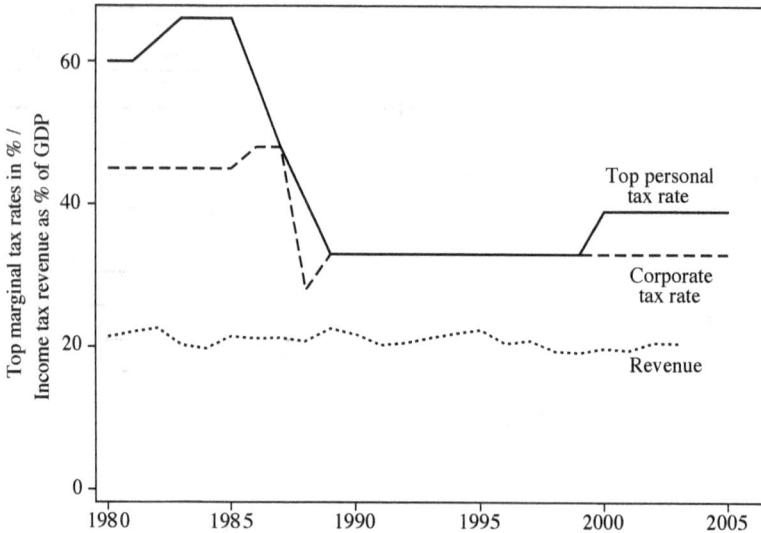

Note: Tax revenue includes corporate and personal income taxes.
Sources: See appendix.

New Zealand started its first major income tax reform in 1984, after the Labour government under Prime Minister Lange had gained office (see Table 5.2). While tax reform was an integral part of the government's program of economic restructuring, stabilisation, and liberalisation, tax reform itself was influenced neither by foreign example nor by external (competitive) pressure (Sandford 1993: 70). Instead, it was a radical effort to tackle the trade-offs in domestic income taxation. The reform was a response to several reports indicating the shortcomings of the tax system (New Zealand Planning Council 1981; McCaw 1982; Treasury 1984). They all criticised the existing (income) tax system with respect to its revenue-raising potential, as well as on efficiency and equity grounds (Stephens 1993: 46–7). The McCaw Report also stressed the need for reducing double taxation of company dividends, and rigorously scrutinizing business tax incentives (*cf.* Sandford 1993: 63).

Like these reports, the resulting tax reform, outlined in November 1984 and implemented over a period to October 1986, attempted to make income taxation more comprehensive and symmetric. A fairly broad-based Goods and Services Tax (GST), which is essentially a value-added tax, was introduced at a rate of 10 per cent. While the GST replaced a diverse range of wholesale sales taxes, it increased the overall share of all goods and services taxes (including excises) in GDP from around 8 per cent in 1985 to almost 13 per cent in 1990. This rise in consumption taxes was intended to bring down the public deficit and to create elbow room for significant cuts in marginal income tax rates. Personal income tax rates were cut across the board. The number of tax brackets was reduced from five to three and the top personal income tax rate from 66 to 48 per cent. To achieve neutrality in business taxation, the corporate tax rate was actually increased to 48 per cent and a full imputation system was introduced, which gave shareholders a full credit for the taxes already paid at the corporate level (see Figure 5.1). The corporate and personal income tax bases were broadened significantly. Most notably, fringe benefits (on the value of company cars, etc.) were included in the tax base, various tax reliefs for private (pension) savings were reduced or abolished, a five-year rebate for interest payments on first home mortgages was abolished, depreciation allowances were reduced or abolished, and a number of sectoral tax concessions were withdrawn (Sandford 1993: 53–5).

The reform process was straightforward from a veto player perspective because the government had a stable majority in parliament. There also existed a broad societal consensus that tax cuts and base broadening were balanced in a way that would increase both efficiency and equity. It was a 'model' of tax reform, with tax policy changes integrated to commence in October 1986, carefully explained to the public, with details openly changed in the policy process in response to submissions (Stephens 1993: 48).

1986 to 1999: right-wing tax reform
The nature of the reform process changed dramatically in 1987, it was 'tax reform in disarray' (Stephens 1993: 49). This change was driven by both general economic crisis and competitive pressures. The Labour Government was returned to office in August 1987 (Table 5.2). Following a stock market crash in October, the Minister of Finance announced a reduction of the corporate tax rate to an 'internationally competitive level, but not less than the personal rate' (Sandford 1993: 55). '[A]nti-avoidance measures on foreign source income became necessary with the freeing of exchange rate; and, in adopting low company income tax rates, Douglas showed his recognition of the dangers of a high rate in an international market...' (Sandford 1993: 70).

The Finance Minister also wanted to reduce the top personal rate to the corporate rate. For Douglas this was not much of a sacrifice. He was opposed to direct progressivity anyway and proposed a flat personal income tax rate of 24 per cent together with the removal of most personal tax allowances and deductions.[1] Despite the base broadening such a rate cut would have required cuts in social expenditures. Not surprisingly, therefore, the Cabinet was deeply divided over the distributional consequences of the flat tax proposal (Stephens 1993: 49, fn. 4). The proposal led to a deep political crisis, which eventually led to the Prime Minister Lange's sacking of Douglas (Chapman 1992). Lange won the fight with the Finance Minister and the top personal rate descended only to 33 per cent (in 1989). Although the additional 33 per cent bracket enabled health care and housing benefits to remain uncut, there was a remaining element of deficit built into the tax cuts that required a rise in the Goods and Services Tax from 10 per cent to 12.5 per cent in 1989. The corporate tax rate temporarily fell to 28 per cent in 1988, but was realigned with the top personal rate in 1999 (Figure 5.1).

The tax reform had far-reaching consequences for New Zealand's tax-and-transfer system (Toder and Himes 1992: 350–1). First, while average tax rates (net of benefits) increased for most groups in the population, including some who received substantial cuts in marginal tax rates, very high income earners, who benefited from the halving of the top marginal income tax rate, were an exception. Second, changes in marginal rates on labour income were similarly distributed: marginal rates remained constant or increased slightly for most groups in the population because the small reduction they received in the statutory marginal rate on cash income was more than offset by the effects of GST and fringe benefit taxation; marginal rates confronted by high-income employees on wage and salary income and taxable interest income 'declined dramatically' (Toder and Himes 1992: 351); finally, marginal rates increased for many low-income families because of the greater reliance on a means-testing or targeting approach towards social security (see also Quiggin 1998a; see also Boston 1999: 9; 1999). As Toder and Himes (1992: 351) summarise: 'Thus, while the decline in the top marginal tax rate substantially increased the incentives to work at the top end of the income distribution, marginal tax rates affecting labour supply did not decline for most of the population.'

At the end of the 1980s, New Zealand probably had the most 'comprehensive' income tax system in the OECD world. Even private pension savings, strongly privileged in most OECD countries, had been subjected to standard income tax treatment. Some exceptions remained nevertheless. New Zealand did not have a capital gains tax, and it did not tax the imputed return to owner-occupied housing—even though housing accounts for more than 70 per cent of total savings of New Zealand's households (TaxReview 2001: 29).[2] These two types of income were considered too sensitive to be taxed under the general tax rate schedule.

Given the 'neo-liberal' profile of Labour's income tax reforms, there was little left to do for the National Party. In 1990, Labour was voted out of office and replaced by National, which governed for the next nine years, first alone and later mainly in coalition with the centrist New Zealand First. National continued, and partly intensified, the market liberalisation begun by Labour, but left the basic features of the income tax system unchanged.

1999 to 2005: centre-left rebalancing

The 1999 election campaign was characterised by the more traditional left-right cleavage on tax policy that had previously been absent in New Zealand (Vowles 2002: 136). The remodelled Labour party under Helen Clark promised to raise the tax rate for the top 5 per cent of income earners in order to pay for better social and health services and a higher level of social assistance. In contrast, the National Party under Jenny Shipley promised to reduce income taxes in general.

Labour won and formed a coalition with the Alliance, which saw itself as the true Labour party and preferred a steeply progressive tax regime (Miller 2005: 40). While the government was in a minority position, it received stable support from another left-wing party, the Greens. Tax experts and the Treasury were critical of the tax increase, because they feared downstream problems and wanted to retain a strict equality of the corporate and top personal tax rates (Whitehead and Oliver 1999). Nevertheless, the government was committed and introduced a new 39 per cent top personal rate on incomes of NZ$ 60,000 in 2000 (Figure 5.1). This move was estimated to indeed affect only 5 per cent of taxpayers but the money raised was seen as essential to the government's social and economic spending program. Given the left-wing majority in parliament, it was passed without problems.

With revenue-raising and progressivity re-established as important policy goals of the Labour Party, the trade-off between tax rate symmetry (equal corporate and top personal tax rates) and progressivity resurfaced. For this reason among others, the government appointed an expert committee to review the tax system from a technical perspective. The committee's mandate was very broad but restricted to the structure (as opposed to the level) of taxation. There was a tacit understanding that the review team would not propose a flat income tax, as Douglas had done in the 1980s. Finance Minister Michael Cullen tried to forestall concerns about a new flat tax debate by pointing to the Nordic dual income tax systems as an alternative reform model. The OECD had previously mentioned the dual income tax model as the most obvious comprehensive alternative to a further flattening of the income tax:

> Maintaining a comprehensive tax system in the long term probably requires base broadening in the personal tax system.... This would allow tax rates to be sufficiently low to avoid capital flight and excessive emigration of highly skilled labour.... Otherwise, a dual tax system may be the better option since it would not impose the same straight-jacket on the top personal rate (on wage income).
>
> (OECD 2000d: 163–4)

Yet the committee did not even consider a dual income tax. It was convinced of the superiority of proportional income taxation and noted that the fiscally-neutral proportional tax was 25 per cent. As a purely political concession it nevertheless suggested a two-tier system with a top rate of 33 per cent. It argued that the 39 per cent rate sends 'a negative signal to mobile, high-skilled taxpayers, and also creates a gap between top personal rates and the tax rate on entities such as companies' (TaxReview 2001: 58). While the committee also noted concerns about New Zealand's statutory and average effective corporate tax rate being too high, especially with respect to the Australian rate of 30 per cent (from 2002), it proposed to move back to and maintain a rate alignment at 33 per cent (TaxReview 2001: 66–7). Not surprisingly, while the right-wing opposition parties ACT and National saw the report as a big victory for them and an embarrassment for the government, the Finance Minister was reserved about the report's recommendations, pointing out that Labour favoured a more progressive regime. As a result, the Labour-led minority coalitions did not make basic structural changes in the income tax system.

In the run-up to the 2005 general elections, the basic trade-off between progressivity and symmetry resurfaced. There was widespread agreement on a further cut in the corporate tax rate to 30 per cent in order to match the Australian rate. Even the left-wing coalition partner of Labour (after 2002), the Progressive Party, embraced this policy. The political conflict once more concerned *personal* income taxation. While the Alliance, which did not win any seats in 2002, proposed to move back to a top rate as high as 54 per cent (for income over NZ$100,000), ACT envisioned a top rate of 25 per cent. Of course, the more realistic options were in between. The coalition parties want to maintain the status quo rate of 39 per cent. Their main antagonist, the National Party, had the hardest time committing to a policy stance. In the past it had repeatedly embraced the goal of reducing the top personal rate to the corporate rate as well as the medium-term target of 25 per cent for both rates. With the 2005 election approaching, however, it became increasingly unclear whether the party would really cut the top personal rate or whether they would give priority to tax relief for people in the middle-income brackets. The latter option was chosen by the right-leaning parties in Australia, which probably left its mark on the discussions in New Zealand. It is to the Australian experience that we now turn.

AUSTRALIA

Introducing the actors and the status quo ante

As discussed in Chapter two, Australia differs from New Zealand in that the government faces a Senate as an additional institutional veto player. The government usually does not command a majority in the Senate, which is elected under a proportional (single transferable vote) system. As a result, governments have to seek the support of minor parties and independents.

Table 5.3 lists those parties — together with their tax-*vs*-spend scores — that either gained representation in the House of Representatives or were potential support parties in the Senate during the period under consideration. The two major parties are the Australian Labor Party on the one hand and the Liberal Party on the other (Singleton *et al.* 2000: 261).[3] The third party that has had continuous representation in the House of Representatives since 1919 is the National Party (formerly Country Party). This party is a 'faithful ally' (Lijphart 1994: 129) and permanent coalition partner of the Liberal Party. When these two parties are in office, they are often referred to as 'the Coalition'. Since both parties limit policy differences to the party room and have had rather similar tax policy preferences, it is not very important whether they are treated as one party or two parties. The important minor parties in the Senate are the Australian Democrats, the Greens, and Pauline Hanson's One Nation, a populist, right-wing and anti-immigrants party.

Table 5.4 summarises the composition of government as well as its seat share in the Senate in the period under consideration. Until early 1996 Australia was governed by the Labor Party, which lacked a majority in the Senate. In 1996 Labor

Table 5.3: Important parliamentary parties in Australia, 1984–2005

Name	Abbreviation	Tax-vs-spend late 1980s	Tax-vs-spend early 2000s
(Australian) Greens	Greens	na	3.5
Australian Democrats	AD	7.7	7.4
Australian Labor Party	ALP	10.1	8.7
(Pauline Hanson's) One Nation	ON	na	11.1
National Party of Australia	NP	14.4	12.9
Liberal Party (of Australia)	LP	15.3	17.0

Notes: na = non-available. Tax-vs-spend scores refer to party leadership and range from 1 to 20.
Sources: Laver and Hunt (1992), Benoit and Laver (2006).

was replaced by the Coalition, which was in a stronger position in the Senate but also fell short of a majority. Only in 2004 did a re-elected Coalition government win a Senate majority. In the area of tax reform, the most important minor party was the Australian Democrats. Both the Greens and the Democrats were to the left of the major parties. Independents alone held the balance of power between 1996 and 1998 but no major tax reform was passed in this period.

Australia's income and total tax burden in the mid-1980s was smaller than in New Zealand. The total tax/GDP ratio was slightly below 30 per cent (compared to 33 per cent), the corporate and personal income tax/GDP ratio around 16 per cent (compared to 23 per cent). The main structural defects—high tax rates, narrow base—were nevertheless the same, as were the resulting policy debates. A Treasury official spoke of the 'Australian symptoms of the international disease' (Evans 1988: 16). The situation was compounded by the absence of a comprehensive indirect consumption tax (Porter and Trengove 1990: 57).

Table 5.4: Governments in Australia, 1984–2005

Begin	Prime Minister (Party)	Type	Parties	Government seat share in Senate	Senate total
13.12.1984	Hawke II (ALP)	majority	ALP	34	76
22.07.1987	Hawke III (ALP)	majority	ALP	32	76
03.04.1990	Hawke IV (ALP)	majority	ALP	32	76
27.12.1991	Keating I (ALP)	majority	ALP	32	76
24.03.1993	Keating II (ALP)	majority	ALP	29	76
11.03.1996	Howard I (LP)	majority	LP, NP	37	76
21.10.1998	Howard II (LP)	majority	LP, NP	35	76
26.11.2001	Howard III (LP)	majority	LP, NP	35	76
09.10.2004	Howard IV (LP)	majority	LP, NP	39	76

Sources: Woldendorp et al. (2000), Kaiser (2002), Mackerras (2002).

One core concern of policymakers was the corporate tax system. Australia operated a 'classical' system that taxed distributed corporate profits twice (at least those
not flowing to tax-exempt shareholders): at the level of the corporation and once
more in the hands of the shareholder. Tax experts and policymakers believed that
this system created serious economic distortions (e.g., Evans 1988: 17), for it lacked
neutrality between different entity structures (incorporated versus unincorporated
businesses) and between different types of finance (debt versus equity). Indeed, with
a corporate tax rate of 46 per cent and a top personal rate of 60 per cent (Figure
5.2), distributed corporate profits were taxed more heavily than any labour income:
for example, a shareholder on the highest marginal income tax rate faced a total tax
burden of up to 78 per cent on distributed dividends: 46 per cent at the corporate
level plus up to 32 per cent at the personal level ([1–0.46] * 0.60).

These concerns about the absence of neutrality in business taxation were to
a large extent motivated by the potential for tax avoidance. Tax avoidance was
generally an important issue in Australia after avoidance-friendly judgments of
the High Court had facilitated the rise of a huge tax avoidance industry in the
1970s (Levi 1988: Chapter seven; Quiggin 1998b: 7). The differentiation of tax
rates provided strong incentives to avoid taxes by shifting taxable income into the
'sectors' of lenient taxation, opportunities that were particularly numerous prior
to the capital gains tax reforms of 1985 (Vann 1997: 16–17).

Figure 5.2: Top income tax rates and income tax revenue in Australia, 1980–2005

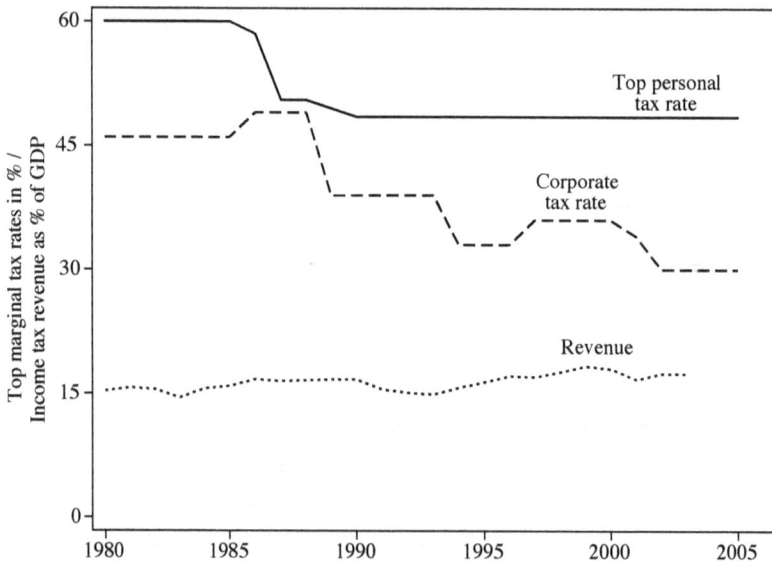

Notes: Tax revenue includes corporate and personal income taxes. Top personal income tax
rate includes Medicare levy (see appendix).
Sources: See appendix.

Reflecting these concerns, the Hawke Labor Government embraced the cause of tax reform in 1984, releasing a Draft White Paper in 1985. The basic features of this initiative so far as direct taxation was concerned included broadening the income tax base through the inclusion of realised capital gains and income taken as fringe benefits, while reducing the top personal income tax rate from 60 to 49 per cent. Later in 1985 it was announced that the classical corporate tax system would be replaced with a 'full imputation system', which gave shareholders a tax credit for taxes paid at the level of the corporation. A significant feature of the reform was that it increased the corporate rate in order to align it with the reduced top personal rate. The rationale of this symmetric imputation system was that even for taxpayers in the top income tax bracket there was no tax-incentive to adopt a particular entity structure or to retain profits that would otherwise be distributed. The system was therefore regarded as a major achievement that set Australia apart from almost all other OECD countries (Evans 1988). While the new corporate tax regime involved increasing the statutory rate from 46 to 49 per cent, business was generally supportive of the proposal on the basis that ending double taxation was expected to reduce net revenue yield by approximately four per cent (Keating and Dixon 1989: 39).

It is also important to note that these reforms did not aim to completely remove investment incentives from the corporate tax base. With respect to the accelerated depreciation of investment in particular, the government argued that it was necessary to provide inflation-adjustment (Porter and Trengove 1990: 66; Jones 1993: 60). There was no intention at that point to move toward a regime of 'real economic depreciation'.

The Labor government had no problem ensuring the passage of the 1985 reform bill in the Senate. The important player in the Senate was the Australian Democrats, whose policy preferences were similar to those of the government. The changes in the tax structure were seen as beneficial for both equality and efficiency. Negotiations between the government and the Democrats only led to minor concessions, mainly affecting capital gains tax and an anti avoidance identity card issue (Sandford 1993: 85; Eccleston 2004: Chapter four).

As part of its ambitious reform agenda of the mid-1980s the Hawke Government had planned to further reduce marginal and average income tax rates by shifting the tax mix onto indirect taxes. Treasurer Keating was determined to introduce a broad-based 12.5 per cent retail sales tax, but the Government failed to win support for broad-based consumption tax and was forced to abandon this proposal (Eccleston 2004). This failure had significant ramifications for tax reform between 1985 and 1998. More specifically, by restricting the growth of the indirect tax base it made the revenue-raising function of the income tax base (both corporate and personal) more important and thus income tax cuts more difficult to achieve.

1986 to 1996: centre-left tax reform

The reforms announced in September 1985 had not even been implemented when Treasury experts and policymakers expressed concerns about the increasing pressure of tax competition. Initially, there was a hope that foreign corporate investors would carefully assess the overall corporate tax system and the effective level of taxation rather than focus on the high statutory 49 per cent rate (Evans 1988: 30–7), but bureaucrats and policymakers clearly understood the mechanisms of tax competition and anticipated future tax cuts.

> At present there is a major incentive for resident corporations to maximize their taxable deductions in Australia while minimizing reported income. Income may instead be recognized in a low-tax country so that the total tax liability can be minimized on a worldwide basis, with the major loser being the Australian revenue. My understanding is that the recent reductions of the US and UK corporate tax rates have raised concerns in other countries that this type of practice will become widespread. (...) The only effective reaction seems to be for other countries to follow the lead of the United States by lowering their corporate tax rates through a process of base broadening.
>
> (Evans 1988: 30–7)

The US reform and its repercussions thus changed actors' policy preferences. Partly as a result, tax reform continued to play an important role in the campaigns for the 1987 federal elections. This election returned Labor into office. Since then there has been a reasonable consensus across partisan lines that the corporate tax rate needs to be competitive. After the 1987 federal election, the Labor government cut the rate to 39 per cent (Figure 5.2). Given the government's budgetary and macroeconomic policy goals, revenue-neutrality was essential. Hence, the only way to achieve a competitive corporate tax rate was to broaden the corporate tax base. Under the prevailing circumstances the government had no alternative other than to wind back existing accelerated depreciation provisions. Given that these provisions had historically been justified as implicit inflation adjustment, removing depreciation provisions and embracing a 'real economic depreciation' regime should have been associated with the indexation of the tax base. Yet given the costs of establishing real economic depreciation, the Treasurer now argued that cuts in depreciation allowances were a trade-off to fund a lower corporate tax rate (Porter and Trengove 1990: 66; Jones 1993: 60). It thus appears that the 1988 cuts to accelerated depreciation allowances were not motivated by the policy preferences of domestic actors but were necessitated by international tax competition. '[T]he driving force behind the abolition of 5/3 [i.e. accelerated] depreciation has been the perceived need to reduce the company tax rate of 49 per cent in line with recent reductions in corporate tax rates overseas' (Head 1989: 13).

That the cuts in corporate tax allowances did not reflect fundamentally changed beliefs about the usefulness of these allowances also showed in 1993, when the Labor Party, confronting a persistent recession and waning electoral support,

increased corporate tax allowances again in order to stimulate domestic investment (Sandford 1993: 105; Chennells and Griffith 1997: 104–6). These increased
concessions were combined with a further cut in the corporate tax rate to 33 per
cent, resulting in a significant reduction of corporate tax revenue. In the face of
persistent budget deficits such an approach was not sustainable and, in 1996, the
corporate tax rate was increased to 36 per cent while depreciation allowances were
either maintained or increased (Hobson 2003: 11).

Tax competition on statutory corporate tax rates also had an indirect effect on
the *personal* income tax. The government now faced the choice between cutting
the top personal income tax rate in line with the corporate rate or abandoning the
goal of equal top tax rates in order to defend the progressivity and revenue-raising
potential of the income tax system. As we have seen above, The Labor government's more neo-liberal counterparts in New Zealand chose the first option and
reduced the top personal rate to 33 per cent, thereby constraining public spending and delivering the greatest cuts to the well-off. For the Hawke Government,
this option was out of the question. Not only would it have been difficult to win
support for regressive tax cuts among the ALP's rank and file membership and
in the Senate but such cuts would also have contradicted Labor's fiscal priorities:
to maintain a balanced budget and the progressivity of the income tax base (*cf.*
Head 1989). As a result, the government had little choice other than to implement
an isolated cut in the corporate tax rate and accept a widening gap between the
corporate and the top personal income tax rate. As shown in Figure 5.2, the only
reduction in the highest income tax rate was from 49 to 47 per cent in 1991 (48.5
per cent including a Medicare levy introduced in 1986 as part of the income tax)
where it has remained since. Various changes were made to the intermediate rates
and tax thresholds but the detail owed more to wages policy than to structural tax
reform (Sandford 1993: 81, 103–5).

Getting the Democrats' approval of an isolated corporate tax cut was once
more no problem, because their policy preferences were not far apart from those
of the government. The Democrats considered a competitive corporate tax rate to
be a necessity and they clearly valued revenue-neutrality and progressivity higher
than the 'technical' goal of tax rate symmetry. Bicameral politics could have been
different if the Liberal-National coalition had controlled the Senate majority. This
majority could then have used its veto power to make additional cuts in personal
income tax rates conditional upon cuts in the top personal rate—just like the
Bundesrat majority in Germany did in the late 1990s (Chapter eight).

1996 to 2005: centre-right rebalancing
The time of the Coalition came in 1996, when Labor lost the 1996 general elections to a Coalition government under the leadership of Prime Minister John
Howard and Treasurer Peter Costello (Table 5.4). Tax reform was a non-issue in
the election campaign. The Coalition specifically ruled out a Goods and Services
Tax. Howard said: 'It's dead. Never ever. It's dead' (Mackerras and McAllister
1999: 323). This 'never ever' stance was due to the lesson learned in the 1993

federal elections. In 1993 the Labor party had 'orchestrated a sophisticated scare campaign' (Mackerras and McAllister 1999: 323) against introducing GST, a campaign that significantly contributed to the Liberals' loss of what had been portrayed as an 'unlosable' election.

Without additional GST revenues, however, the government had little elbow room for income tax cuts. During its time in opposition, the Coalition parties had planned to reduce tax rates on high incomes and thus to reduce the tax rate gap. In the *Fightback!* proposal of 1991, the Liberals had proposed to reduce the top personal rate from 47 to 42 per cent and to increase the respective income threshold from A$50,000 to A$75,000. The intermediate marginal rate was to fall from 46 to 36 per cent for those in the A$50,000–75,000 bracket, and the corporate tax rate was to be increased to at least restore the corporate-personal rate alignment at this intermediate level (Quiggin 1992; Eccleston 2004). Given limited elbow room, though, the central features of the income tax rate schedule remained unchanged during the Howard government's first term.

The re-established tax rate gap between corporate and top personal rate was nevertheless an issue, because it had the anticipated adverse consequences. The increased tax rate gap served to 'reintroduce some of the worst distortions and inequities of the classical system of company tax which dividend imputation was supposed to eliminate' (Head and Krever 1997: xxix). It created serious new problems of tax avoidance with the use of private company structures to shelter the investment portfolios of the wealthy and the labour incomes of self-employed professionals and consultants (for details and data, see Quiggin 1998b: 35; Ganghof and Eccleston 2004: 528).

In 1997 the government, desperately trying to establish its economic reform credentials, championed the cause of tax reform, with a Goods and Services Tax as its centrepiece (Eccleston 2004). While the decision was largely a response to pressures from business and industry for comprehensive tax reform, the need for further income tax cuts certainly played a role as well. The objective was to broaden and modernise Australia's consumption tax base and to use some of this revenue to finance cuts in personal income tax rates. This GST-plus-income-tax-cut package was referred to as 'A New Tax System' (ANTS). With respect to income tax rates, the Coalition pursued a moderated strategy compared to the *Fightback!* proposal. Most importantly, it resisted reducing the top marginal tax rate from 47 per cent but wanted to align the intermediate personal rate (which would apply to 80 per cent of taxpayers) with the corporate rate of 30 per cent (Harris 1999: 252; Kobetsky 2000: 73). That the Coalition stepped back from its earlier proposal to reduce the top rate can be explained in three related ways. First, the Howard Government certainly *anticipated* that it would be difficult to win a Senate majority for such cuts. Second, the government was acutely aware of the electorate's sensitivity to the overall distributional impact of its entire tax reform agenda. This is because income tax cuts were inexorably linked to the very contentious introduction of the GST. Since a major complaint about the GST was its regressive effect on the tax system (Eccleston 2004), it was certainly prudent for the

Coalition to postpone further cuts in income tax rates until after the introduction of GST was completed. Finally, even if one neglects the GST issue, it is likely that many in the Coalition camp were worried that large tax cuts for the very well-off would give the government too rightist a profile and thus alienate the middle classes.[4]

In addition to 'A New Tax System', the government pursued a business tax reform that included further cuts in the corporate tax rate. The more technical parts of the reform were prepared by the so-called Ralph Committee (Review of Business Taxation 1999). Business tax reform and ANTS were distinct but closely connected. Most notably, the government constantly threatened that if GST was not implemented then the corporate income tax rate could not be further reduced (Eccleston 2004).

In October 1998, the government called elections, earlier than required under the constitution, thereby asking the voters for an explicit electoral mandate for introducing a GST. The election result was a very poor vote for the government in both houses of parliament. Yet the majoritarian electoral system translated less than 40 per cent of the votes into a House majority of 12 seats and returned the government to office. Despite the poor vote, the Coalition interpreted the election as giving it a clear mandate.

The next hurdle for the government's tax reform plans was the Senate. Welfare groups like ACOSS (Australian Council of Social Service) made the criticism that Howard's proposals would help rich people and leave those on lower incomes worse off; but they were in favour of a modified GST (*Economist* 22.8.1998). In contrast, the Labor Party as the major opposition party remained implacably opposed to the GST and argued that over half of the government's proposed income-tax cuts would benefit the top one-fifth of earners. The government therefore needed the support of minor parties or independent senators. Initially, the government hoped to circumvent negotiations with the Democrats. While the October 1998 election resulted in a loss of two Senate seats (Table 5.4), the new Senators would not take their seats before July 1999 (Mackerras and McAllister 1999: 323–4). Hence, the government could still rely on its 'old' 37 Senate seats, only two seats short of a majority. In addition, the government was supported by a disgraced former Labor senator, Mal Colston, who had been convicted of fraud but still held a seat in the Senate.

After Colston agreed to support tax legislation in return for extra funding for his home state of Queensland, the Coalition only needed the support of one independent Senator, Brian Harradine. In May 1999, though, after much thought, Mr. Harradine decided he would vote against the legislation—a decision that threw the government into turmoil (Quiggin 1999). In theory, the government could have provoked a double dissolution election, hoping to change the composition of the Senate. In practice, however, the Coalition itself would have been unlikely to survive such an election because political support for the Coalition had weakened considerably since 1998—partly as a result of the Senate's critical inquiry into the government's tax package (Eccleston 2004). Harradine's rejection of the tax reform package thus established the Democrats as a veto player. They had previously made it known that they would not entertain a GST unless basic food was free of the tax, there was a greater compensation package for the disadvantaged, and the income tax reductions for the wealthy were reduced (Ferrers 2000: 31).

Detailed and protracted negotiations extended for more than a week until the government struck a deal with the Australian Democrats in the Senate, so that the new tax system could take effect from July 2000.[5] In the present context, the most important concessions made to the Democrats were to increase the threshold for the top personal income tax rate only to A$60,000 (instead of the originally envisaged A$75,000) and to establish an intermediate rate of 42 per cent (instead of 40 per cent) for those in the $50,000–60,000 bracket.[6] Altogether, personal income taxes were cut by A$12 billion per annum. As part of the wider agreement on tax reform, with GST as the central pillar, the Australian Democrats also agreed to reducing the corporate tax rate from 36 to 30 per cent (effective July 2001). Democrats embraced the goal of a lower company tax in return for an investigation of the possibility of instituting a 20 per cent minimum corporate tax rate (Head 1999).

The further cut in the corporate tax rate was a testimony to strong (perceived) competitive pressure (*cf.* Ganghof and Eccleston 2004). From a domestic perspective, a further corporate tax cut was seen as a problem, not a solution. One problem was that, given budget constraints, the cut would have to be funded by a further worsening of depreciation rules. Hence there was a trade-off between a lower tax rate and quicker depreciation. The Ralph committee found this trade-off to be the 'most difficult of all', one that demanded a 'judgment call' (Review of Business Taxation 1999: 24–5). The reason was that it continued to embrace accelerated depreciation as an important policy tool. The second problem of a lower corporate tax rate that worried the Ralph Committee was the implied rise in the tax rate gap by 6 percentage points (Harris 1999: 252). From a domestic perspective, given the distributional and political problems of cutting the top personal rate, it would have been rational to *increase* the corporate rate. Given tax competition, however, this was out of the question (Harris 1999: 251; Ferrers 2000: 32). The corporate had to fall in order to 'make the headline rate of corporate tax internationally competitive, both in terms of the Asia Pacific region and compared to the corporate tax rate operating in capital exporting countries' (Review of Business Taxation 1999: 425). Hence the depreciation of business assets had to be further decelerated (except for small business) and the tax rate gap had to increase.

After the GST deal, the voices within the Coalition that wanted to do something about the tax rate gap, preferably by reducing the top personal income tax rates, did not soften (Ganghof and Eccleston 2004: 529). However, partly in order to not give the opposition cheap political opportunities, the government did not cut the top personal rate. Instead, it decided to continue the policy of increasing the income thresholds for upper tax brackets in order to decrease the percentage of taxpayers facing a marginal personal tax rate higher than the corporate rate of 30 per cent. This was possible despite the explicit disagreement of the ALP and the

Democrats because the threshold increases were passed as part of the annual budgets and because there is a norm in Australian politics against the Senate majority blocking supply (Young 1999; Ganghof and Bräuninger 2006). In addition, as a result of the 2004 Senate elections, the Coalition parties had a majority in the Senate from July 2005. In the 2005–6 budget bill the government raised the 42 per cent threshold to A$70,001 from July 2006 and the 47 (48.5) per cent threshold to A$125,001. This implied that the percentage of taxpayers facing the top marginal tax rate fell to three.[7]

In sum, Australia displays the two principal consequences of corporate tax competition at the same time. On the one hand, this competition led to a tax rate gap of 17 per cent (18.5 per cent if the Medicare levy is included), as compared to a zero (1.5) per cent gap in 1988 (Figure 5.2). On the other hand, corporate tax competition nevertheless spilled over into personal income taxation and contributed to cuts in the marginal tax rates of middle-higher income earners. Australia differs from New Zealand—and the other countries covered in this study—in that the political right increased the income threshold for the top income tax rate rather than decreasing the rate. However, there is significant pressure from within the government to cut the top rate to 40 or even 30 per cent, and Prime Minister Howard has indeed expressed his commitment to further cuts in the top rate if the budgetary situation allows this (*The Australian* 26.8.2005).

CONCLUSION

My comparison of Australia and New Zealand supports the explanation advanced in Chapters three and four. First, corporate tax competition was clearly of major importance. Second, tax policy choices were influenced by the interaction of party ideology, economic constraints, and veto power in a rather straightforward manner. The competitive imperative of corporate tax cuts was so strong that neither party ideology nor the number of veto players significantly retarded or reduced corporate tax cuts. However, partisan ideology and veto players did shape how governments reacted to the multiple trade-offs in income taxation. In New Zealand, ideologically 'compact' right-wing governments moved towards a flat income tax with significantly reduced progressivity, while the subsequent left government shifted the balance back towards more progressivity and less 'neutrality' in capital income taxation (differentiated income taxation). In Australia, ideologically compact governments both on the centre-left and the centre-right sacrificed 'neutrality' between corporations and non-corporations to some extent but the degree of income tax progressivity was clearly influenced by the partisan 'centre of gravity'. Most notably, the Australian Democrats used their influence in the Senate to defend the goals of revenue-raising and progressivity.

In both countries, the normative attachment to the idea of uniform income taxation was so strong that the actual choice was between flat and differentiated income taxation. Only in recent years has the dual income tax model received some attention, but without being considered an actual reform option. The next chapter analyses the Nordic countries, where this model was invented and in which it has played a crucial role.

NOTES

1 The very low level of 24 per cent had no competitiveness rationale. It is well established in the literature on international taxation and tax competition that a domestic corporate tax rate much lower than that in the relevant foreign countries may stimulate little additional inward investment but result in a transfer of tax revenues to foreign countries. The reason is that foreign investors would receive a tax credit against their foreign tax liability for tax already paid in the source country, in this case New Zealand. Thus, if New Zealand's tax rate was much below that of foreign countries, foreign investors would simply pay a larger share of their overall tax burden to their home country rather than to New Zealand. The treasuries of foreign countries would capture much of the benefit of a lower corporate tax rate in New Zealand. The New Zealand Treasury (1987) used precisely this argument to try to persuade the Finance Minister of a corporate tax rate of 35 rather than 23–4 per cent.

2 Note, however, that New Zealand denies a deduction for mortgage interest.

3 To differentiate itself from the British Labour Party the ALP uses the American spelling.

4 Hobson (2003: 57) argues that the aforementioned tax avoidance strategies employed by high-income earners, which were facilitated by the tax rate gap, contributed to 'middle income taxpayer revolts', which in turn contributed to the Coalition government's tax reform agenda.

5 The tax package included a number of other features, including lower marginal effective tax rates for low-income working families (OECD 2000b: 121–3; 2001b: 70–73, 181).

6 In addition, basic food was to be exempted from GST, pension beneficiaries' compensation was increased and a diesel fuel rebate (except for farmers) was reduced (Ferrers 2000: 31). In the 2002–3 budget, the income thresholds were increased to A$52,000 and A$62,000, respectively.

7 Note that the 2005–6 budget was passed *before* the government controlled a Senate majority and that the ALP in this case decided to vote against the income tax cuts and propose their own, which emphasised cuts to lower-middle income earners. However, the Democrats supported the budget, again despite their own disagreement with the tax cuts.

chapter six | income tax reform in scandinavia[1]

This chapter compares the tax reform experiences of Denmark, Finland, Norway and Sweden. On the one hand, these countries resemble each other in many ways, including important aspects of their tax systems, and policy ideas flow freely between them. As a result, all four countries have experimented with the 'Nordic-style' dual income tax. On the other hand, during the core period under consideration (mid 1980s to early 2000s) there was significant variation in partisan-institutional configurations as well as in income and total tax burdens (see Chapter four), which helps us to draw causal conclusions.

The sequence of the four case studies is based on the point in time when dual income taxes were introduced. I shall start with Denmark, where such a tax was introduced in 1985, as an alternative reform model rather than a reaction to the US reform of 1986. I shall then deal with Sweden and Norway, where dual income tax reforms were passed in 1989–91 and 1991, respectively. The Finnish reform was passed in 1992.

DENMARK

Introducing the actors and the status quo ante

Denmark is a parliamentary system with a unicameral parliament.[2] As explained in Chapter two, we can focus on parties at the central government level as the relevant actors. During the core period under consideration (mid 1980s to early 2000s) more than ten parties (excluding independents) gained parliamentary seats. The important parties' names and their scores on the tax-versus-spend dimension are displayed in Table 6.1. On this dimension one can roughly divide the party system into three blocs:

- the *left* (Social Democrats, the Socialist People's Party and, since 1990, the Unity List, which is an alliance of the former Left Socialists and Communists);
- the *centre* (Centre Democrats, Social Liberals, Christian People's Party and since 1998 the Danish People's Party);
- the *right* (Conservatives, Liberals and Progress Party).[3]

Between 1982 and 2005 only one government, for a period of 21 months, had

Table 6.1: Important parliamentary parties in Denmark, 1984–2005

English name	Danish name	Abbreviation	Tax-vs-spend late 1980s	Tax-vs-spend early 2000s
Unity List (formerly Left Socialists)	Enhedslisten	UL (LS)	3.4 (LS)	3.8
Socialist People's Party	Socialistisk Folkeparti	SPP	6.7	4.8
Social Democrats	Socialdemokratiet	SD	9.1	7.4
Centre Democrats	Centrum-Demokraterne	CD	11.8	9.2
Christian People's Party	Kristeligt Folkeparti	CPP	12.7	9.5
Danish People's Party	Dansk Folkeparti	DPP	na	10.0
Radical (Social) Liberals	Radikale Venstre	RL	12.5	10.4
Liberals	Venstre, Danmarks liberale Parti	Lib	17.4	14.8
Conservatives	Konservative Folkeparti	Con	16.0	15.3
Progress Party	Fremskridtspartiet	PP	19.4	17.8

Notes: na = non-available. Tax-vs-spend scores refer to party leadership and range from 1 to 20.
Sources: Laver and Hunt (1992), Benoit and Laver (2006).

majority status (Table 6.2). From the early 1980s to the early 1990s, Denmark was governed by centre-right minority governments under the Conservative Prime Minister Poul Schlüter. There were originally four coalition parties but this number was later reduced to three and then two. In 1993, the fifth Schlüter government was replaced by a Social Democratic-led government under Prime Minister Poul N. Rasmussen, which also lost coalition partners over time. At the end of 2001 a

Table 6.2: Governments in Denmark, 1984–2005

Begin	Prime Minister (Party)	Type	Parties	Gov.'s seats	Total seats
01.1984	Schlüter II (Con)	minority	Con, Lib, CD, CPP	78	179
09.1987	Schlüter III (Con)	minority	Con, Lib, CD, CPP	70	179
06.1988	Schlüter IV (Con)	minority	Con, Lib, RL	68	179
12.1990	Schlüter V (Con)	minority	Con, Lib	60	179
01.1993	P.N. Rasmussen I (SD)	majority	SD, RL, CD, CPP	91	179
09.1994	P. N. Rasmussen II (SD)	minority	SD, RL, CD	76	179
10.1996	P. N. Rasmussen III (SD)	minority	SD, RL	71	179
03.1998	P.N. Rasmussen IV (SD)	minority	SD, RL	71	179
11.2001	A.F. Rasmussen I (Lib)	minority	Lib, Con	73	179
02.2005	A.F. Rasmussen II (Lib)	minority	Lib, Con	70	179

Notes: Of the 179 members 2 come from the Faroe Islands and 2 from Greenland.
Sources: Damgaard (2000), Bille (2002).

Figure 6.1: Top income tax rates and income tax revenue in Denmark, 1980–2005

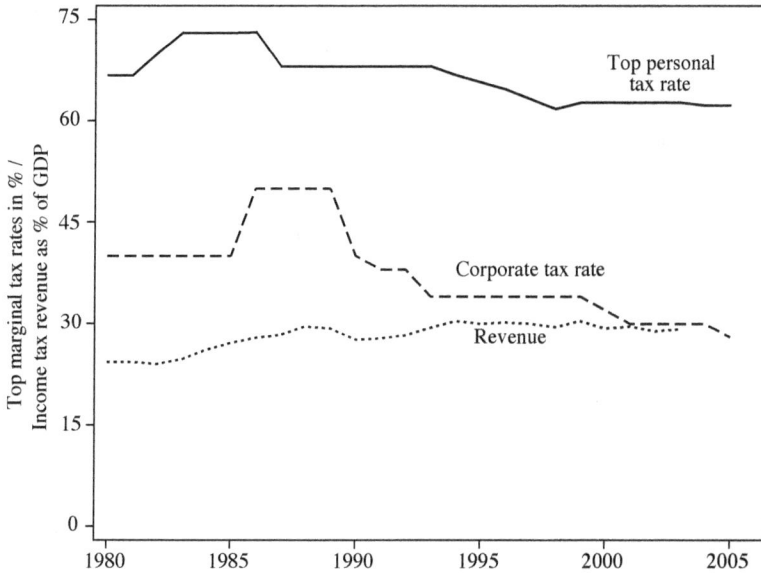

Notes: Tax revenue includes corporate and personal income taxes.
Sources: See appendix.

new Liberal-Conservative minority government gained office, which was re-elected in 2005.

Denmark's income tax system in the 1970s and early 1980s was similar to that of most OECD countries. The income taxation was built on the principle of uniform income taxation, but only formally so. The most important types of personal capital incomes were taxed at preferential rates or not taxed at all (Drejer 1988; Andersson *et al.* 1998: 116–7; Ervik 2000: Chapters eight and nine). For instance, many types of capital gains were tax-exempt, imputed rents of owner-occupiers were taxed at a level considerably below the true market rent, and pension savings were taxed at a very low level. The corporate tax rate stood at 40 per cent (Figure 6.1) but the corporate tax base had always been fairly narrow and eroded further in the late 1970s and early 1980s. Double taxation of dividends was only moderately reduced by a partial imputation system, which granted shareholders a credit for a certain percentage of the dividend received.

Of course, this highly differentiated system of income taxation was partly a consequence of Denmark's large income tax ratio (Ganghof 2005b). In 1985 corporate and personal income taxes amounted to 28 per cent of GDP and the top marginal tax rate was 73 per cent (Figure 6.1).[4] It is understandable, therefore, that sensitive types of capital income received special treatment. On the other hand, the high marginal tax rates on labour income were themselves, in part, a result of differentiated tax treatment. The combination of lenient interest deductibility rules, high marginal tax rates, and low taxation of most capital income was an invitation for massive tax arbitrage (e.g., Sørensen 1993; 1994; Andersen *et al.* 1999: 18–19). Tax planning became an important 'industry', the basic purpose of which was to transform earned income and highly taxed capital income into low-taxed capital income. High-income taxpayers could purchase real estate with borrowed funds and, due to high marginal tax rates, pass on much of their interest expenses to the fisc; as property values rose, the assets could then be sold at a vast profit liable to very little tax. As a result, capital income taxation was inefficient, the redistributive profile of the income tax was undermined and *higher* taxes on wages were necessary.

1985 to 1992: Consensual tax reform

In response to these problems, Danish reform committees in the early 1980s developed the idea of a dual income tax, with a flat uniform tax rate on all capital income and progressive tax rates on labour. Such a system was to reduce the value of interest deductions, simplify capital income taxation, reduce tax arbitrage and introduce implicit inflation adjustment. By formally differentiating between capital and labour incomes, tax reformers wanted to effectively make income taxation more uniform. Parties' policy preferences converged fairly quickly around the dual income tax model because it promised a clear improvement over the status quo in virtually all aspects of tax policy: more efficiency, more equity, higher household savings and higher income tax revenue.

In June 1985 the bourgeois minority government (Schlüter II) struck a deal with the Social Democrats and Social Liberals on a reform to take effect from 1987 (Drejer 1988; Lotz 1993). The parties agreed to introduce a uniform capital income tax rate of generally 50 per cent and reduce the top marginal tax rate on labour from 73 to 68 per cent. Capital income was defined as interest, dividends, imputed rents from owner-occupied housing, imputed returns to capital invested in unincorporated businesses and certain capital gains.

The reform did not abolish progressive capital income taxation entirely. Indirect progressivity by means of a basic tax allowance was retained. More concretely, the 50 per cent flat rate and the basic tax allowance applied jointly to capital and labour incomes and the value of the basic allowance was reduced to 50 per cent for labour incomes as well (Drejer 1988: 80–2). In other words, the basis of the Danish dual income tax was actually an indirectly progressive flat tax, the revenues of which went to national government and local authorities collectively. On top of the flat tax, an additional income tax was payable to the national government at the rates of 6 and 12 per cent of the part of the personal income exceeding certain thresholds. In this way the marginal tax rate on personal income ran as high as 68 per cent. In addition to the basic allowance Danish policymakers also retained an element of direct progressivity by applying the 6 per cent national surtax to capital income as well. This was largely as a concession to Social Democrats. This surtax was a 'gross tax', i.e. interest payments typically had a tax value of only 50 per cent.

Corporate taxation was also included in the reform. In contrast to other countries, academic debates about the adverse effects of high corporate tax rates and narrow bases on the quality of investment had not really reached policymakers. There was not much domestic political pressure to lower the corporate tax rate. Instead, the debate about dual income taxation had highlighted the usefulness of aligning the corporate rate with the tax rate on personal capital income. Therefore, and probably also to capture some revenue, the corporate tax rate was *increased* from 40 to 50 per cent (Andersson *et al.* 1998: 117). Parties also agreed on abolishing the double taxation of dividends by 1990 in order to increase neutrality between equity- and debt-financing.

Given proximate policy preferences, the tax reform was generally not contentious. However, the Social Democrats used their influence as an opposition party to establish the 6 per cent surtax on higher capital income. This concession is interesting because the Social Democrats were not actually needed to pass the reform. The government, which commanded 77 seats in parliament, was supported by three members from Greenland and the Faroe Islands as well as two defectors from the Progress Party and could therefore have relied on the 10 seats of the Social Liberals to gain a majority (Damgaard and Svensson 1989: 736; Green-Pedersen 1999: 255).[5] The government's commitment to including Social Democrats in the legislative coalition on tax reform is therefore explained, in part, by the Danish tradition to manufacture broad consensus on fundamental (tax) reforms.

Rather complicated rules were designed to keep unincorporated businesses and closely held corporations from reclassifying labour income as capital income (Hagen and Sorensen 1998: 61–3). The profits of unincorporated businesses were split into their capital and labour components, based on an imputed rate of return to their net assets (equal to the average market interest rate on bonds). In addition, these businesses were given the opportunity to accumulate income within the business on the same tax terms as corporations. That is, 'labour income' was not immediately taxed at the progressive tax rates, but the part of it that was retained in the business was subject to a preliminary flat tax rate equal to the corporate tax rate. Only if retained profits were subsequently distributed were they added to the owner's personal income and taxed as such, with the previous preliminary tax being deducted from the final tax bill. This regime did not apply to closely held corporations with active shareholders. However, these companies' opportunities for tax arbitrage were reduced by the fact that total tax burden on dividends was slightly *higher* than the top marginal tax rate on labour income.

Very sensitive types of capital income were not fully subjected to the capital income tax rates—which is not surprising given the high marginal rates of 50–56 per cent: Private pension savings were not part of the dual income tax, some types of capital gains remained tax-exempt. Owner-occupied housing was included in capital income but the assessed value of the imputed rent was generally too low.

While policymakers perceived the new dual income tax system as working rather well, there were also important problems. On the one hand, many experts and observers worried that the capital income tax rate was *too low* (Lotz 1993). The new system was criticised for being too complicated and for establishing too large a gap between capital and labour income taxation (Drejer 1988: 91; Pedersen 1992). In addition, the cuts in the capital income tax rate greatly reduced the tax value of interest deductions, which was capitalised in prices and led to a drop in the value of real estate. As a result, a considerable number of home owners went bankrupt because the market value of their real estate no longer covered the mortgage (Nannestad and Green-Pedersen: forthcoming). On the other hand, experts and policymakers also believed the uniform capital tax rate to be *too high*, especially with respect to corporate tax competition. Already at the time of the reform many observers had argued that the rate increase from 40 to 50 per cent would 'worsen the competitiveness of Danish business and make it harder for Denmark to attract foreign investment' (Koch-Nielsen 1988: 93), and such concerns increased after the 1987 reform (Andersson *et al.* 1998: 118).

Because the two types of concerns pointed in different directions, policymakers were unable to maintain the rate alignment between corporate and personal capital income taxation. The corporate tax rate was cut in isolation: to 40 per cent in 1989, 38 per cent in 1991 and 34 per cent in 1992 (Figure 6.1). The cuts had to be revenue-neutral so that the corporate tax base had to be broadened significantly, mainly by reducing investment incentives (Andersson *et al.* 1998: 118). Because tax cuts were revenue-neutral, they were passed by parliament without problems. As in Australia, corporate tax competition thus forced policymakers to abolish tax rate equality in capital income taxation shortly after it had been instituted. But Danish policymakers, in contrast to their Australian counterparts, could at least defend some degree of neutrality in business taxation because the *retained* profits of unincorporated businesses continued to be taxed at a rate equal to the corporate tax rate.

1992 to 2001: Centre-left rebalancing

By 1992 the government (Schlüter V) had become convinced of the need for another systematic tax reform attempt. It appointed a tax reform committee that was to design a model for a new personal income tax system involving lower marginal tax rates, especially for labour income. The committee was split between proponents of uniform and dual income taxation, but neither of the two models was realistic. The switch to a uniform income tax would only have been possible if marginal income tax rates had been cut drastically. Otherwise the tax value of interest deductions would have *increased* again, leading to revenue losses for the fisc and weakened savings incentives for households (*cf.* Sørensen 1998: 23). But cutting the top personal income tax rate to 50 per cent or even 34 per cent (the level of the corporate tax rate) was completely out of the question for reasons of 'intra-labour equity' (revenue-raising and wage-tax progressivity).

The return to a consistent dual income tax was equally unrealistic, though, mainly due to tax competition. For if the uniform capital income tax rate had been levelled down to the corporate tax rate of 34 per cent, this would have reduced the tax benefits to home-ownership and thus caused a significant fall in the prices of owner-occupied dwellings. 'Since the Danish housing market was already in a state of serious depression—partly as a result of the 1987 tax reform—and since the Committee's mandate required it to pay particular attention to the housing market, it was not realistic to align the capital income tax rate with the corporate income tax rate' (Sørensen 1998: 23). This implied that the simplification advantages of a purely proportional capital income tax rate were unavailable, which rendered the dual income tax model much less attractive.

Hence the reform committee ended up proposing, in autumn 1992, a modernised version of a differentiated income tax. This proposal was turned into law (in a modified form), but not by the centre-right coalition. The government resigned over a scandal in January 1993 and was replaced by a *majority* coalition of Social Democrats, Social Liberals, Centre Democrats, and the Christian People's Party (Table 6.2). Tax reform was a central issue in the coalition agreement, and the reform was passed by the coalition in the spring of 1993 (Damgaard 2000: 245).

Positive 'income from capital' was re-included as far as possible into progressive income taxation. This capital income was defined to include interest income, the rental value of owner-occupied dwellings and capital gains on shares held less than three years. One reason for re-including this income into progressive taxation was to increase voter support; it 'had been difficult to gain popular acceptance of a tax system which taxes large positive income from wealth at a considerably lower marginal rate than income from labour' (Sørensen 1998: 23). Another reason was to increase tax revenue, which could be used to reduce marginal tax rates on labour income. In fact, marginal tax rates were cut across the board, with cuts being phased in over a five-year period starting in 1994; from 1998 the top marginal tax rate was 58 per cent (Figure 6.1). Capital gains on shares held at least three years were lumped together with dividends as 'income from shares' and subjected to a separate two-bracket schedule. Share income below an indexed limit was taxed at 25 per cent, income above that limit at 40 per cent.[6] Together with a corporate tax rate of 34 per cent, these rates implied overall marginal rates on corporate-source income ranging from 50 to 60 per cent and hence not (far) below the top rate on wages (Andersson *et al.* 1998: 99).[7] Finally, *negative* capital income was not re-included into progressive income taxation; interest payments were deductible at a rate of around 46 per cent.

While the reform was deliberately underfinanced in 1994—in an attempt to stimulate the economy—it was intended to be revenue-neutral in the longer term (OECD 1996a: 46; Nannestad and Green-Pedersen: forthcoming).[8] Taxes on personal incomes were planned to be strongly reduced, by around 4.5 per cent of GDP (OECD 1996a: 46). To make up for these revenue losses, green taxes, including excise taxes on energy and water use, were introduced. In addition, a proportional tax on gross labour income was introduced, earmarked to finance labour-market policy measures.[9] This gross tax financed almost half of the cuts in personal income taxes (OECD 1996a: 46). Hence the reduction of marginal tax rates within the income tax was partly made possible by increasing *proportional* wage taxation *outside* of the income tax.

The period from 1994 to 1998 brought some changes in the composition of the governing coalition. As a result of the 1994 elections the coalition lost one partner, the Christian People's Party, which did not win any seats. This ended the short period of majority government. In 1996 the Christian Democrats also left the government, which reduced the government's strength to 71 seats, a situation that remained unchanged after the 1998 election (Table 6.2). In contrast to government composition and strength, income taxation changed little during this period.

Tax reform came back on to the policy agenda as a matter of macroeconomic policy. Shortly after the 1998 election, it was clear that a tightened fiscal policy was necessary to prevent the booming Danish economy from over-heating. Yet the government did not just want to increase taxes. The necessity of reducing consumption demand spending in the short-term offered the opportunity of further reducing the tax value of interest deductions. The goal was to reduce the increase in property prices and thus dampen consumption by reducing private consumer wealth. The resulting tax reform, based on the so-called 'Whitsun' agreement with the left opposition parties, was passed in 1998 and implemented in 1999 (Fitzmaurice 2001; Nannestad and Green-Pedersen, forthcoming). It reduced the tax value of the interest deductibility from approximately 46 per cent in 1998 to 32 per cent from 2001 onwards (Andersen 1998; OECD 2000a: 86–9). In addition, the reform increased progressivity in three main ways: by reducing the lowest income tax rate at the central government level in steps from 8 per cent in 1998 to 5.5 per cent (in 2002), by abolishing a tax allowance for positive capital income taxed at the top marginal tax rate and by increasing the top personal tax rate from 58 to 59 per cent. The cut in the bottom income tax rate was partly financed by further increases in 'green taxes'.

The tax reform also introduced a municipal property tax on the 'accommodation value of an owner-occupied home', which replaced, in the vast majority of cases, the taxation of the rental value of owner-occupied houses. This replacement was not a substantive change of the tax burden but a reaction to the general public resentment of income taxes on owner-occupied housing.

Opposition parties' veto power had a clear but moderate effect on the shape of tax reform. The government had 71 of 179 seats and thus needed the approval of either both parties on the left (Unity List [5 seats] and Socialist People's Party [13 seats]) or three centre-right parties (Christians [4 seats], Centre [8 seats], Conservatives [17 seats]) (Damgaard 2000: 234–35). The government negotiated with both sides and tried to win the support of the centre-right parties by proposing to cut the corporate tax rate to 26 per cent in a revenue-neutral manner. These parties nevertheless rejected the reform because they were opposed to the idea of further reducing interest deductibility and because they wanted a significant net reduction of the corporate tax burden.[10] The government thus had to find a compromise with the two left opposition parties, who wanted a higher top personal income tax rate and rejected a cut of the corporate tax rate. A higher top rate was difficult to accept for the Social Liberals, but because the Danish top rate was already the highest in the OECD world it was clear that any increase could not be large. The eventual small increase of one percentage point was acceptable to the Social Liberals, given the other improvements of the tax package that they had long favoured: the further cut in the value of interest deductions and tax cuts for lower wages.

In sum, in 1998 the centre-left coalition more-or-less completed Denmark's turn (back) to a differentiated income tax. Less sensitive types of capital income were taxed jointly with labour income under a progressive rate schedule, while more sensitive types of capital income were taxed at much lower marginal rates. Examples include owner-occupied housing, private pension savings and retained corporate profits. In fact, the corporate tax rate was subsequently reduced further, to 32 per cent in 2000 and 30 per cent in 2001, and the corporate tax base was broadened somewhat. The gap between the corporate rate and the top rate on personal capital income thus increased from around 6 percentage points in 1987 to around 30 points in 2001. Capital income taxation as a whole is thus far from 'market-conforming' in Denmark, but policymakers have tried to defend some degree of 'organisational neutrality'.

2001 to 2005: Centre-right rebalancing

In spring of 2000, the 'Danish Economic Council' proposed a rather pure dual income tax, which included the returns to pension saving and owner-occupied housing. The proposed capital income tax rate was 20–25 per cent. In 2001, the government mandated a new tax reform committee to investigate the future challenges of economic internationalisation and make adequate reform proposals. This committee would most likely also have proposed a pure dual income tax. Yet after the 2001 general elections a new Liberal-Conservative minority government took office (Table 6.2) and immediately dissolved the tax reform committee and imposed a tax freeze. The tax freeze committed the government to abstain from raising any tax or duty either as a percentage rate or as a nominal amount. It also applied to local governments; while it did not prevent individual municipalities and counties from adjusting tax rates on income and land, tax rates set either by municipalities or counties could not on average exceed the 2002 level.

The Conservative People's Party also pushed for tax *cuts* in addition to the freeze. It was clear that support for tax cuts would have to come from the Danish People's Party which had become much more centrist after its inaugural national congress in 1996, generally opposing tax cuts and the tax freeze. The People's Party used its influence to reduce the overall size of the tax cut, to focus tax cuts on low-income groups and to make sure that the cuts would not reduce the resources allocated to certain welfare measures, e.g. so-called 'seniors' cheques' for the poorest pensioners (Bille 2004: 990–1). Eventually, the income tax reductions, implemented from 2004–7, were indeed rather moderate, rising to 0.75 per cent of GDP. The main elements were an increase in the threshold for the medium tax bracket and an earned income tax credit; the top personal rate of around 63 per cent remained unchanged (Figure 6.1). From 2005 the corporate tax rate was cut to 28 per cent, so that the tax rate gap increased to 35 per cent. Nevertheless, the government declared the 2004–7 tax reform to be historic in that a reduction in the taxation of work was not accompanied by increases of other forms of taxation or duties.

SWEDEN

Introducing the actors and the status quo ante

Sweden is a parliamentary system with a unicameral parliament. As explained in Chapter two, we can focus on parliamentary parties at the central government level as the relevant legislative players. The important parties' names and their scores on the tax-versus-spend index are displayed in Table 6.3. Until 1988 the Swedish party system was made up of five established parties; these parties were joined in the Riksdag by the Green Party in 1988 and by the Christian Democratic Party and the New Democracy Party in 1991. New Democracy is an anti-tax party. After gaining 25 seats (7 per cent of the vote) in 1991, it did not manage to return to parliament in 1994 and 1998. One noteworthy difference to Denmark is that the Swedish Liberal Party, whose parliamentary base significantly weakened after the mid 1980s, has a more centrist profile than its Danish namesake.

During the period under consideration (mid 1980s to early 2000s) all governments were in a minority position (Table 6.4). Social Democrats governed alone during the whole period, with the exception of three years between the end of 1991 and the end of 1994 when a bourgeois coalition was in office. They had traditionally relied on the passive support of the Communist/Left Party without offering major policy concessions (Bergman 2000: 218–19), but from the early 1980s this became more difficult (Arter 1999: 208). From the mid-1990s a form 'contract parliamentarism' developed in which the cooperation between minority

Table 6.3: Parliamentary parties in Sweden, 1984–2005

English name	Swedish name	Abbreviation	Tax-vs-spend late 1980s	Tax-vs-spend early 2000s
Left Party-Communists	Vänsterpartiet	Com	3.6	3.3
Social Democrats	Arbetarepartiet-Socialdemokraterna	SD	7.6	7.1
Environmental Party	Miljöpartiet de Gröna	Green	7.4	7.2
Centre Party	Centern	Ce	10.8	11.4
Liberal Party	Folkpartiet Liberalerna	Li (FP)	13.6	13.5
Christian Democrats	Kristdemokraterna	CD	12.2	13.7
Conservative Party	Moderata Samlingspartiet	Co	17.0	17.7
New Democracy	Ny Demokrati	New Dem	na	na

Notes: na = non-available. Tax-vs-spend scores refer to party leadership and range from 1 to 20.
Sources: Laver and Hunt (1992), Benoit and Laver (2006).

Table 6.4: Governments in Sweden, 1984–2005

Begin	Prime Minister (Party)	Type	Parties	Gov.'s seats	Total seats
08.10.1982	Palme IV (SD)	Minority	SD	166	349
04.10.1985	Palme V (SD)	Minority	SD	159	349
01.03.1986	Carlsson I (SD)	Minority	SD	159	349
04.10.1988	Carlsson II (SD)	Minority	SD	156	349
03.10.1991	Bildt (Co)	Minority	Co, Ce, CD, Li	170	349
06.10.1994	Carlsson III (SD)	Minority	SD	161	349
21.03.1996	Persson I (SD)	Minority	SD	161	349
20.09.1998	Persson II (SD)	Minority	SD	131	349
02.10.2002	Persson III (SD)	Minority	SD	144	349

Sources: Bergman (2000), Widfeldt (2003).

governments and support parties resembled that between members of majority coalitions (Bale and Bergman: forthcoming).

In Sweden, the share of income taxation in GDP was substantially lower than in Denmark (21 per cent in 1985) but the basic pathologies of hybrid income taxation were the same (Ljungh 1988: 192–9; Lindencrona 1992; 1993; Södersten 1993; Mutén 1996: 7–10; Andersson *et al.* 1998: 124–7). Marginal tax rates were high (Figure 6.2), but the tax base was narrow due lenient interest deductibility

Figure 6.2: Top income tax rates and income tax revenue in Sweden, 1980–2005

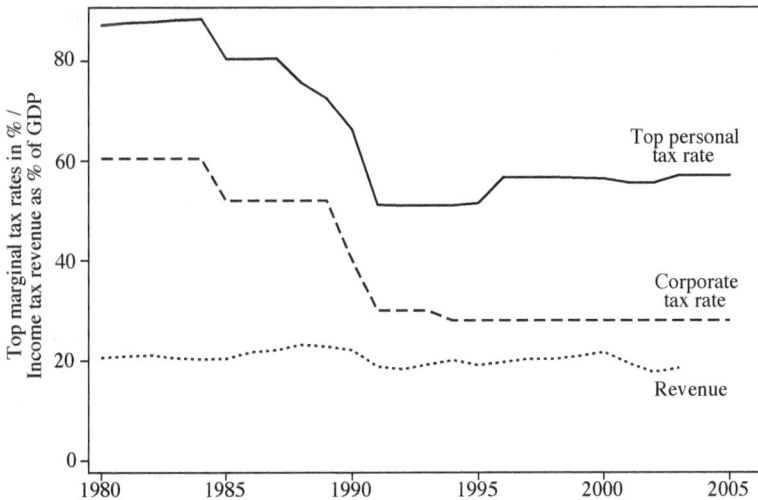

Notes: Tax revenue includes corporate and personal income taxes.
Sources: See appendix.

rules, low taxation of capital gains, low taxation of owner-occupied housing, tax privileges for retirement savings and generous investment incentives for businesses. The result was massive tax arbitrage that led to 'a continuing battle between the tax planners and the tax authorities' (Agell *et al.* 1998: 9). Capital income tax revenues were negative, income taxation as a whole was slightly regressive (SOU 1986; Salsbäck 1993: 200; Andersson and Mutén 1998: 347) and private saving was low (Ljungh 1988: 197).

1986 to 1991: Centre-left tax reform

The first Swedish response to the state of the income tax system started in the early 1980s and drew on ideas that had been developed by official reform committees in Norway (Ljungh 1988: 189–91). The most important reform, passed in the spring of 1981 and implemented from 1983 to 1985, was the so-called 'Wonderful Night' reform, which reduced marginal tax rates by up to twenty percentage points and limited the value of interest deductions to a maximum of 50 per cent (Edlund 2000: 42). The reform was not passed by the bourgeois majority coalition of Centre Party, Liberals, and Conservatives but an issue coalition that excluded the Conservatives and included the Social Democrats. The latter were willing to accept cuts in marginal tax rates in exchange for limitations on the deductibility of interest payments (Steinmo 1993: 184). The Conservatives vigorously opposed the limiting of interest deductions and, as a result of the tax reform deal, left the government, which continued as a minority coalition (Bergman 2000: 196, 221).

According to Steinmo (1993: 184) the political confusion over the reform and the consequent fall of the government were central components of the Social Democratic party's electoral victory in 1982 (Table 6.4). The resulting government's tax reform efforts were triggered by the tax reform activities in the US and Denmark. In autumn of 1986 Finance Minister Kjell-Olof Feldt decided to champion comprehensive income tax reform (Salsbäck 1993: 200–1). While the policymakers around Feldt as well as most tax experts were convinced that much flatter broader income taxation was needed, the left as a whole was reluctant to embrace this project (Steinmo 1993: 186; 2002: 849). The reform ideas were not too well received by the more traditionalist elements in the labour constituency (Sainsbury 1993; Arter 1994: 77; Edlund 2000: 41). Nevertheless, Social Democratic elites were able to receive a mandate for tax reform. A discussion paper proposing drastic cuts in marginal tax rates was accepted by the 1987 party congress. In June 1987 Feldt set up three official reform committees which issued tax reform recommendations. These were presented two years later and turned out be 'more far reaching than the mandate given by the party congress' (Feldt 1991: 380; cited in: Edlund 2000: 41). Nevertheless, they provided the basis for the so-called 'Tax Reform of the Century'.

The bulk of the reform was passed between 1989 and 1991 and based on a detailed agreement between the governing Social Democrats and the Liberals (Salsbäck 1993; Steinmo 1993: 187–190). The basic features were as follows (Andersson and Mutén 1998; Strand 1999): The central government income tax was split into a tax on capital income at a 30 per cent proportional rate, and a tax on other income, notably labour income, at a 20 per cent proportional rate. This latter tax was levied only on incomes above an indexed threshold corresponding to 110 per cent of the gross wage of an average production worker. Together with an additional municipal tax on labour income of around 32 per cent (on average), this made for a top marginal tax rate on earned income of 52 per cent (Figure 6.2). In contrast to the Danish dual income tax capital and labour taxation were separated (almost) completely; no basic allowance could be deducted from capital income. Progressivity in capital income taxation was thus completely abolished, which foreclosed tax arbitrage opportunities within the family (Lindencrona 1992: 366; 1993). The corporate tax rate was reduced from 52 to 30 per cent; and to maintain 'unchanged revenue from corporation tax, this rate reduction presupposed a substantial base-broadening' (Andersson *et al.* 1998: 125). The existing system of reducing the double taxation of dividends at the level of the corporation ('Annell deduction') was maintained.

Tax competition was clearly a driving force behind the reform (e.g., Mutén 1988; e.g., Lindencrona 1992: 367; Norrman and McLure 1997: 147), but domestic reasons were also important. Most notably, the dual income tax was defended as a step towards a *more equal* treatment of capital income and wages (Lindencrona 1993: 168). One main objective was to achieve a better correspondence between intended and actual taxation of labour income by reducing the possibility of affecting the taxation of labour income by interest expenses (Norrman and McLure 1997: 120). Another was to achieve implicit inflation adjustment—an important topic given inflation rates of consistently above 4 per cent in the 1980s and 10.4 per cent in 1990 (OECD 2001a: 246).

One of the most important effects of tax competition was probably that maintaining the statutory corporate tax rate of 52 per cent was impossible. If that rate could have stayed unchanged, it would have been equal to the reduced top rate on wages, thus helping to reduce tax avoidance. Negative effects on domestic investment could have been avoided by applying the high corporate rate only to above-normal profits (see Chapter three). In the presence of corporate tax competition, though, this option was out of the question.

The reform was sold as being revenue-neutral, but the financing estimates were 'unduly optimistic' and made 'little sense' even considering only the information available at the time (Agell *et al.* 1998: 160). The tax cuts for personal income, together with additional outlays for housing and child allowances to cushion the distributional effects of the reform, were to reduce revenues by between 6 and 7 per cent of GDP, as against 1 to 2 per cent of GDP in the 1986 US tax reform (Strand 1999: 13). Estimates suggest that the reform was underfinanced by 2 to 3 per cent of GDP. In addition to this net reduction, part of the income tax burden was shifted on to consumption taxes. A broadening of the value-added tax (of an unchanged 23 per cent) to include goods and services previously exempted, or granted lower rates, was to yield additional revenue on the order of 30 per cent of the budget loss projected by the Ministry of Finance (Agell *et al.* 1998: 23).

As to the politics of the reform, it was rather clear from the beginning that 'the only possible partner for the government was the Liberal party' (Salsbäck 1993: 208). For the type of tax reform proposed by the government, the Left Party was obviously 'not an option' (Steinmo 1993: 187). This allowed the Liberals to extract significant concessions from the Social Democrats (Steinmo 1993: 235, n. 49). While there was little conflict about the capital income tax rate, the Liberals kept the government from responding to trade union pressure to limit the reduction of the top personal tax rate on wages. When the Prime Minister wanted to give in to these demands, the Liberals threatened to abort the negotiations and had at one point already summoned a press conference to announce negotiation failure. As a result, the cut in the top rate remained unchanged and other means were found to change distributional effects in favour of the low-income earners, if only very slightly (Salsbäck 1993: 209).

1991 to 1994: Centre-right rebalancing

In 1991 general elections were held and the Social Democrats lost power with a large margin—a loss that many observers attributed to the government's economic policies including the dual income tax reform. Two new political parties entered parliament for the first time: the Christian Democrats and the anti-tax party New Democracy. New Democracy enabled the other non-socialist parties (Conservatives, Centre, Liberals and Christian Democrats) to form a minority government under the leadership of Prime Minister Carl Bildt (Table 6.4). The government needed the support of either the Social Democrats or of New Democracy. Because New Democracy was hesitant to enter into agreements with the government, Social Democrats were a powerful actor.

The government started with ambitious tax-cutting plans but these had to be shelved quickly in the face of a brewing economic recession—average growth between 1991 and 1993 was minus 1.5 per cent—and the urgent need to reduce a large budget deficit. The unfortunate timing of the implementation of the dual income tax contributed to the economic downturn. The reduced tax subsidies for borrowing and an increased value-added tax rate on housing investment stimulated indebted households to sell off assets and contributed to the collapse of the construction sector (Agell et al. 1998: Chapter six; Huber and Stephens 1998: 382–3).

Social Democrats had not been able to complete the dual income tax reform, especially with respect to the taxation of unincorporated businesses and closely held corporations. This task was taken on by the centre-right coalition (Andersson and Mutén 1998: 430). The rules implemented are far too complex to discuss here (see Sørensen 1998) but the basic approach was similar to that in Denmark. First, a 'normal return' on business assets was administratively determined (with respect to the interest rate on ten-year government bonds) and all income beyond this was taxed as wages. Second, in order not to discriminate against non-corporations, policymakers allowed them to tax the 'labour' component of income as capital income as long as it was retained in the business. Only if this set-aside was brought back to account, did the regular 'labour' tax apply. The tax already paid was then refunded (Mutén 1988: 216; Andersson and Mutén 1998: 331).

But the Bildt government was also keen on achieving further tax cuts. For one thing, it intended to reduce the capital income tax from 30 to 25 per cent. For another, it wanted to abolish double taxation of dividends and capital gains by exempting dividends and reducing the tax rate on capital gains from shares to 12.5 per cent (thus assuming that about one half of capital gains were due to retained profits that had already been taxed). Finally, the government wanted to scrap the net wealth tax, which would have implied a significant reduction of the capital income tax burden. Due to the powerful position of the Social Democrats, however, the government had to make significant concessions. The exemption of dividends, the reduction of the tax rate on capital gains from shares and a cut of the corporate tax rate to 28 per cent became effective in 1994. However, the 5 per cent cut in the capital income tax rate and the scrapping of the net wealth tax were postponed (Andersson and Mutén 1998: 328, 337, 342, 350; Strand 1999: 31).

1994 to 2001: Centre-left rebalancing
Social Democrats won the 1994 general elections, gaining 161 of 349 seats in parliament. The Liberals (with 26 seats) signalled their interest in entering a majority coalition, but Social Democrats preferred minority status. One of their main tasks ahead was to reduce the budget deficit (11 per cent of GDP in 1994) and they did not want to rely only on lowering expenditure—as the Liberals would likely have demanded. Social Democrats wanted more flexibility in finding a majority (Boston 1998: 81). Tax increases could be passed with the support from the Left Party (22 seats) or the Greens (18 seats).

The government also wanted to deal with increasing public concerns about tax equity. Part of these concerns was simply due to the large visible tax rate gap between capital and labour taxation, which was subject to heated debate. In addition, low inflation rates undermined the justification of the dual income tax system as implicit inflation adjustment. Finally, official reports showed that while the overall redistributive potential of income taxation had not changed much, this result did not take the reform's under-financing into account. If revenue losses—now visible in the budget deficit—were to be compensated mainly by regressive tax hikes or cutbacks in social spending, the result would be reduced redistribution (Agell *et al.* 1998: Chapter seven).

With the support of the left parties the government adopted the following measures (Andersson and Mutén 1998: 350). First, the top tax rate on wages at the central government level was increased from 20 to 25 per cent, making for a total rate of 56–57 per cent (Figure 6.2). Second, instead of re-aligning the corporate tax rate with the capital income tax rate at the lower level of 25 per cent—as planned by the Bildt government—the government left the corporate tax rate at 28 per cent and cancelled the reduction of capital income tax rate. Third, the double taxation of both retained and distributed corporate profits was reinstated: the tax rate on capital gains from shares was re-increased from 12.5 to 30 per cent and the exemption of dividends was scrapped. Finally, the abolition of the net wealth tax was also cancelled.

Despite these increases of tax rates on capital, most of the consolidation-related tax hikes fell on labour. One reason was that, in addition to the increase in the top marginal tax rate on wages, indexation clauses were partially abandoned so that the number of wage earners facing the highest marginal rate (as a share of all full-time workers) increased from 30 per cent in the early 1990s to 40 per cent in 1998 (Strand 1999: 14). Another reason was that labour taxes were also increased outside of the income tax system, by means of introducing employees' social security (pension) contributions. By 1998 these had reached close to 7 per cent. In total, consolidation-related tax hikes represented an income loss to households amounting to 3 to 4 per cent of GDP; and taxes paid out of wage income, which had started to fall relative to other countries after the 1991 reform, turned upwards again.

However, the dual income tax system not only facilitated tax hikes for labour incomes, it also made it easier for the government to focus subsequent tax reductions—made possible by structural budget surpluses—on lower and medium wage earners. This focus was explicitly justified in terms of justice and efficiency. The efficiency aspect was that labour supply may be more elastic at lower levels of earnings (Strand 1999: 38), the justice aspect that personal social security contributions 'constitute a disproportionately heavy burden on low and medium wage earners' (Swedish Ministry of Finance 2002: 22). Hence the increased top marginal rate on wages was maintained, and in 2000 the government embarked on a multi-year program of reducing the tax burden on wages. One main measure was to give wage earners income tax compensation for their personal pension insurance contribution. In 2004 75 per cent of it was deductible from assessed income and 25 per cent from the tax itself. The other main measure was to increase the threshold for the state income tax. The government reaffirmed the ambition, already stated in connection with the 1990–91 tax reform, that the state tax should not be paid by more than 15 per cent of wage earners. In 2004 the threshold for the 20 per cent rate increased to SEK (Swedish Krona) 291,800 (SEK 441, 300 for the 25 per cent rate).

Social Democrats also implemented various reforms in capital taxation. For example, property taxes were reduced in response to rising prices of houses, the income splitting rules for small companies were reformed, the exempt amount for the wealth tax was increased and, finally, the inheritance and gift tax was abolished as from 2005. However, these were rather incremental reforms. The dual income tax system is perceived as working rather well, and it has certainly increased the government's flexibility in responding to policy challenges.

The government plans to begin a major review of the entire tax system in 2006—the election year—fifteen years after the basic 1990–91 reform (Swedish Ministry of Finance 2005: 34). It is unlikely, though, that this reform will lead to a substantial reduction of the overall tax burden. In 2005 Social Democrats actually started a debate about tax *increases*, and both the Liberals and the Conservatives—trying to target the rather 'Social Democratic' median voter—reacted to this by *reducing* their zeal for tax cuts (*Economist* 13.8.2005).

NORWAY

Introducing the actors and the status quo ante

As explained in Chapter two, we can treat the Norwegian Storting as a unicameral parliament and focus on parliamentary parties at the central government as the relevant legislative actors. During the core period under consideration (mid 1980s to early 2000s) more than ten parties gained parliamentary seats. The names of the most important parties and their tax-versus-spend scores are given in Table 6.5.

Table 6.5: Important parliamentary parties in Norway, 1984–2005

English name	Norwegian name	Abbreviation	Tax-vs-spend score 1992	Tax-vs-spend score 2005
Socialist Left Party	Sosialistisk Venstreparti	SV	4.1	3.6
Centre Party	Senterpartiet	SP	9.8	6.3
Labour Party	Arbeiderpartiet	A	6.4	6.6
Christian People's Party	Kristelig Folkeparti	KRF	9.6	9.7
Liberal Party	Venstre	V	9.4	12.2
Progress Party	Fremskrittspartiet	FRP	18.4	15.3
Conservative Party	Høyre	H	14.3	16.8

Notes: na = non-available. Tax-v-spend scores refer to party leadership and range from 1 to 20.
Sources: Laver and Hunt (1992), Benoit and Laver (2006).

As shown in Table 6.6, after 1986 all governments were in a minority position. In addition to the parties in the government coalition, opposition parties can become very influential players under minority governments. The Labour Party

Table 6.6: Governments in Norway, 1984–2005

Begin	Prime Minister (Party)	Type	Parties	Gov.'s seats	Total seats
06.1983	Willoch II (H)	majority	H, SP, KRF	79	155
09.1985	Willoch III (H)	majority	H, SP, KRF	78	157
05.1986	Brundtland II (A)	minority	A	71	157
10.1989	Syse (H)	minority	H, SP, KRF	62	165
11.1990	Brundtland III (A)	minority	A	63	165
10.1993	Brundtland IV (A)	minority	A	67	165
10.1996	Jagland (A)	minority	A	67	165
10.1997	Bondevik I (KRF)	minority	KRF, SP, V	42	165
03.2000	Stoltenberg (A)	minority	A	65	165
10.2001	Bondevik II (KRF)	minority	KRF, H, V	62	165

Sources: Woldendorp *et al.* (2000), Narud and Strøm (2000).

Figure 6.3: Top income tax rates and income tax revenue in Norway, 1980–2005

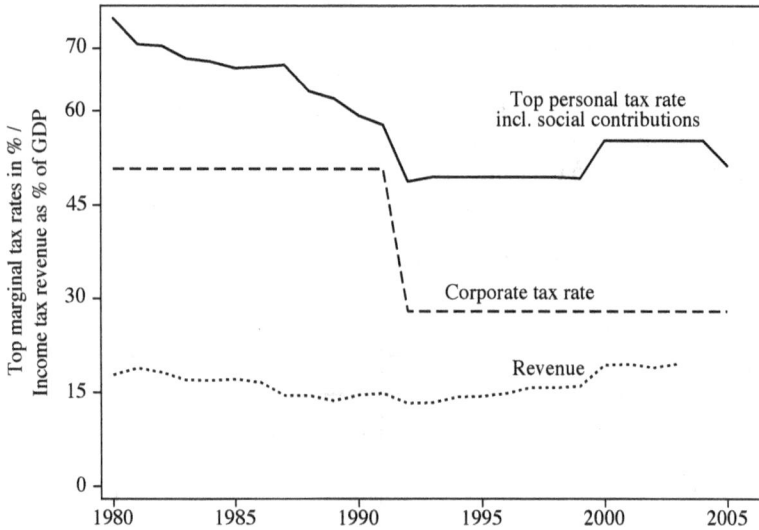

Notes: Tax revenue includes corporate and personal income taxes.
Sources: See appendix.

governed through most of the period under consideration, but its reign was inter-rupted by two centrist coalition governments. At the end of 2001, the Labour government was replaced by a new bourgeois coalition government that included the Conservatives and had a more rightist profile.

Norway's tax system in the 1970s and early 1980s was very similar to that in the other Nordic countries. Tax rates were high (Figure 6.3), the income tax base was narrow, with lenient interest deductibility rules and preferential treatment of many types of positive capital income. Corporate investment was stimulated with a multitude of tax incentives and a full deduction of dividend payments from the base of the national corporate income tax (Andersson *et al.* 1998: 86, 122–4).

1986 to 1989: Centre-left (incremental) tax reform

In May 1986 a centre-right coalition government that had governed from 1981 to 1986 was replaced by a Labour minority government (Table 6.6). The reason was that the Progress Party had voted with Labour against the government's proposal to increase taxes on petrol (Heidar 1993: 68). The Labour government, which had to rely on the support of the Centre Party or the Christian People's Party, started the tax reform process more-or-less immediately. This was less a response to the US tax reform of 1986 than triggered by the oil price collapse during the winter of 1985–86. Tax reform was part of Labour's broader macroeconomic reform package known as the 'turning operation' (Fagerberg *et al.* 1990: 85; Moses 2000: Chapter seven).

However, the underlying problems of domestic tax structure had been long known and discussed. Until the mid 1980s, Norway maintained low interest rates. This policy combined with high inflation rates, full tax deductibility of interest payments, and high marginal taxes on net incomes to make loan-financed investment in real estate highly profitable (Koren 1993: 127). In the late 1970s and early 1980s, this led to growing concern about overinvestment in the housing sector. The severity of the problem became obvious in the first half of the 1980s, when financial liberalisation and a rapid development of credit markets induced a debt-financed consumption spree and a housing bubble (van den Noord 2000: 7). There were also equity concerns. As those in the higher income brackets borrowed more money than low-income groups, high marginal tax rate no longer contributed substantially to income redistribution. The magnitude of tax relief from interest payments led to a realisation that an equalisation of real loan costs after taxes between income groups could contribute more towards an equitable income distribution than would the maintenance of high marginal tax rates (Koren 1993: 127).

The search for policy responses to these concerns had already started in the 1970s. In the early 1980s, a reform committee with a very broad representation both in political and academic respects worked for several years and finally arrived at a fairly extensive agreement in their final report (NOU 1984). One of the main ideas was to introduce a gross tax on higher labour incomes, i.e. a progressive surtax against which interest payments would not be deductible. Both centre and left parties aimed at giving increasing weight to this type of tax. In contrast, Conservatives and the Progress Party opposed it (Fagerberg *et al.* 1990: 86; Ervik 2000: 228). In fact, the Conservatives had already blocked a reduction of the tax deductibility of interest payments during the centre-right coalition (Fagerberg *et al.* 1990: 81).

The Labour government was able to pass tax reform in 1987 with the help of the Centre Party (Fagerberg *et al.* 1990: 86). A gross income surtax was introduced in 1988 at a rate of 8.5 per cent, increased to 9.5 per cent in 1991 (Messere 1993: 238; van den Noord 2000: 9). The tax base of individuals was broadened and the top marginal tax rate against which interest deductions were allowed was gradually reduced. As in Denmark and Sweden, tax reform triggered an unwinding of the housing bubble, which had adverse consequences for the economy. But this did not mean that the gross tax idea was wrong, only that the timing of reform—financial liberalisation preceding tax reform—was unfortunate (Moses 2000: 170; van den Noord 2000: 7).

1989 to 1993: Consensual tax reform
In 1988 the government appointed the so-called 'Aarbakke Committee' to develop a comprehensive reform proposal (NOU 1989). The work of the Committee led to a further convergence of policy preferences on the dual income tax model. The Committee's proposal was presented in 1989 and submitted to parliament in 1990 (van den Noord 2000: 8).

After the 1989 general elections the Labour government was replaced by the former centre-right coalition (Table 6.6). By that time, the Conservatives had changed their attitude towards the idea of a gross surtax, so that in May 1990 the coalition announced a new tax reform involving larger reductions in the value of interest deductibility than those implemented by the 1987 reform (Fagerberg *et al.* 1990: 86). However, the coalition could not actually pass tax reform, because it broke apart at the end of 1990 over the issue of EU membership (Narud and Strøm 2000: 185). Labour returned to office—as always in minority position—and passed the tax reform in 1991, drawing heavily on the proposal of the Aarbakke Committee. After many years of negotiations and committee work, the reform was passed with almost unanimous agreement in parliament (Gjelsvik 1998: 182; van den Noord 2000: 8).

Effective from 1992, a dual income tax was introduced with significantly lower rates and a broadened tax base. A basic rate flat rate of 28 per cent was levied on income from all sources, called 'general income', in principle including all capital income, while an additional two-step 'surtax' applied to labour income (including pensions). The top personal rate was reduced to 49.5 per cent (41.7 per cent excluding social security contributions). All allowances and the costs of earning income were only deductible from 'general income', that is, at the rate of 28 per cent (Cnossen 1999: 22).[11] The Norwegian dual income tax was thus designed differently from the Swedish: instead of separating capital and labour taxation completely and abolishing any progressivity in the former, Norwegian policymakers essentially introduced an indirectly progressive flat income tax supplemented by a directly progressive gross tax on wages.

The most important reform goal was to achieve competitive and more uniform capital income taxation. '[I]t was considered that the Norwegian capital tax rate could not be higher than in comparable countries' (Zimmer 1992: 351). Given the basic trade-offs in income taxation, the emphasis on low and uniform capital income taxation made it necessary to compromise capital-labour equity (equal treatment of capital and labour) and/or reduce intra-labour equity (high revenues and wage progressivity). Policymakers' choices were clear:

> [H]igher taxes on earned income were considered necessary both for fiscal and equity reasons: the revenue was needed, and it was considered politically impossible to introduce a tax reform which gave significantly greater tax advantage to well-off taxpayers than to the less well-off.
>
> (Zimmer 1993: 143)

Other justifications for the dual income tax system were given as well. Most notably, the lower rate on capital income was defended partly as implicit inflation adjustment as well as compensation for the net wealth tax. However, the corporate wealth tax was abolished as part of the reform, and the top rate of the (progressive) personal wealth tax was reduced from 2.3 to 1.3 per cent in 1992 (Zimmer 1992: 358–9; Gjems-Onstad 1993: 112).

In line with the strong orientation towards intersectoral neutrality, corporate taxation was fully included in the dual income tax system. The corporate tax rate was almost cut in half, from 50.8 to 28 per cent (Figure 6.3). The previous system of dividend deduction at the corporate level was replaced by a full imputation system, i.e., Norwegian shareholders were entitled to a full tax credit on dividends received. This system was equivalent to the exemption of dividends but there was 'a widespread feeling that the Norwegian public would not accept personal tax exemption for dividend income, despite the economic equivalence between such a measure and the full imputation system which was actually adopted. Public perceptions rather than economic realities seemed to be governing the design of tax policy' (Andersson *et al.* 1998: 94).

To avoid double taxation of *retained* profits—to the extent these are reflected in capital gains on shares—the so-called 'RISK' method was introduced. This method assumes that retained profits are in fact deferred dividends that are reflected in the share values, so that the associated capital gains are already taxed at the company level. Therefore, only capital gains that exceed the increase in the stock of retained earnings of the company were taxed (van den Noord 2000: 14).

To match neutrality at the level of tax rates with approximate neutrality with respect to tax bases, policymakers scrapped virtually all types of tax reliefs with 'almost merciless consistency' (Andersson *et al.* 1998: 122). Most notably, they tried to achieve rough correspondence between depreciation for tax purposes and 'true economic depreciation'. Instead of allowing all machinery and equipment to be written down annually by some percentage (traditionally 30 per cent), the new Norwegian tax code divided assets into eight different categories with different depreciation rates to reflect the differences in economic lifetimes across asset types.

As in all dual income tax countries, policymakers had a hard time finding a regime to divide the income from unincorporated businesses into its capital and labour components. At one point this problem even 'threatened to topple the entire tax reform process' (Zimmer 1993: 148). The final solution, the so-called 'split model', was in principle a purer separation of the two types of income than in Denmark and Sweden (Zimmer 1993: 149–52; Hagen and Sørensen 1998: 59–60). Capital and labour incomes of unincorporated businesses and closely held corporations were separated, with capital income being computed as the value of business assets multiplied by some 'capital yield rate'. This imputed rate of return was set equal to the market interest rate on five-year government bonds plus a risk premium.

There were important modifications of this general rule, however, which resulted in regressive taxation of very high incomes. If the estimated capital income of a proprietor exceeded NOK (Norwegian Kroner) 1.25 million (1993 level), the excess amount was taxed as capital income. As Gjems-Onstad (1993: 113) observed: 'A young lawyer making NOK 300 000 a year has to pay an extra tax of 52.4 per cent if the income is increased by NOK 100 000, i.e. a tax of NOK 52 400. An established lawyer making NOK 1 300 000 will only have to pay 28 per cent, i.e. NOK 28 000, on the same increase in income.' Not surprisingly, this regressive element invited derision from the political Right (Willoch 1995: 179).

All in all, Norway implemented a very consistent type of dual income tax, making it '[t]he leading nation in the field...' (Mutén 1996: 19). The dual income tax was not 'pure' (van den Noord 2000: 6), however, because a number of important tax expenditures remained. Most importantly, owner-occupied housing as well as retirement savings continued to receive preferential tax treatment (Ervik 2000: Chapters eight, eleven and twelve; Bye and Åvitsland 2003).

1993 to 2001: Centre-left rebalancing

Between 1993 and 1997 the basic income tax system remained unchanged but there was more-or-less constant criticism of the rules for splitting the income of small businesses. They were seen as too complicated and administratively costly (Gjelsvik 1998: 182; van den Noord 2000). As a result, calls for abolishing the surtax, which had already been voiced immediately after the 1992 reform (Zimmer 1993: 152–3), became louder. The political right, most notably the Progress Party, called for reducing the tax rate gap or the abolition of the progressive surtax on labour income altogether (Ervik 2000: 227). In fact, a flat income tax was a more credible reform option in Norway compared to Denmark or Sweden because income tax revenue was significantly lower than in these countries. On the basis of econometric estimates, it was argued that a flat tax would lead to significant efficiency gains while leaving a majority of households better off (Aaberge *et al.* 2000, see also Strøm and Wiig 1995).

As a result, Norway's tax policy debate reflected the trade-off structure discussed in Chapters three and four: If the tax rate gap between capital and labour had been reduced by reducing the top tax rate on wages, the resulting reduction in progressivity and/or revenue would have been difficult to sell politically. If the gap had been reduced by increasing the uniform capital income tax rate, the efficiency losses of taxing sensitive forms of capital income would have increased significantly. Finally, the increase of the capital income tax rate could have been restricted to less sensitive capital income, but this would have compromised the goal of a level playing field. This trade-off structure is what van den Noord (2000: 28) refers to when he writes:

> the dual income tax system applies a uniform income tax by all forms of capital, mobile and immobile capital alike, and therefore carries an important dead-weight loss [*differentiation efficiency*]. The efficiency advantages [*non-differentiation efficiency*] stemming from Norway's dual income tax may have more than outweighed this drawback so far, but an increase in the rate of capital taxation from its present level of 28 per cent, an issue which has remained on the political agenda, would tend to accentuate the disadvantages.

Not surprisingly, the Labour government made no attempt to abolish the split model. It was only changed at the margins. For example, in 1995 the rules for identifying active shareholders were eased and the taxation of the liberal professions (doctors, etc.) was tightened by increasing the ceiling above which wages were taxed as capital income (van den Noord 2000: 10–11).

After the general election of 1997, the three centre parties formed a mini-coalition headed by Mjell Magne Bondevik, which controlled only about a quarter of the seats in parliament (Table 6.6). Although Labour had lost only two seats (65 versus 67), Prime Minister Jagland had announced beforehand that the government would step down if it failed to get at least the same vote as in 1993 (36.9 per cent). So Labour decided to leave office, arguing that 'sound government of the country needed more executive authority' (Heidar 2001: 165). Obviously, parliament was an important veto point for the new Bondevik government. Bondevik did not want to rely exclusively on the support of the Conservative and Progress parties but the Labour Party initially adopted a 'non-accommodating' stance on most issues, so that, throughout 1998, the Bondevik government was typically forced to negotiate its support from right-wing parties.[12]

During this period minor adjustments in the split model were made. Most notably, for liberal professions the income ceiling above which labour income was taxed as capital income was entirely abolished in 1998. This led to a higher marginal tax burden and hence also to greater incentives for avoiding taxes, e.g. by incorporating and subsequently trying to qualify as a 'passive' company owner (van den Noord 2000: 10–11, 28).

But the centrist coalition also wanted to tackle the problem of the tax rate gap. In February 1998 it appointed a public tax reform committee with the task of considering the scope for reductions in the difference between the maximum marginal tax rate on wage income and capital income, with at least one of the resulting proposals being revenue-neutral. The committee's report, published in January 1999, argued that the likely welfare impact of a small increase in the capital income tax rate combined with a reduction in the income surtax would generally be small but positive (NOU 1999). The subsequent discussion once more revealed the underlying trade-offs. Most of the groups and organisations' consultative statements on the report endorsed the goal of reducing the tax rate gap but the 'adequate' levels of tax rates were quite controversial. For example, the Norwegian Central Bank called for a cut in the surtax but strongly rejected the proposed increase in the capital income tax rate. It emphasised that the committee did not take sufficient account of the effect of taxes on enterprises' locational choices (Norges Bank 1999).

The discussion about the split model shows how competitive pressures may in the long run create a bias towards less progressive taxation of wages. A low corporate tax rate tends to increase the incentives and opportunities for tax avoidance, which may in turn increase voter support for a smaller tax rate gap and hence less progressive wage taxation. In the short run, however, the political game in Norway was a different one, reflecting the power structure in parliament. In 1999 Labour changed its strategy towards the centrist mini-coalition and adopted a more accommodating stance. It went into serious budget negotiations with the government, which urgently needed Labour to accept a reform of cash benefits for families with small children. Both sides disagreed about the balancing of the budget. Despite the recommendations of the tax reform committee, Labour demanded an *increase* in the tax rates on higher labour incomes in order to fund some of the party's priorities on the spending side of the budget; the government opposed this increase. After protracted negotiations, the government eventually gave in on the tax issue and the parties reached a budget compromise on 30 October 1999 (Narud and Valen 2000: 485). As from 2000 a third bracket for the income surtax was introduced, increasing the top rate on labour by 6 percentage points to 55.3 per cent (47.5 per cent excluding social security contributions).

But this was not the only adjustment of the dual income tax system driven by equity and revenue considerations. In March 2000, the Bondevik government lost a vote of confidence in parliament and was replaced by a Labour minority government, now with Jens Stoltenberg as Prime Minister (Table 6.6). Back in power, the Labour government tackled another issue that had gained increasing attention in the years after 1992: the perceived tax exemption of shareholders. Even though Norwegian policymakers had chosen the imputation system rather than dividend exemption, public perception was that the income taxes on dividends 'were removed altogether' (Moses 2000: 172) or that dividends were 'barely taxed at all' (Aalberg 1999: 214). In addition, since dividends were very unevenly distributed between households, the 1992 tax reform was seen as having 'contributed to the increased income for the top ten per cent' as well as to 'the decreased progressivity in the tax system' (Aalberg 1999: 214–15). In 2000, the Stoltenberg government responded to these types of concerns and introduced a 11 per cent income tax on dividends received by Norwegian personal taxpayers—with a basic deduction—in order to 'enhance the distributional profile of the tax system' (Norwegian Ministry of Finance 2000: 18–19). However, the Ministry of Finance (2000: 19) also made clear that this move to a partial double taxation of dividends was a provisional solution. The government intended to introduce a new system of business taxation from 2002, which would only subject *above-normal returns*—i.e. return in excess of a specified share of a company's capital stock—to a higher tax rate.

2001 to 2005: Centre-right rebalancing
It was not to be up to Labour to implement more systematic reform, however. The government changed once more in October 2001, after the Labour Party had suffered a big defeat in the general elections. A more rightist coalition formed that included the Conservatives (Table 6.6). The government announced that it would scrap the highest bracket of the surtax pushed through by the Labour Party (in opposition) in 1999, and it abolished the dividend tax already in 2002. The government stated its commitment to the basic pillars of the 1992 reform—highlighting the broad political support for the dual income tax principles—but appointed a tax reform committee ('Skauge Committee') to prepare a comprehensive reform of the income tax. The mandate for the committee included proposals for reducing the tax rate differential between labour and capital income and reforming the income splitting rules for small businesses. The committee was also requested to review the net wealth tax.

The proposals of the Skauge Committee were presented in February 2003. In addition to a phase-out of the net wealth tax and an increase of real property and inheritance taxes, the committee made two central proposals, which are exemplary for the problems of progressive income taxation in the face of strong competitive pressure on statutory corporate tax rates. First, the committee worked out the idea already hinted at by the Labour government, i.e. to tax *above-normal* corporate profits at the normal capital income tax rate (28 per cent) *at the level of domestic personal shareholders*, based on the value of their shareholdings (Sørensen forth-coming-b). For the committee, however, the main reason for this 'shareholder tax' was not to increase the tax burden on dividends but to reduce the tax avoidance incentives that closely held corporations had under the existing income splitting rules. The tax rate on above-normal returns on shares would increase from 28 to 48.16 per cent [28 per cent + (72 x .28) per cent]. This would reduce the difference between the tax rate on labour income and on capital income and thus reduce the scope for tax planning of businesses.[13]

While we do not have to get into the details of the shareholder model, it is important to note that it is very complex. In fact, its administrative complexity led many tax experts and administrators to reject the model, arguing that it is 'good in theory but too complex to implement in practice' (OECD 2004b: 108). Administrative complexity could probably be greatly reduced if the taxation of above-normal returns happened *at the level of the corporation* rather than the level of domestic personal shareholders. This was essentially the solution adopted by the Italian-style dual income tax discussed in Chapter three. As also discussed there, however, this option was not available anymore in the face of strong cor-porate tax competition. In fact, that Tax Committee explicitly acknowledged that a system with a high corporate tax rate might deter profitable multinational enterprises and should therefore be avoided (Sørensen forthcoming-b). Hence the shareholder model can be seen as the second-best model, but one that might be compatible with tax competition. It is perhaps the last line of defence for proponents of a systematic and efficient alternative to flat taxes (Chapter three). Not surprisingly, therefore, in the context of the Norwegian discussion about the complexities of the shareholder model, quite a few tax experts highlighted the administrative advantages of the flat income tax (OECD 2004b: 107).

The aim of the shareholder model was to reduce tax arbitrage *given a large difference between the top marginal tax rates on capital income and on labour income*. However, the Committee also argued that, even with the shareholder model, the tax rate differential would also need to be *reduced*. It was highlighted in the reform discussions that that difference between the marginal tax rates on capital and on earned income (*including* employers' and employees' social secu-rity contributions) had increased from 27.6 to 36.7 percentage points between 1992 and 2003. This was mainly due to the increase of the top marginal income tax rate discussed above as well as the introduction of a supplementary employer's social security contribution on top wage earners in 1993 (OECD 2004b: 89, 105). The committee proposed to reduce marginal income tax rates and remove the sup-plementary contribution.

The government followed the two main recommendations of the Skauge Committee (OECD 2004b; Gjems-Onstad 2005). In connection with the 2005 budget, and with the support of the Progress Party, the minority coalition introduced the shareholder model and reduced marginal tax rates on labour income. Most notably, the top marginal tax rate was reduced by 4 percentage points (Figure 6.3) and the maximum marginal tax rate including employer's social security contributions was lowered from 64.7 to 61.5 per cent. The basic allowance for wage income was also increased. Furthermore, the wealth tax burden was reduced, with a view to its full abolition. It is also noteworthy that the tax on imputed income on owner-occupied housing was abolished, despite the fact that this greatly increased intersectoral tax distortions (Bye and Åvitsland 2003). As noted earlier, however, the right-wing parties had long defended tax privileges for housing (Ervik 2000: 236). A large part of the tax cuts were financed by increases of the general rate for value-added tax from 24 to 25 per cent and of the low rate from 6 to 7 per cent. Hence, despite a small overall net reduction, the reform represented mainly a shift from labour income to indirect consumption taxation.

The logic of the new system adopted in Norway is one that severely constrains the setting of marginal tax rates on labour income. As Sørensen (forthcoming-a: 26) observes:

Under the new Norwegian tax scheme...[t]o ensure that active owners of closely held corporations cannot gain from transforming labour income into capital income (or vice versa), [the] total effective tax rate [on shareholder income] will have to be kept close to the top marginal tax rate on labour income. Clearly this will severely constrain the choice of tax rate structure. In particular, if future increases in capital mobility force a reduction in the tax rates on corporate income and capital income, the marginal tax rate on labour income will also have to come down. Hence a major advantage of the dual income tax—that it allows a separation between the marginal tax rates on capital and labour to account for differences in factor mobility—would seem to be lost.

In line with this view, the Skauge Committee recommended that the marginal tax rate on labour incomes (also including *employer's* contributions) be scaled back to 54.3 per cent, which implied a further cut in the top marginal income tax rate of up to 5 percentage points. However, it is unclear whether further cuts will materialise, however, because the general election in September 2005 was won by the left-wing opposition parties, which had criticised the tax reform. It remains to be seen, therefore, whether the most recent tendency towards a lowering and flattening of the personal income tax was the short-term result of the political power distribution or a small step on a long way toward a flat income tax.

FINLAND

Introducing the actors and the status quo ante

As explained in Chapter two, we can treat the Finnish parliament (*Eduskunta*) as unicameral and focus on parliamentary parties at the central government as the relevant legislative actors. Table 6.7 shows the nine most important parties that gained parliamentary representation during the period under consideration as well as their tax-versus-spend scores. The largest parties were the three traditional ones: Social Democratic Party, Centre Party (formerly Agrarian Union), and Conservative Party.

Table 6.7: Important parliamentary parties in Finland, 1984–2005

Party	Finnish name	Abbreviation	Tax-vs-spend late 1980s	Tax-vs-spend early 2000s
Left-wing Alliance	Vasemmistoliitto	VAS	na	4.3
Green League	Vihreä Liitto	GR	7.4	7.1
Social Democratic Party	Suomen Sosialidemokraattinen Puolue	SDP	5.9	8.4
Christian League	Suomen Kristillinen Liitto	CHR	13.7	8.5
True Finns	Perussuomalaiset	PS	na	9.4
Centre Party	Suomen Keskusta	KESK	11.2	9.5
Swedish People's Party	Ruotsalainen Kansanpuolue (Finnish); Svenska Folkepartiet i Finland (Swedish)	SW	14.7	12.9
National Coalition Party (Conservatives)	Kansallinen Kokoomus	CON	14.3	15.8
Finnish Rural Party	Suomen Pienviljelijäin Puolue	FRP	10.4	na

Notes: na = non-available. Tax-v-spend scores refer to party leadership and range from 1 to 20.
Sources: Laver and Hunt (1992), Benoit and Laver (2006).

Table 6.8 displays the governments that formed during the period under consideration. The 'supermajoritarian' rules that characterised Finnish politics until the late 1980s/early 1990s (see Chapter two) contributed to oversized coalition governments. While some of these coalitions had a very large 'ideological range' in terms of tax-versus-spend scores, we will see that the range of *policy* preferences in fiscal policy was often much narrower (see also Jungar 2000: 2002).

Finland's income tax system was similar to that of the Scandinavian countries (Joumard and Suyker 2002): Personal income taxation was formally based on the principle of uniform income taxation with steeply progressive tax rates (Figure 6.4). However, most important types of capital income were strongly tax-advantaged. For instance, interest income was completely tax-exempt until 1991, when

Table 6.8: Governments in Finland, 1984–2005

Begin	Prime Minister (Party)	Type	Parties	Gov.'s seats	Total seats
05.1983	Sorsa (SDP)	surplus	SDP, KESK, FRP, SW	123	200
04.1987	Holkeri I (CON)	surplus	SDP, CON, SW, FRP	131	200
08.1990	Holkeri II (CON)	surplus	SDP, CON, SW	122	200
04.1991	Aho I (KESK)	surplus	KESK, CON, SW, CHR	115	200
06.1994	Aho II (KESK)	majority	KESK, CON, SW	107	200
04.1995	Lipponen I (SDP)	surplus	SDP, CON, VAS, SW, GR	145	200
04.1999	Lipponen II (SDP)	surplus	SDP, CON, VAS, SW, GR	139	200
05.2002	Lipponen III (SDP)	surplus	SDP, CON, VAS, SW	128	200
04.2003	Jäätteenmäki (KESK)	surplus	KESK, SDP, SW	117	200
06.2003	Vanhanen (KESK)	surplus	KESK, SDP, SW	117	200

Sources: Nousiainen (2000), Sundberg (2004).

it was subjected to a 10 per cent withholding tax (15 per cent in 1992), and long-term capital gains on shares were tax-exempt. Home-owners were also privileged. Interest deduction rules were favourable; and while there existed a tax on the imputed rent of owner-occupiers, most of them did not in practice pay any taxes because houses were valued well below market rates (Tikka 1982; Saarimaa 2005: 7–8). As

Figure 6.4: Top income tax rates and income tax revenue in Finland, 1980–2005

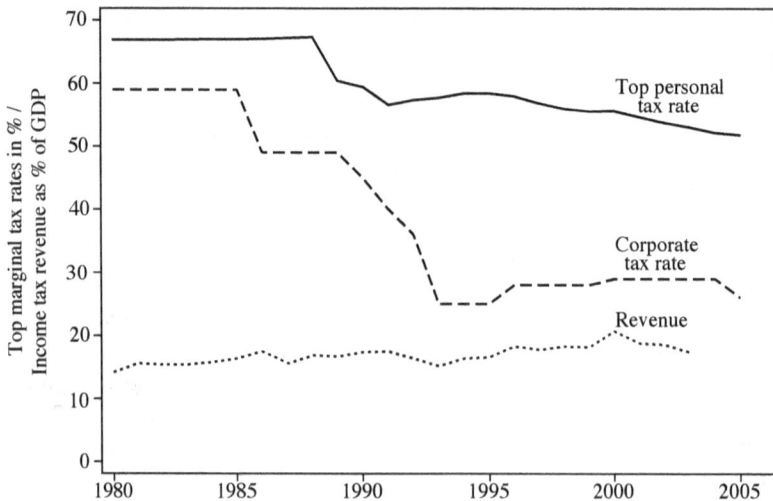

Notes: Tax revenue includes corporate and personal income taxes.
Sources: See appendix.

a result, the government paid for a large share of taxpayer's interest costs and capital income taxation of individuals yielded no tax revenue (Tikka 1993b: 94).

The pattern in corporate taxation was similar (Andersson et al. 1998: 120). The statutory corporate tax rate was high, the tax base very narrow. Double taxation of distributed profits was alleviated at the corporate level by allowing dividends to be deducted, to various extents, from the corporate tax base. This system turned out to create major distortions and revenue losses because the granting of the deduction was not predicated on the taxability of dividends in the hand of the recipient and because around two-thirds of the distributions were in fact received by shareholders who paid no or few dividend taxes, such as foreigners or tax-exempt domestic investors (Tikka 1989: 108–9; Andersson 1993: 68). The average effective tax burden on corporations was estimated to be 16.5 per cent in 1980–5 and 8 per cent in 1986–9 (Government Institute for Economic Research 1995: 35).

1985 to 1995: Dual income taxation as a response to tax competition
While tax experts and policymakers became increasingly dissatisfied with the income tax system, the domestic policy debate was less intense than in Norway and Sweden. Tax reform in the second half of the 1980s was not only reinforced but actually triggered by the international tax reform wave; competitiveness considerations were crucial (Andersson et al. 1998: 121; Joumard and Suyker 2002: 6). Base-broadening was less something that policymakers had wanted anyway than a requirement of the combination of tax competition and budgetary tension: 'As there was no possibility of reducing total income tax revenue, the cost of reducing tax rates had to be covered by broadening the tax base, as in most other countries' (Andersson 1993: 64). The US reform of 1986 was perceived as much more attractive than the Danish dual income tax. For it proved to Finnish policymakers that it was in fact possible to stop the continuous erosion of the income tax base. Initially, therefore, Finnish policymakers were guided by the ideal of uniform rather than dual income taxation.

Soon after a new four-party government (Holkeri I), including Conservatives and Social Democrats as the two major parties, had formed in April 1987, it appointed two one-person reform committees to propose reforms of capital income taxation. Based on these proposals, a reform was passed in the fall of 1988 and implemented in steps between 1989 and 1992 (Tikka 1989; Andersson 1993; Andersson et al. 1998: 120–1). Corporate and personal income tax rates were cut at the central government level and the tax base was broadened. A full imputation system was introduced in 1990 to make business taxation more neutral (Tikka 1989). The overall reform was designed to be revenue-neutral but business taxes were expected to rise, which they did. Starting from a very low level, around 6 per cent of total *income* taxation in 1987, revenues increased by 44 per cent after the introduction of the imputation system (Andersson 1993: 69).

The government used the 'trick' of passing a series of one-year tax laws to get around the oversized majority requirements in parliament (see Chapter two)

(Tikka 1989: 107). Within the government, however, there was not much political conflict. That the tax reform was less radical than elsewhere—and, in part, less radical than the experts' reform proposals—had less to do with conflicting policy preferences than with *uncertainty*. The government also liberalised the Finnish financial market in the second half of the 1980s and was strongly concerned about competitiveness. However, the government did not yet know the precise nature and extent of tax reforms in other countries and therefore wanted to postpone the next steps of the tax reform process (Tikka 1989: 112; Andersson 1993: 67).

This process continued under increasingly dramatic economic circumstances. Between 1990 and 1993 Finland experienced the deepest post-war recession in the OECD area, with a real GDP growth of minus 6.3 per cent in 1991. Unemployment and public expenditures soared. The time of budget surpluses was over, at least temporarily, and public debt increased. What is more, by 1991 uncertainty about the tax reforms of other countries no longer existed. Sweden and Norway had introduced dual income taxes with strongly reduced statutory rates on capital income, and policymakers had no doubt that Finland had to follow suit to maintain its competitiveness: 'A great risk was foreseen that capital would flow out from Finland.... For...external reasons it was not possible to tax capital income more heavily than it is generally taxed abroad' (Andersson 1993: 69). As a result, policymakers had to abandon their normative attachment to the idea of uniform income taxation and switch to the dual income tax blueprint.

The reform was carried out by a new government. The Centre Party was the main winner of general elections in March 1991 and formed a government with Conservatives, Swedish People's Party and Christian League, which took office in April (Table 6.8). Already in May a tax reform committee was established, which delivered its report in January 1992. On this basis a dual income tax was enacted in December 1992 and became effective from January 1993 (Andersson 1993: 70). A very low capital income tax rate of 25 per cent was chosen. Capital income comprised interest income, dividends, rental income, capital gains (regardless of the holding period), timber sales proceeds, and a share of the profits of unincorporated businesses. The corporate rate was also reduced to 25 per cent and the full imputation system maintained in order to achieve neutrality (Tikka 1993a: 96).[14] The corporate tax rate was further broadened. Labour tax rates did not fall, so that a very large tax rate gap emerged between the two types of income (Figure 6.4). The top marginal tax rate was set at around 57 per cent. The overall reform was supposed to be revenue-neutral but turned out to increase tax revenues slightly (OECD 2001c). Despite the low statutory tax rate, the effective tax rate on businesses did not change significantly as a result of the reforms.

As in Norway, income of unincorporated businesses and certain corporations was split into capital income and labour income, based on an imputed rate of return on business assets (18 per cent in 2002). However, the Finnish splitting regime was characterised by various unique features. First, policymakers did not actually define a category of closely held corporations but simply applied the splitting regime to all businesses not listed on any stock exchange. Second, for these companies splitting took place only when profits were distributed; retained profits leading to capital gains were taxed completely as capital income (Hagen and Sørensen 1998: 60–1; Cnossen 1999: 23). Third, the economically important and politically powerful agriculture and forestry sector was privileged because income from forestry is in practice taxed completely as capital income (Tikka 1993a: 100). During a long transition period, 1993 to 2005, farmers were also able to choose taxation under the very favourable old system.

Although Finnish policymakers adopted the dual income tax model somewhat reluctantly, and merely as a 'defensive...reaction to international tax competition', the reform was carried out 'without a vigorous political debate' (Tikka 1993a: 91). There was little conflict in government and in parliament and broad 'political consensus for introducing a flat rate tax' on capital income (Tikka 1993a: 92). The only bone of contention was the exact level of this tax rate (Koskenkyla 1992; Tikka 1993a: 107). Given tax competition as well as the previous under-taxation of capital income for example, the political right as well as some tax experts called for a rate lower than 25 per cent. The left opposition proposed a 30 per cent level for the flat rate.

The Finnish dual income tax was of course also 'impure'. In order to avoid adverse political or economic consequences of increasing the capital income tax burden, a number of exemptions and transition regimes were established, e.g. in the area of interest income (Tikka 1993a: 97). With respect to owner-occupied housing, policymakers tried to prevent the adverse consequences of devaluing interest deductions experienced in the other three countries by introducing, for a five-year period, an additional deduction (Joumard and Suyker 2002: 39, n. 27). The usual privileges for retirement savings and owner-occupied housing existed as well. The rental value of owner-occupied housing was completely exempted. While this exemption was partly compensated by a property tax, the resulting taxation was so low that it hardly lessened the favoured tax treatment of house-ownership (Joumard and Suyker 2002: 24). The deductibility of voluntary pension insurance payments was curtailed marginally to increase neutrality between different types of savings (Tikka 1993a: 101).

1995 to 2005: Marginal adjustments
In April 1995 general elections led to a change of government. Social Democrats achieved a clear election victory and formed the broad 'Rainbow Coalition', including the Left-wing Alliance and Greens on the left and the Swedish People's Party and the Conservatives (National-Coalition) on the right. This government was re-elected in 1999 but from May 2002 did not include the Greens anymore who had been outvoted in a decision to build a new nuclear power plant in Finland (Table 6.8)

On the assumption that all members of the Rainbow Coalition were true veto players and that their very diverse tax-versus-spend scores (Table 6.7) translated into equally diverse policy preferences, one could have expected the Rainbow Coalition to lead to deadlock and inefficient decision-making (*cf.* Tsebelis 1999).

As discussed in Chapter two, however, this assumption is misleading. Parties' power was reduced by *simple majority rule* in parliament and parties' short-term policy preferences converged strongly due to severe *socio-economic constraints* (i.e. high budget deficits, high unemployment and international competition). In tax policy, as elsewhere, differences between the parties were minor, and there was broad consensus to *focus on budget consolidation* without further *increasing* an already high tax burden (Jungar 2000: 313–14).

As to capital income taxation, there was agreement to increase the capital income tax rate in order to bring in more revenues and to improve the distributional profile of the tax system. This agreement was facilitated by three factors. First, the Finnish capital income tax rate was the lowest among the Scandinavian countries, giving policymakers some elbow room. Second, the inflation rate had come down considerably, from an average of 6 per cent prior to the 1992 reform (1989–91) to an average of 1 per cent (1994–9); and since high inflation had been an important argument for the move to the dual income tax, low inflation became an argument for an increase in the capital income tax rate. Third, there were widespread public concerns about tax equity due to the low taxation of capital income. They were reinforced by the fact that tax information is public in Finland, so that everyone could read about the low effective tax rates of wealthy capital owners in the papers.[15] Hence the capital income tax rate was increased to 28 per cent from 1996 and to 29 per cent from 2000 (Figure 6.4). In addition, the taxation of some types of capital income, e.g. interest on bank deposits, was tightened (Joumard and Suyker 2002: 39, n. 27).[16]

As to the taxation of labour income, all parties wanted labour tax cuts but realised that the budgetary room to manoeuvre was very small. The main conflict was that the Conservatives wanted to cut taxes across the board, while the left parties preferred cuts targeted to the lowest incomes. Eventually, the coalition eventually agreed to give 'special consideration' to lower and medium incomes (Jungar 2000: 314; Finnish Ministry of Finance 2002: 10). While the top marginal tax rate only fell marginally (Figure 6.4), a number of more targeted tax reliefs were implemented (Laine 2002; Sinko 2002). For instance, an earned income tax credit was introduced in 1997, with its coverage and generosity steadily increasing, and in 2001 the lowest tax bracket was abolished, effectively raising the threshold below which labour income is not taxable (from 7,900 to 11,100 EUR). These measures helped to lift labour market participation, which is high by international comparison (Joumard and Suyker 2002: 10).

In 2003 the Rainbow Coalition was voted out of office, but the Social Democrats and the Swedish People's Party continued to govern in a new coalition with the Centre Party (Table 6.8). The new government pursued the same policy of continuous but moderate cuts in marginal tax rates on wages. The Swedish People's Party and the Centre Party preferred somewhat deeper cuts in marginal tax rates on high wages, but Social Democrats only agreed to marginal cuts (*Helsingin Sanomat International Edition* 14.11.2003) (Figure 6.4). The more important topic, however, was the reform of capital taxation. There were two main reasons for reform. The first was tax competition; it was felt that Finland had to react to tax cuts in other countries. The second reason was the anticipated 'veto' of the European Court of Justice (ECJ). Because the Finnish imputation tax credits did not extend to foreign shareholders, the imputation system constituted a discrimination against foreigners and a barrier to the free movement of capital in the European Common Market (e.g. Helminen 2001). Both reasons were related, because other countries such as Germany had partly financed their cuts in the corporate tax rate by shifting the tax burden on to shareholders, and this policy had itself been justified with respect to the ECJ (see Chapter seven). It was rather clear at this point that imputation systems would not have a future in the European Union.

Hence, despite a certain public pressure to *increase* the capital income tax rate further (Joumard and Suyker 2002: 22), it was clear that the corporate tax rate would have to be cut and that a certain degree of double taxation of dividends would be allowed for. Political conflict concerned only the details of the proposal (*Helsingin Sanomat International Edition* 7.11.2003): the Centre Party wanted a general cut in the capital income tax rate to 26 per cent, while Social Democrats wanted to cut only the corporate rate to this level. The compromise was to cut the capital income tax rate to 28 per cent and the corporate tax rate to 26 per cent from 2005. Dividends were made taxable in the hands of shareholders, but to alleviate double taxation 30 per cent of the dividend remained tax-exempt. In addition, non-listed corporations were made tax-exempt up to a limit of 70,000 Euros (Sørensen forthcoming-a: 25). Finally, the government also decided to abolish the wealth tax.

All in all, Finnish policy resembled the Swedish: the dual income tax model was retained and used for focusing reductions in labour income taxation on to lower and medium wages. Pragmatic changes were made in response to the trade-offs between different equity and efficiency goals. Political conflicts were basically the same as in the other Nordic countries, but their severity was reduced by tight socio-economic constraints. Most notably, unemployment has been substantially higher in Finland than in the other Nordic countries (around 9 per cent in 2004), so that the left parties find it much more difficult to defend high tax rates on labour and discount the usual threats of the business sector to move headquarters and research departments abroad (Tikka 2001). As a result, the former Social Democratic Prime Minister Lipponen gradually moved away from the idea that Finland would maintain a total tax rate significantly above the EU average in the medium and long run. In June 2000 Lipponen pronounced for bolder labour tax cuts and for setting the long-term goal of bringing the tax burden down to the EU level (OECD 2000c: 132).

CONCLUSION

The comparison of the Nordic countries supports the explanation advanced in Chapters three and four. First, corporate tax competition was clearly of major importance. Second, tax policy choices were influenced by the interaction of party ideology, economic constraints, and veto power in a rather straightforward manner. The competitive imperative of corporate tax cuts was so strong that neither party ideology nor the number of veto players significantly retarded or reduced corporate tax cuts. However, partisan ideology and veto players did shape how governments reacted to the multiple trade-offs in income taxation. Social Democratic and Socialist parties defended the goals of progressivity and revenue-raising, even if this meant to restrict progressivity to the taxation of wages, while centre-right and right parties were more likely to push for flatter taxation of (wage) income and smaller tax rate gaps between the taxation of capital and labour income.

The debates in the Nordic countries reflected the trilemma structure explicated in Chapters three and four more fully than Australia and New Zealand: Sweden and Finland essentially maintained the dual income tax model, Denmark moved (back) to a differentiated income tax, and in Norway (partly due to the lower income tax burden) the flat tax has been discussed as a realistic alternative. The next chapter analyses Germany, another case that fully reflects the trilemma structure. On the one hand, Germany shared Australia's and New Zealand's attachment to the idea of uniform income taxation and thus reacted to tax competition in similar ways. On the other hand, here has been so much resistance in Germany to the idea of differentiated income taxation that dual income tax recently emerged as an important competitor to the flat tax model.

NOTES

1   Note that in the Nordic languages, the word 'Scandinavia' only includes Sweden, Denmark and Norway (and sometimes Iceland) but not Finland.

2   The *Folketing* (People's Diet) has 179 members, 175 members and two representatives each of the Faroe Islands and Greenland.

3   The Danish People's Party is a right-wing party on many non-economic issues (most notably immigration), but has come to accept the high level of taxation in Denmark (Table 6.1) (Bille 2004: 991).

4   The total of national income tax and local tax rates is subject to an overall limitation (tax ceiling). If the total of national and local income tax rates exceeds this 'top marginal rate', the national tax rate is reduced by the excess percentage.

5   Table 7.2 denotes 78 seats for the government because it already includes one of the government's supporters from the islands.

6   The partial imputation system had already been replaced by a separate two-bracket tax schedule for dividends in 1991.

7   Quite a few concessions and exemptions were included in the tax bill. See e.g. (OECD 1994a: 43).

8   While the reform was probably also underfinanced in the long run, the budget situation nevertheless improved considerably after 1994 due to the performance of the Danish economy.

9 The contribution rate for employees increased from 5 per cent in 1994 to 8 per cent in 1997, while an employers' contribution was introduced in 1997 at a rate of 0.3 per cent, increasing to 0.6 per cent in 1998 (OECD 1994a: 42).

10 In fact, a proposal of the non-socialist parties to lower taxes on house-owners had received public attention in the last days of the 1998 election campaign and provoked a counter-campaign by trade unions (Nielsen 1999: 71–3).

11 However, there were exceptions for unincorporated businesses (Cnossen 1999: 22, n. 6).

12 See Ganghof and Bräuninger (2006) for a discussion of 'non-accommodating' behaviour of opposition parties.

13 Gjems-Onstad (2005: 143) notes that another reason for the shareholder model was that imputation tax systems were increasingly be seen as problematic in member states of the European Economic Area (EEA, i.e. the EU member states, Iceland, Liechtenstein and Norway). I shall discuss this issue in more detail in the next section, which deals with the Finnish case.

14 However, the dual income tax included no double tax relief for capital gains from shares (Cnossen 1999: 39). This was partly to reduce the tax incentive for owners of closely held corporations to transform labour income into capital gains (Sørensen Forthcoming-a: 25).

15 Equity concerns were also reinforced by a unique 'loophole' built into the Finnish dual income tax (Tikka 1993a; Mutén 1996: 20). Because the income splitting regime was not applied to closely held companies listed on the stock exchange, these companies had ample room for transforming highly taxed earned income into lowly taxed capital income. In addition, since for unlisted companies the splitting regime is only applied to distributed profits, these companies, too, had the opportunity of transforming labour income into lowly taxed capital gains.

16 The imputed rate of return has been adjusted several times as well as differentiated in order to reduce the tax burden on unlisted corporations. In 2002, the imputed rate of return was 18 per cent for partnerships and proprietors, and 13 per cent for unlisted corporations (Joumard and Suyker 2002: 23).

chapter seven | income tax reform in germany

As explained in Chapter four, the German case study could in principle have been included in the comparison of Australia and New Zealand. Prior to the heating up of corporate tax competition in the second half of the 1980s, all three countries had implemented an ambitious type of uniform income tax that implied the strict equality between the corporate tax rates and the top tax rate on personal income. Therefore, policymakers in the three countries faced rather similar decision problems in adjusting to tax competition. However, we have also seen that German case differs in many important respects. For example, the country's level of *income* tax revenue was significantly lower than in Australia and New Zealand, which meant that a flat income tax would be easier to achieve. On the other hand, Germany's *total* tax burden was higher, mainly due to a heavy social security tax burden, so that the 'progressivity adjustment' function of the income tax was more important. Finally, the analysis of the politics of income tax reform is complicated by Germany's unique federal structure, the veto power of the Bundesrat and the existence of a powerful and activist constitutional court. For these reasons, among others, Germany deserves a chapter of its own. The structure of the analysis, however, is the same as before: I shall introduce the relevant actors, characterise the status quo ante of the German income tax system and then provide a condensed history of tax reform between the mid 1980s and the early 2000s.

INTRODUCING THE ACTORS AND THE STATUS QUO ANTE

The actors

During the period under consideration, five parliamentary parties were represented in Germany's federal parliament, the Bundestag. Their names and scores on the tax-versus-spend dimension are displayed in Table 7.1. The 'ideological' development of the Greens, which started out as a left party, is noteworthy. By the time they became an influential player in German legislative politics (from October 1998 onwards) their position on the tax-versus-spend dimension was to the right of the Social Democrats.

Table 7.2 shows the German governments during the period under considera-

Table 7.1: Important parliamentary parties in Germany, 1984–2005

Party	German name	Abbreviation	Tax-vs-spend score late 1980s	Tax-vs-spend score early 2000s
Socialist Party	Partei des demokratischen Sozialismus	PDS	na	3.0
Social Democratic Party	Sozialdemokratische Partei Deutschlands	SPD	6.5	9.3
Greens	Bündnis90/Die Grünen	GR	5.2	11.0
Christian Democratic/ Social Union	Christlich Demokratische / Soziale Union	CDU / CSU	13.5	14.4
Liberal Party	Freiheitlich Demokratische Partei	FDP	15.7	18.7

Notes: na = non-available. Tax-vs-spend scores refer to party leadership and range from 1 to 20.
Sources: Laver and Hunt (1992), Benoit and Laver (2006).

tion. The Christian-Liberal coalition under Chancellor Helmut Kohl governed for sixteen years. Only in 1998 was it replaced by the so-called Red-Green coalition of Social Democrats and Greens. All governments had majority status in the Bundestag.

However, governments did not always control a majority in the Bundesrat. As explained in Chapter two, it is state *governments* that are represented in the Bundesrat. Three types of governments which can be distinguished: (1) *congruent* governments that only include parties that are part of the governing coalition at the federal level, (2) *opposition* governments that only include parties that are not part of the governing coalition at the federal level, and (3) *mixed* governments that include both types of parties. Mixed state governments usually abstain in the Bundesrat if the coalition partners cannot find agreement. In the case of 'manda-

Table 7.2: Governments in Germany, 1984–2005

Begin	Prime Minister (Party)	Type	Parties	Gov.'s seats	Total seats
03.1983	Kohl II (CDU)	majority	CDU/CSU, FDP	278	498
03.1987	Kohl III (CDU)	majority	CDU/CSU, FDP	269	497
10.1990	Kohl IV (CDU)	majority	CDU/CSU, FDP	370	663
01.1991	Kohl V (CDU)	majority	CDU/CSU, FDP	398	662
11.1994	Kohl VI (CDU)	majority	CDU/CSU, FDP	341	672
10.1998	Schröder I (SPD)	majority	SPD, GR	345	669
10.2002	Schröder II (SPD)	majority	SPD, GR	306	611

Notes: In Oct. 1990, 144 new members elected by the German Democratic Republic (GDR) People's Chamber joined the Bundestag. The eastern German DSU (German Social Union) was incorporated into the coalition. Sources: Saalfeld (2000), Poguntke (2003).

Table 7.3: German governments' strength in the Bundesrat, 1984–2005

Government coalition			Bundesrat seats			
Parties	Begin	Status	Congruent	Oppositional	Mixed	Total
(CDU/CSU/FDP)	01.10.1982	majority	26	15	0	41
	09.04.1985	majority	23	18	0	41
	23.04.1987	majority	27	14	0	41
	02.09.1987	majority	27	11	3	41
	31.05.1988	majority	23	15	3	41
	16.03.1989	majority	23	15	3	41
	21.06.1990	minority	18	24	3	45
	03.10.1990	minority	20	26	3	49
	27.10.1990	minority	27	26	3	56
	01.11.1990	minority	27	26	7	60
	2.11.1990	minority	31	26	7	64
	08.11.1990	majority	35	26	7	68
	24.01.1991	majority	35	22	11	68
	04.04.1991	minority	31	26	11	68
	21.05.1991	minority	27	26	15	68
	26.06.1991	minority	27	29	12	68
	11.12.1991	minority	27	26	15	68
	11.06.1992	minority	21	26	21	68
	15.12.1993	minority	21	23	24	68
	22.07.1994	minority	17	27	24	68
	11.10.1994	minority	17	31	20	68
	30.11.1994	minority	13	31	24	68
	09.12.1994	minority	10	31	27	68
	18.01.1996	minority	10	32	27	69
	12.06.1996	minority	16	32	21	69
	12.11.1997	minority	16	35	18	69
(SPD, Greens)	27.10.1998	majority	35	16	18	69
	07.04.1999	minority	30	21	18	69
	29.09.1999	minority	27	24	18	69
	01.10.1999	minority	27	28	14	69
	13.10.1999	minority	23	28	18	69
	16.06.2001	minority	27	28	14	69
	31.10.2001	minority	24	28	17	69
	17.01.2002	minority	20	28	21	69
	16.05.2002	minority	16	32	21	69
	04.03.2003	minority	10	38	21	69
	10.11.2004	minority	10	37	22	69
	28.05.2005	minority	6	37	28	69
	22.06.2005	minority	0	43	28	69

Notes: The 'status' column refers to the seats of congruent state governments. Until 1990, West Berlin sent non-voting delegates to the Bundesrat. Sources: Leunig (2005).

tory' legislation, abstentions count as rejections because the government needs an absolute majority of votes in the Bundesrat.

The status quo ante

Germany's income tax system in the 1970s and early 1980s was similar to that of the six countries analysed in Chapters six and seven. While the top tax rates on corporate and personal income were somewhat lower than in these other countries—both rates stood at 56 per cent after 1977 (Figure 7.1)—this was not because Germany had a significantly broader income tax base but because the German income tax raises *less revenue*. During the 1970s, income tax revenue (corporate and personal) averaged around 12.5 per cent of GDP, roughly half of Denmark's income tax ratio during the same period. Many types of capital income received very favourable tax treatment, as did specific types of labour incomes; the rules for determining taxable profits were very favourable for businesses and investment incentives such as accelerated depreciation of assets were quite generous (e.g., Shonfield 1965; Dengel 1987).

Where Germany differed from the other countries was a stronger emphasis on 'organisational neutrality'. Academics and policymakers were strongly concerned about equal tax treatment of corporations and unincorporated businesses. One important reason for these concerns was that most German businesses (around 85

Figure 7.1: Top income tax rates and income tax revenue in Germany, 1980–2005

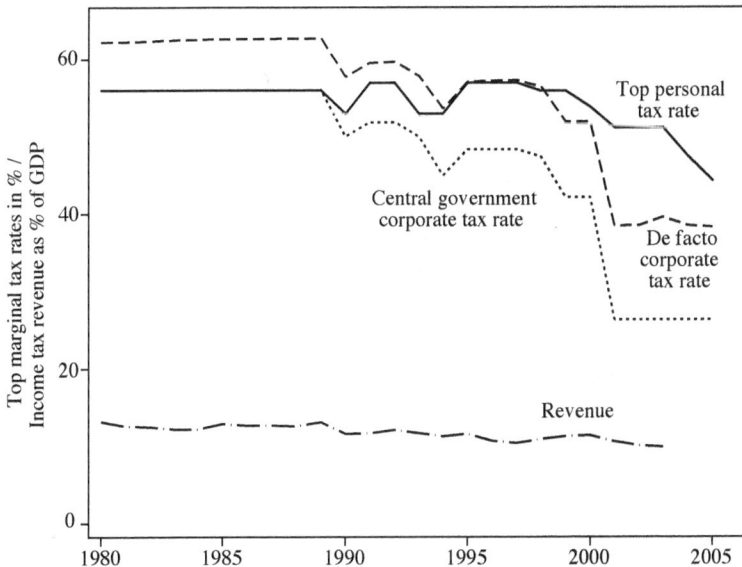

Notes: Tax revenue includes corporate and personal income taxes. 'De facto' corporate tax rate includes local business tax and all tax rates include solidarity surcharge (see appendix).
Sources: See appendix.

per cent at the time of writing) are partnerships and sole proprietorships; and in contrast to most other OECD countries these unincorporated businesses include *large* firms whose main competitors are domestic and foreign *corporations* (OECD 1994b: 25, Table 3.1).

Concerns about organisational neutrality led to the corporate tax reform of 1977, which was an integral but eventually postponed part of a comprehensive income tax reform of 1975. This reform was passed by a SPD-FDP government and its supreme goal was *tax justice* (Krüer-Buchholz 1982; Muscheid 1986: 142–58). Finance and Economics Minister Karl Schiller, who had initiated the reform in 1971, wanted the reform to 'realise as much social justice as at all possible' (cited in Muscheid 1986: 143). The effective tax burdens on low incomes, workers, and families decreased; that on high incomes increased. The top personal income tax rate was increased from 53 to 56 per cent, and the deductibility of the wealth tax from the income tax base was abolished. The reform would have been more redistributive, and the increase of the top personal rate more pronounced, had the SPD been the only veto player. Yet Social Democrats had to compromise both with their coalition partner and with a CDU/CSU-controlled Bundesrat (Muscheid 1986: 144, 150).

The 1977 reform increased the corporate tax rate from 51 to 56 per cent and domestic shareholders were granted a full credit for taxes paid at the corporate level—as proposed by the Canadian 'Carter Committee' (Chapter three).[1] This system was to abolish double-taxation of distributed profits completely and establish neutral treatment of different legal forms and different types of financing. The 5 percentage point gap between corporate and top personal tax rates prior to the reform would probably have been considered negligible in most other OECD countries; but it was perceived as 'wide' in Germany (Muscheid 1986: 166). The rate alignment achieved by the reform was seen as crucial in levelling the playing field between incorporated and unincorporated businesses.

The 1977 corporate tax reform thus established the same system that Australia and New Zealand briefly established in the mid 1980s—a system that tried to tax corporate-source income only once, at the marginal tax rate of the individual shareholder. However, Germany differed from Australia and New Zealand in that it also operated a local business tax on profits (*Gewerbeertragsteuer*), payable by incorporated and unincorporated businesses.[2] This tax was *de facto* an income tax but not in a technical sense. In addition, income from self-employment, agriculture, and forestry was exempted. It was mainly a tax on *large* businesses, because tax allowances—which increased over time—exempted a large share of unincorporated businesses from paying any tax at all. The tax increased the *de facto* corporate tax rate, as illustrated in Figure 7.1: in 1980, the local tax rate was around 6 per cent in the average community, so that the corporate tax rate of 56 per cent led to a *de facto* rate of around 62 per cent.[3]

1986 TO 1994: INCREMENTAL ADJUSTMENT OF THE CENTRE-RIGHT

In 1982 the Liberal Party left the coalition with the Social Democrats and entered a coalition with the Christian Democrats, which was to govern Germany for the next 16 years. This centre-right coalition, led by Chancellor Helmut Kohl and with Gerhard Stoltenberg as Finance Minister, wanted to reduce the tax burden. Initially, however, big tax cuts were out of the question, as the coalition gave priority to consolidating the budget. Only some minor reductions were implemented with respect to the wealth tax and the local business tax on capital. In addition, some special depreciation allowances were introduced, especially for small and medium-sized firms (Krause-Junk 1993; Leibfritz *et al.* 1998).

Consolidation came sooner than expected, which provided elbow room for tax reductions. The government embarked on a multi-year tax reform. My focus is on the third and final reform stage, which included Germany's first response to competitive pressures on the corporate tax rate. The first two stages were passed in the summer of 1985 and focused on personal income taxation (Dengel 1987). The reform (re-)introduced a child allowance, increased the basic tax allowance and reduced tax rates. The tax base was not broadened but narrowed further by granting a special depreciation allowance to small and medium-sized enterprises (Leibfritz *et al.* 1998: 154). The net tax relief was almost DM (German Mark) 25 billion.[4]

The debate about the third tax reform step played an important role in the run-up to the elections in January 1987, which was won by the incumbent coalition. The basic outline of the reform was agreed upon during the coalition negotiations in February 1987. The core of this reform was introduction of the so-called 'linear-progressive' tax schedule. While most countries have income tax brackets so that marginal tax rates increase in steps, Germany's marginal tax rates were based on a formula and increased continuously over a large range of incomes. This formula was 'linearised' by the reform in order to reduce the tax burden of medium incomes.

For competitiveness reasons the coalition also wanted to cut the corporate tax rate. Finance Ministry officials were well aware that the US tax reform would result in a race toward lower tax rates among OECD countries (McLure *et al.* 1990: 45), and there had been an increasingly heated debate about the exceptionally high *statutory* tax burden on German businesses. The coalition parties agreed, therefore, that the high corporate tax rate would have to come down. However, this goal created a trade-off with which German policymakers would struggle for the next 20 years: if the cut were achieved by reducing the *federal* corporate income tax rate, this would imply either cutting the top personal income tax rate or giving up tax rate equality. Both of these options were problematic: the rate alignment, introduced in 1977, had become a cherished feature of the German income tax system, and parts of the CDU were reluctant to accept any cuts in the top personal income tax rate.

Alternatively, the government could have reformed or abolished the local business tax. This would have reduced the *de facto* corporate tax rate without requiring a cut in the top personal rate. One option was to scrap this outdated and rather inefficient business tax altogether and compensate local governments by giving them a share of the revenues from value-added or income taxation. Birgit Breuel (CDU), then Finance Minister of Lower-Saxony, advanced this proposal in order to avoid a cut in the top personal rate. Such a cut, she argued, would favour a well-earning minority and waste financing options for targeted tax cuts and for strengthening the labour market. Agreeing on this kind of reform within the coalition seemed possible. A number of CDU politicians were in favour of it, and the FDP had long proposed to scrap the local tax. However, fiscal compensation for local governments would have implied a revision of the German fiscal constitution and thus necessitated qualified majorities in both Bundestag and Bundesrat. Mustering these majorities was impossible. The SPD categorically rejected the scrapping of the local tax because it feared a shift of the tax burden away from 'big industry' and on to small and medium-sized businesses. What is more, local business tax reform would have given Social Democrats veto power over the entire tax reform project, which they also rejected (Zohlnhöfer 2001: 89). Finally, many Länder governments, both SPD- and CDU-led, were against local business tax reform.

The issue of the local business tax was not completely removed from the agenda. The second-best reform option was to 'neutralise' some of the local business tax burden by making the tax partially creditable against the federal income tax or the value-added tax. This would also have reduced the tax burden for businesses without necessitating cuts in top personal rate. The local business tax had already been *deductible* from the federal income tax base (as well as its own base). The new proposal intended to make the local business tax *creditable*, in part, against the income tax burden, to which extent it would not add to the overall tax burden. This type of proposal had been made early in the reform debate by the CDU-led government of Rhineland-Palatinate (Burger 1996: 138–42) but resurfaced in 1987. The Federation of German Industries (*Bundesverband der deutschen Industrie*) made a similar proposal because it feared deadlock and saw a partial crediting of the local business tax against the federal income tax as the 'last chance for an effective and specific relief for businesses' (Mann 1994: 232). Chancellor Kohl was open toward the proposal but both the CSU and FDP rejected it, referring to 'strong misgivings with respect to constitutional law by the Ministry of Interior and the Ministry of Justice' (Stoltenberg 1997: 298). The industry representatives had anticipated these misgivings and cited a constitutional lawyer's expert opinion arguing for the constitutionality of the proposal (Mann 1994: 232). Yet the lawyers in the ministries disagreed and the reform proposal was rejected.

Reforming the local business tax thus turned out to be impossible due to the veto positions of the SPD in parliament, the Bundesrat (majority) and the Constitutional Court. The search for a reform compromise therefore continued in a constrained policy space (Findling 1995; Zohlnhöfer 2001: 83–104). Tax policy experts and the Finance Minister insisted on symmetric cuts in the (top) tax rates on corporate and personal income. They feared that a de-alignment of tax rates, however small, would open the floodgates for unsystematic tax policy in the future. But, cuts in the top personal income tax rate were very controversial. While CSU and FDP preferred a reduction of both top tax rates to below 50 per cent, this was fiercely opposed by large parts of the CDU, especially the labour-wing and many state prime ministers. After protracted negotiations, and after Chancellor Kohl had put his foot down, a compromise was found (Stoltenberg 1997: 299): the corporate tax rate on retained profits was cut to the desired (and still very high) level of 50 per cent and the top personal rate fell to 53 per cent, thus implying a tax rate gap of 3 percentage points (see Figure 7.1).

This reform compromise was also accepted by the (congruent) Bundesrat majority (Table 7.3). However, the congruent state governments used their influence to the effect that base-broadening measures ended up raising only DM 14 billion instead of DM 20 billion (*cf.* Zohlnhöfer 2003: 139). This increased the originally planned net reduction of DM 25 billion and forced the government to later increase various indirect taxes (Leibfritz *et al.* 1998: 155).

1990 TO 1994: DIVIDED GOVERNMENT AND INCREMENTAL ADJUSTMENT

A more thorough response to tax competition was tried in 1992. The reform was initiated by the fourth Kohl government, with Finance Minister Theo Waigel, in a political and economic situation that was fundamentally changed by re-unification: congruent state governments lacked a majority in the Bundesrat after April 1991 (Table 7.3), and re-unification created strong fiscal pressures that shifted the policy agenda from tax cuts to tax hikes. In addition, during the reform process Germany plunged into a recession, with real GDP growth dropping from above 5 per cent in 1990 and 1991 to minus 1.1 per cent in 1993.

Re-unification made the trade-offs in income taxation much more severe. To react to conflicting imperatives, the Kohl government did the opposite of what other OECD countries had been doing after the US reform in 1986: it allowed for a slight *increase* of marginal income tax rates and *narrowed* the tax base. The government introduced a surcharge on corporate and personal income tax of 3.75 per cent in 1991 and 1992, thereby increasing the *de facto* corporate tax rate by about two percentage points (see Figure 7.1). In addition, tax incentives were introduced to stimulate investment in East Germany. For instance, an investment tax credit was introduced and accelerated depreciation allowances were granted with a maximum depreciation rate of up to 50 per cent of construction/acquisition cost (Leibfritz *et al.* 1998: 150–1).

Yet this accustomed strategy did no longer fit the international context. Between 1986 and 1992, most OECD countries achieved large cuts in their corporate tax rates (see Chapters one and eight), and there was mounting evidence that German companies became increasingly responsive to low tax rates in other countries (Weichenrieder 1996; Ganghof 2000: 161). As a result, concerns about the de factor corporate tax rate increasingly became the 'focal point' of German tax policy (BMF 1999b: 79).

This is also shown by the fact that Social Democrats' policy preferences changed. The SPD had previously not called for a lower statutory corporate tax rate but changed its position in the early 1990s. Social Democrats still considered the *effective* tax burden on the corporate sector to be 'adequate' but acknowledged that the corporate tax rate would have to be cut in order to increase foreign direct investment (Poß 1992: 449). Because the Social Democrats were unwilling to accept any revenue loss, they also adopted a 'level playing field'rhetoric. As we will see below, however, this rhetoric would prove to be short-lived.

Of course, concerns about the corporate tax rate led to the same trade-off as before: corporate tax cuts implied either a cut in the top personal income tax rate or a larger gap between the two rates. Because Christian Democrats and business associations believed that the former option was politically infeasible, they looked for ways to combine a large tax rate gap with organisational neutrality (e.g., Faltlhauser 1988: 245–248; Willemsen 1991: 110–11). However, such a solution was disliked by the Liberals, and it would have given away a powerful rationale for a future flattening of personal income taxes. Not surprisingly, therefore, the coalition again turned to the local business tax and proposed a different way to 'neutralise' its burden: an isolated reduction of the top personal income tax rate *for those businesses that bore the local business tax.*[5] This proposal was politically very powerful but, not surprisingly, its constitutionality was questioned (e.g., Wendt 1993: 8; Tipke and Lang 1998: 451–2). There was a high probability that the Constitutional Court would sooner or later nullify a special top tax rate for businesses. This time, however, coalition policymakers discounted this possibility, and the main reason seems to be that they had run out of alternatives. Because they were unwilling to accept the revenue losses associated with a general cut in top income tax rates, they *had* to embrace the special tax rate model as a second-best solution. Hence the government, in early 1993, proposed a revenue-neutral reform that would reduce both the corporate tax rate and the top rate for business income (which bore the local business tax) from 50 to 44 per cent while leaving the general top personal rate at 53 per cent. To finance the reform, the tax base was to be broadened, most notably by reducing the depreciation rate for movable business assets and buildings (*degressive Absetzung für Abnutzung [Afa]*) from 30 to 25 per cent.

In discussing the policy preferences of the Bundesrat as a veto player, we can focus on the policy preferences of the Social Democrats. After all, the issues on which SPD-led Länder governments might have disagreed with the party line—net revenue losses and a reform of the local business tax—had been kept off the agenda. The SPD also proposed a cut in the corporate rate on retained profits, from 50 to 45 per cent, but was against any cuts in the top personal income tax rate. It denounced the idea of a special top tax rate for businesses as a breach of the principle of uniform income taxation and thus unconstitutional. Instead, Social

Democrats adopted the proposal—implemented in countries like Denmark and previously embraced by tax policy experts of the Christian Democrats—to tax the *retained* profits of unincorporated businesses at the same rate as the corporate tax rate (Poß 1992: 449–51). Hence, the SPD wanted a differentiated income tax that achieved organisational neutrality.

As a result, the Bundesrat majority categorically rejected any differentiation of personal income tax rates as inequitable. It argued that the corporation tax was an entirely different type of tax and that an isolated cut in the corporate tax would therefore not undermine the idea of uniform income taxation. The Bundesrat therefore proposed to cut only the corporate rate to 46 per cent. Furthermore, while the Bundesrat welcomed the government's goal of revenue-neutrality, it had misgivings about the proposed cut in depreciation allowances for movable equipment and proposed an alternative list of base-broadening measures. These misgivings were not only due to short-term business cycle concerns but revealed the fact that the 'level playing field'-rhetoric had been just that. Many SPD politicians still strongly believed in the efficacy of investment incentives.

The deadlock had to be resolved in the mediation committee of Bundestag and Bundesrat in July 1993. There was no doubt that an agreement would be found because short-term policy preferences had been converging in response to the deepening recession. Most economists criticised the deceleration of depreciation due the adverse effects on domestic investment incentives. In fact, the Advisory Council of the Ministry of Finance advised to shelve the entire reform if a net reduction of the tax burden was not possible (BMF 1999b: Chapter six). In addition, a number of coalition politicians, including Economics Minister Günther Rexrodt (FDP), joined the ranks of the critics. Two days before the negotiations in the mediation committee, therefore, the coalition agreed on shelving the planned cuts in depreciation rules for movable business assets (Zohlnhöfer 2001: 221). This set the stage for the following compromise: depreciation rules remained unchanged and the resulting revenue 'loss' of about DM 5 billion was financed by reducing the top personal tax rate on business income only to 47 per cent and the corporate rate to 45 per cent. Additional base-broadening measures were included in the agreement. The compromise was passed by the Bundestag and, almost unanimously, by the Bundesrat in July 1993 and most of the reform became effective at the beginning of 1994. The model of 'neutralising' the local business tax was thus not implemented consistently but the special top rate on personal business income allowed at least a minor reduction of the corporate income tax rate.

1994 TO 1998: DEADLOCK

In October 1994 the centre-right coalition was re-elected by a slim margin. The election weakened the position of the FDP within the coalition, as the party's vote share fell from 11 to 6.9 per cent. In addition, the party did not win any seats in three parallel state elections (Mecklenburg-Western Pomerania, Thuringia,

Saarland). Another result of these state elections was that the majority of the opposition states in the Bundesrat increased (Table 7.3).

The FDP had been the only party calling for far-reaching income tax cuts in their election campaign but failed to commit its coalition partners to an ambitious tax reform agenda in the coalition agreement. The fundamental problem was tight budgetary constraints: unification-induced fiscal pressure continued to be strong; the generous investment incentives in the eastern States were eroding the income tax base, the run-up to European Monetary Union was sure to necessitate further deficit reduction, and the Federal Constitutional Court made a number of expensive judgments (Leibfritz *et al.* 1998: 155–7). In short, the fiscal room to manoeuvre was tiny.

That tax cuts nevertheless remained on the government's policy agenda had a lot to do with tax competition, in which Germany's position had further deteriorated. The hard won tax reduction of 1994 had already been lost by 1995 because local governments had increased local business tax rates and because the solidarity surcharge of 7.5 per cent was reinstated (see Figure 7.1).[6] In contrast, many other OECD countries—such as the Nordic countries discussed in the previous chapter—had used the 1990–4 period for radical overhauls of their income tax systems. As a result, all parties' policy positions, except that of the PDS, converged on a federal corporate tax rate of 35 per cent (Kraeusel 1997).

However, parties' positions with respect to the *corporate* tax rate had not been the problem in the past. The gnawing problem was that of the 'tax rate gap'. In fact, after the 1994 tax reform there were two distinct problems. First, many experts believed the gap *within* personal income taxation to be unconstitutional — the gap created by the special top tax rate for personal business income. The government therefore had good reason to fear that this special rate would sooner or later be scrapped by the Constitutional Court. Second, the gap *between* the corporate tax rate and special top rate on personal business income was also increasingly discussed as a constitutional issue (see also Wendt 1996; Bareis 2000; Lang 2001: 54, 103–4). The coalition emphasised the importance of the second gap, Social Democrats that of the first.

At the time of coalition bargaining, the government perceived general income tax cuts as much too expensive and therefore launched a new effort to reduce the local business income tax. Again, however, this effort was thwarted by the Bundesrat.[7] Part of the problem was surely that Social Democrats favoured the model of a differentiated income taxation plus organisational neutrality, which would have allowed for a large tax rate gap between corporate and personal taxation. Therefore, they saw no necessity to use local tax reform as a means of adjusting to corporate tax competition.

Given the government's beliefs about the likely preferences of the Constitutional Court, the failure of local business tax reform had far-reaching consequences. To increase competitiveness, the corporate income tax rate had to be cut; and to cut this rate in a constitutional manner, the top personal income tax rate had to be cut, too. More and more coalition politicians therefore called for general income tax cuts, so that the tax reform debate shifted. The issue of competitiveness could no longer be separated from the issue of general income tax reform.

Of course, competitiveness considerations were not the only driving force of the shifting tax reform debate. Another important factor was an increasingly intense debate about 'cleaning up' the income tax base after the 1994 elections. This debate was stimulated by a reform proposal of an expert committee, sometimes called the 'Bareis Committee', whose task was to advise the Finance Minister on how to meet a policy challenge created by the Federal Constitutional Court in 1992. The Court had judged that the basic tax allowance was too low because low-income earners, although taxed, might have to apply for social assistance. The Court demanded the introduction of a tax-free subsistence level by 1996, and this demand became a central part of the coalition agreement of 1994, scheduled to cost about DM 15 billion. The Bareis Recommendations, published at the beginning of the 1994–8 legislative term, were very ambitious: in addition to a net reduction of DM 15 billion and an increase of the bottom tax rate from 19 to 22 per cent, it envisaged systematic base-broadening measures worth DM 25 billion (BMF 1995). This combination of painful base-broadening and tax rate *hikes* was fatal. Both the CSU Finance Minister and leading SPD politicians dismissed the expert's recommendations even before they were fully known, and the government eventually adopted a more pragmatic solution: the basic allowance was increased to DM 12, 095 (by 1996), and the resulting revenue loss was compensated by increasing the basic tax rate to 25.9 per cent as well as by making the marginal tax rate curve much more progressive for lower incomes. But even though the Bareis Recommendations had no direct effect on income tax reform, they helped to initiate a broad reform debate.

This debate was also reinforced by the increasingly obvious failure of tax-based investment stimulation in Eastern Germany. The Eastern German experience highlighted the problems of an unsystematic mixture of elements of Income and Consumption taxes (Chapter three). Investment incentives were used for tax arbitrage, enabling well-off taxpayers to generate negative capital income and bring down their labour tax burden (Bork and Mueller 1998). The result was an eroding income tax base, reduced *effective* income tax progressivity and a large number of unoccupied office-blocks in East Germany. In the face of these perverse outcomes, even leading economic tax policy experts who had been keenly opposed to the strategy of tax-cut-*cum*-base-broadening, e.g. Hans-Werner Sinn (1992), now embraced precisely this strategy (Sinn 1997).

The time for a general income tax reform seemed to have come. Many groups drafted reform proposals that (selectively) combined the base-broadening measures listed by the Bareis Committee with more-or-less drastic cuts in statutory tax rates. By April 1996 it was clear that the government would embark on a comprehensive reform. The strategy of tax-cut-*cum*-base-broadening in personal income taxation was now fully embraced by all three coalition parties. As suggested above, it is likely that the debate about the constitutional problems of 'tax rate gaps' contributed to this convergence of policy preferences

The coalition appointed a tax reform committee, headed by the Finance Minister, which prepared a tax reform proposal (BMF 1997). The corporate tax rate and the special top tax rate for personal business income were to be cut to 35 per cent (which would still have led to a '*de facto*' corporate tax rate of around 48 per cent). The top personal tax rate was to fall to 39 per cent, and in order to contain revenue losses, the income threshold for the top rate was to be reduced from DM 120,000 to DM 90,000. In addition, the solidarity surcharge was to be cut to 5.5 per cent. The basic allowance was to increase to DM 13,000 and the basic tax rate to be reduced from 26 to 15 per cent, but only for a small income range. The tax base was to be broadened significantly both in the business and the household sector. Base-broadening measures in the business sector mainly concerned the valuation of assets and the set-up of accruals. The measures in the household sector included the partial taxation of pensions and transfers as well as the scrapping of tax relief for extra payments for Sunday-, holiday- and night-time-work. Some tax expenditures for higher incomes were to remain unchanged, most notably the tax exemption for 'non-speculative' private capital gains—only the 'speculation periods' were to be lengthened: from two to ten years for immobile property, and from six months to one year for financial assets. Finally, in addition to these base-broadening measures, the value-added tax rate was to be increased by one percentage point.

Around DM 30 billion were to remain as a net reduction of the tax burden. Given severe budgetary tension, this target for the net reduction was very ambitious but had a clear economic and political rationale. Economically, a purely revenue-neutral reform would have reduced domestic investment incentives because part of the tax burden would have been shifted from above-normal to normal profits (see Chapter three). As in 1993, therefore, economists advised strongly against revenue-neutrality. The Advisory Council of the Ministry of Economics called for a large net reduction, and some of its members even suggested combining tax rate cuts with an *improvement* of depreciation rules (BMWi 1996: 10–12). The political rationale of a significant net reduction was to reduce the number of groups that were losers as a result of the reform.

The problem was how to make up for the revenue loss. The coalition's somewhat vague strategy was to cut expenditure (in the future) and hope for self-financing through higher economic growth. In addition, there were clear signals to accept higher deficits as the default solution.

Not surprisingly, Social Democrats rejected the government's approach. As before, consensus existed about the need to cut the corporate tax rate to (at least) 35 per cent. However, the SPD rejected the idea that such a cut required a similar cut in the top rate on personal income. Whereas the coalition parties talked about a 'competitive top tax rate', the SPD party leader called this a 'joke' and 'an absurdity on which the SPD will not waste time' (*Der Spiegel* 24.2.1997: 24; 17.3.1997: 27). Social Democrats were not against a cut of the top personal income tax rate *per se*, but opposed a cut whose only purpose was to render a low corporate tax rate 'constitutional'. Lafontaine said:

I have always explained to businesses: if you want lower nominal rates and agree that many exceptions drop out in return, we can do that. However, to obviate lawyer's sophistry, I must also say: if one concludes from this that the income tax rate for private income would then also have to go down because the rates must not fall apart so much, then the tax rate for business income cannot be reduced that much.

(Der Spiegel 17.3.1997: 28)

The SPD's tax reform proposal stated that a (moderate) cut was possible if and only if 'additional tax expenditures are eliminated that have so far mainly benefited top earners' (Kraeusel 1997: 146). In addition, the proposal reaffirmed the party's commitment to 'organisational neutrality'. Social Democrats aimed at a differentiated income tax similar to that in Denmark, i.e. low and proportional taxation of *retained* profits of *all* businesses. However, as a compromise—and partly due to doubts about the practicability of a Danish-style solution—Social Democrats later also signalled their willingness to accept an isolated cut of the special top tax rate for personal business incomes, which the government had introduced in 1994.

Social Democrats were also decidedly opposed to a net reduction of the tax burden. As in 1993, they called for net reduction in the medium term but saw no budgetary elbow room in the short term (Poß 1996; Kraeusel 1997: 144). Their tax reform program included the possibility of a fairly small tax reduction of DM 7.5 billion but this reduction only concerned the cut in the solidarity surcharge, which the government had planned anyway and which did not affect the financial interests of state governments. The SPD proposed focused tax rate cuts for businesses, lower incomes and families: the basic allowance was to increase to DM 14,000, the basic tax rate to reduce to 22 per cent, and child benefits were to be raised. The resulting revenues losses were to be fully compensated by closing 'loopholes' for businesses and high-income earners and by reintroducing a tax on private wealth (Kraeusel 1997: 150). Because they did not want a large net reduction, however, Social Democrats were wary of reducing the depreciation rate for movable business assets (Kraeusel 1997: 147). The government wanted to cut this rate from 30 to 20 per cent, bringing in an additional DM 10 billion of business tax revenue. The SPD rejected this proposal. Finally, the SPD was also unwilling to accept an increase of the value-added tax in order to finance income tax cuts. Instead they wanted to use a higher value-added tax as well as higher excise taxes on energy in order to reduce social security contributions.

Prospects for agreement were thus bleak. The government wanted to move in the direction of a flat income tax with uniform taxation of all incomes, whereas Social Democrats aimed at a differentiated income tax that was *more competitive* but *at least as redistributive* as the status quo. All that would have been possible was agreement on a structural business tax reform in order to achieve a more competitive corporate tax rate but, given the anticipated veto position of the Constitutional Court, the room for agreement in this respect was also quite small.

Not surprisingly, therefore, the negotiations between the government and the SPD/Bundesrat majority, which spanned almost the entire year of 1997, failed (for details see Zohlnhöfer 2001: 236–65). The only measure both sides could agree on was an increase of the value-added tax rate from 15 to 16 per cent in order to reduce social security contributions. In addition, the governing coalition used their majority to reduce the solidarity surcharge by two percentage points (from 1998).

1998 TO 2005: NEOLIBERALISM BY DEFAULT?

With the tax reform finally shelved at the beginning of 1998, income tax policy figured prominently in the run-up to the general elections in October the same year. Both the coalition parties and the SPD stuck to their respective reform proposals and wanted the voters to give them a clear mandate to reform income taxation. Voters gave the mandate to a new centre-left coalition of Social Democrats and Greens (Table 7.2). While this Red-Green coalition was led by the centrist Chancellor Gerhard Schröder, the Finance Ministry was in the hands of the SPD's leftist chairman Oskar Lafontaine—at least initially.

The Greens entered the politics of income tax reform as a new player that generally stood somewhere between the SPD and the opposition parties on economic issues (Table 7.1). Initially the Greens called for strict revenue-neutrality in tax reform but this was to change in the tax reform process. This is not surprising because Green ideas about tax structure were clearly to the right of the SPD (Kaltenborn 1999). The Greens embraced the ideal of uniform income taxation and therefore preferred lower tax rates and deeper cuts in depreciation allowances and tax expenditures for workers than Social Democrats. They aimed at a corporate tax rate of 35 per cent, wanted to abolish the special top tax rate on personal business income and reduce the general top tax to 45 per cent—with the perspective of reducing it further in the future in order to reduce the tax rate gap.

In the coalition negotiations, the Social Democrats asserted themselves on most controversial issues (SPD and Bündnis90/Die Grünen 1998). The top personal rate was scheduled to fall only to 48.5 per cent (from 2002), the special top rate on business profits was not to be scrapped but further reduced to 43 per cent (by 2000), depreciation rules were to remain unchanged, as were tax reliefs for workers. A net reduction of DM 14 billion was planned, but only from 2002. As proposed by the SPD in 1997, tax cuts were to be focused on low and medium incomes, families, and businesses (as opposed to high 'private' incomes).

The SPD also pushed through its idea of a 'uniform business tax' with a tax rate on retained business profits of 35 per cent. Given increasing competitive pressure, however, this 35 per cent target would prove to be short-lived. The coalition agreement did not specify how 'organisational neutrality' could be achieved but delegated this task to a tax reform committee. When this committee started its work in December 1998 most of its members believed that 35 per cent *plus* the local business income would still be too high and that a more adequate target would be 38–40 per cent *including* the local tax (Schaumburg and Rödder 2000: 102).

From October 1998 to March 1999 the government was supported by a majority of congruent state governments in the Bundesrat, and it used this majority to push through initial tax reform measures. The corporate tax rate was cut to 40 per cent (from 1999), the top tax rate on businesses was scheduled to be cut to 43 per cent (from 2000), and the top personal rate was scheduled to be cut to 48.5 per cent (from 2002). The child benefit increased to DM 250 for the first and second child, the basic tax allowance increased to DM 13,067 and the basic tax rate decreased to 23.9 per cent. Base-broadening measures fell largely on businesses and higher incomes. The government revised some of these measures after protracted and heated public debates about their economic consequences. The measures included stricter regulations for the determination of taxable profits as well as creation and valuation of reserves, elimination of special depreciations, and a 50 per cent reduction in a savings allowance. The insurance and energy sectors were forced to release large reserves. All in all, these reform measures were to lead to a net tax reduction of DM 20 billion from 2002 but large businesses actually had to shoulder a higher tax bill.

A further increase of the child benefit to DM 260, although specified in the coalition agreement, was not included in the initial tax reform step. This was due to another intervention of the Federal Constitutional Court. The Court demanded equal treatment of married and single parents, thereby forcing the government to pursue a more comprehensive and quite expensive reform of the taxation of families. The resulting reform increased the child allowance to EUR 154 from 2002, among other measures. The net reduction of this reform alone was put at around EUR 5.8 billion (BMF 2002: 6)—almost the amount that the coalition agreement had envisaged for *all* tax reductions.

But business tax reform was still to come. The tax reform committee published its recommendations in April 1999 (BMF 1999a). By that time the political situation had changed significantly. Because the Red-Green state government in Hesse lost the state elections in February 1999, the federal government lacked, from April 1999 onwards, a majority of congruent state governments in the Bundesrat (Table 7.3). Furthermore, in March Oskar Lafontaine resigned, both as Finance Minister and chairman of the SPD. His resignation was the result of quarrels within the government about the general direction of economic policy. Chancellor Schröder was elected chairman of the SPD and Hans Eichel, former Prime Minister of Hesse, became Finance Minister. This change from Lafontaine to Eichel did not lead to a changed conception of tax reform but Eichel took greater effort to explain publicly the importance of a low corporate tax rate with respect to the behaviour of multinational enterprises.

Because the government had—with the consent of Lafontaine—agreed to a more ambitious target for the *de facto* corporate tax rate of 38–40 per cent, it would have been helpful if local taxes had been included in the reform package. However, this was once more out of the question from the start. The government saw tax cuts as extremely urgent and believed that an inclusion of the local business tax in the reform package would unduly complicate and lengthen the reform process (Eichel 2000: 77). By implication, the federal corporate tax rate had to fall to 25–28 per cent.

The question was how this tax rate could be achieved without further cuts in the top personal rate. The option the coalition seemed to prefer was the one they had already chosen in their initial tax cuts: preserve the special top tax rate on personal business income and accept larger tax rate gaps between the three different top tax rates. The corporate tax rate could have fallen to 25–28 per cent or lower, the special top rate on business income to 35–38 per cent and the general top personal rate to 45–48 per cent. Such a model was sketched by the tax expert to the Greens, for instance. However, this option was rendered unfeasible by a decision of the Federal Fiscal Court published in April. The court argued that, even with the already existing tax rate gap, the special top rate for business income contradicted the constitution's equality principle. The Federal Fiscal Court found fault in the lack of a consistent economic or social rationale behind the measure and particularly objected to the 'indiscriminate privileging of both distributed and retained profits' (BStBl [Federal Tax Gazette] II 1999: 450). For this reason, the court rejected the legislator's claim that the special tax rate was in the public interest and judged it to be unconstitutional. This decision, although it still had to be affirmed by the Federal Constitutional Court, effectively foreclosed the possibility of reaching a competitive corporate tax rate on the basis of the special tax rate model.

This decision of the Federal Fiscal Court threw the government into turmoil. While the SPD had hitherto resisted the Greens' demands for a lower top personal rate, the Ministry of Finance now had to acknowledge that the Court's decision might necessitate further cuts in that rate (Frankfurter Allgemeine Zeitung 30.4.1999). The coalition searched for ways to reduce the federal corporate tax rate to 25 per cent that was not too expensive and did not necessitate large cuts in the top personal income tax rate. In doing that they drew strongly on the recommendations of the tax reform committee.

The committee's first decision was to turn away from the imputation system and establish a modified 'classical' system with partial double taxation of corporate profits. The reasons were those already discussed in the Finnish case study. First, moving away from the imputation system would help to *finance* a further 15 percentage point cut in the corporate tax rate: the tax burden was partly shifted away from the corporation and on to its shareholders. The vice-chairman of the tax reform committee observes that '[i]t was clear to the...committee from the start that a low corporate tax rate could only be financed by turning away from the full imputation system', that maintaining the imputation system was 'not even discussed' and that Germany 'could only stand up against tax competition by turning back towards the classical corporate tax system' (Lang 2000: 27). The second reason was the veto threat of the European Court of Justice. The government argued that the European Court of Justice (ECJ) would sooner or later enforce equal treatment of residents and non-resident shareholders. Hence the government proposed a corporate rate of 25 per cent for both retained and distributed profits and to replace the imputation system by a modified classical system.[8] Under the so-called 'half-income system' the dividends paid by corporations were to be subject to personal income tax but at only 50 per cent of the shareholder's marginal income tax rate. In practice this is achieved by taxing only 50 per cent of the dividends at the shareholder's marginal personal rate.

The reform committee's preference for the half-income system was not unanimous. Most notably, the public economist Helga Pollak, member of the Economic Advisory Council of the Finance Ministry, expressed her opposition to the intended gap between the business tax rate (on retained profits) of 25 per cent and a top personal tax rate of 48.5 per cent (BMF 1999a: 110–12). She proposed a flat income tax—a proposal that was later embraced by the (majority of the) Advisory Council of the Finance Ministry in a letter to the Minister of Finance.

But, of course, a flat income tax was out of the question for the coalition, and— at this point—also for the opposition Christian Democrats. The main question for the government was how to achieve 'organisational neutrality'. The tax reform committee discussed two (potentially complementary) ways to allow unincorporated business to accumulate profits in the business at the corporate tax rate. One way was to give unincorporated businesses the option of being treated like corporations for tax purposes *in all respects* (called the 'option model'). The other was to emulate corporate taxation within the personal income tax by establishing a special tax rate on retained business profits, which I shall call the 'emulation model'. Most members of the tax reform committee were sceptical on both models (Schaumburg and Rödder 2000: 111). The committee therefore proposed to test their practicability in business games, which were implemented by management consultants and whose results were presented in December 1999 (BMF 2000a).

Between April and December 1999 the tax reform plans were heavily attacked from both sides of the political spectrum. Ironically, both the left and right mainly defended the ideal of uniform income taxation but drew different conclusions about what this ideal implied. The right-wing critics, including many economic and legal policy experts and tax lawyers, criticised the structural changes proposed by the government and called for a radical flattening of the income tax schedule. The left side also criticised the structural changes but believed that a radical flattening was unnecessary and that the corporate tax rate could remain at a level of 35–40 per cent. The Greens, too, criticised the reform plans of the Ministry of Finance and called for further (but still moderate) cuts in marginal tax rates. Ironically, therefore, the main supporters of the Finance Minister came out of the business sector, which was keen on benefiting from lower business tax rates. Surveys revealed that a large majority of managers supported a tax rate gap between retained and distributed profits (*Handelsblatt* 17./18.12.1999).

The criticism notwithstanding, the Finance Minister continued to pursue the general tax reform concept that had been devised by his predecessor. This also had fiscal reasons: when the tax reform was being discussed within the coalition, there was also a heated debate about Germany's structural budget deficit. In fact, in the same cabinet meeting that decided on basic elements of the tax reform (23 June 1999), the cabinet also agreed on painful expenditure cuts worth DM 30 billion. Hence it seemed of utmost importance to keep net reductions of the tax burden to a minimum. For this reason, the SPD also had to abandon further aspects of its tax reform program. The cabinet decided to cut the federal corporate tax rate to 25 per cent but to keep the resulting revenue losses to a minimum, depreciation of business assets had to be decelerated much more than the SPD (and many economists) would have liked. The depreciation rate for movable business assets, which the Social Democrats had defended several times in opposition, finally had to descend from 30 to 20 per cent. This cut alone was estimated to bring in around DM 13-14 billion (BMF 2000b: 290). In addition, depreciation periods for different types of assets were to be lengthened, and the cabinet accepted the switch to the half-income system. The overall net reduction of the reform—which was now to start in 2001 rather than 2000 as stated in the coalition agreement—was to be around DM 6 billion (*Frankfurter Allgemeine Zeitung* 24.6.1999).

The cabinet did not make a decision on the taxation of unincorporated businesses because the results of the business games had to be awaited. In evaluating the results of the business games, the Finance Ministry was counselled by an advisory group that included members of the tax reform committee. In November, 'after controversial discussion' (Schaumburg and Rödder 2000: 125), the majority of this group advised against the 'emulation model' and in favour of the 'option model', and the Finance Minister followed this advice. This meant that true 'organisational neutrality' would not be achievable. For it was estimated that the option model would only be attractive for around 10 per cent of all businesses, those with high profits. For the other 90 per cent a different solution had to be found.

The preferred solution had already been sketched by the tax reform committee in April. It was the well-known idea of neutralising the local business tax burden by crediting local business tax against income tax. Recall that this approach had been proposed in 1987 but eventually rejected on constitutional grounds. This time the committee and the government believed it could be made constitutional—a belief that was contested by many legal tax experts. Unincorporated businesses were to subtract a standardised amount of their local business tax from their individual income tax liability. Compared with incorporated firms, unincorporated firms would then pay higher income taxes but lower local business taxes. This solution, which was also favoured by the Greens, meant abolishing the burden of the local business tax for a majority of unincorporated businesses. These businesses would effectively only bear the federal income tax. As a result, the downward pressure on the top personal income tax rate would be reduced. The planned top rate of 48.5 per cent would no longer have to be compared with the federal corporate rate of 25 per cent but with the de facto corporate tax rate of 38–40 per cent. A gap of almost 10 percentage points would remain, however. In addition, businesses whose profits were so small that they did not have to pay the local business tax would benefit from neither the 'option model' nor the crediting of the business tax. The reform plans therefore continued to be attacked by the opposition and, partly in response, also within the governing coalition.

Despite the criticism, the Finance Minister initially tried to keep the floodgates closed. In early December, estimates were leaked from the Finance Ministry that the costs of business tax reform would increase from DM 6 to DM 20 billion—an estimate that led an anonymous SPD finance policy expert to reckon that only obfuscation could prevent intra-party rebellion (*Der Spiegel* 6.12.1999: 113). In fact, the Finance Ministry responded to these press reports that a net reduction of DM 20 billion would make it impossible for the government to continue its consolidation course. It emphasised that nothing had been decided and that the detailed reform plans would not be presented until 5th January 2000 (*Frankfurter Allgemeine Zeitung* 8.12.1999).

However, this announcement was obsolete only a week later. The government changed its strategy and prepared far-reaching income tax cuts, which they now wanted to present before Christmas. There are many potential reasons for this strategy change but the lack of a Bundesrat majority surely was an important one. As we shall see, the government's political strategy was *not* to enter into negotiations with the opposition leaders, which rejected the entire approach of the reform (e.g. the half-income system). Rather, the government aimed at winning the support of a sufficient number of 'mixed' state governments. Therefore, the overall package had to be sufficiently attractive and the Finance Minister had to accommodate the critics.

On the 21st December the government announced a reform plan that would lead to an overall annual tax reduction of more than DM 40 billion by the year 2005. Within only two weeks the Finance Ministry's emphasis on budget consolidation had given way to rhetoric of 'strengthening growth' and 'returning the money to the taxpayers' (BMF 1999d). The main aspects of the tax reforms were as follows: first, the government wanted to bring the final stage of the tax reform already passed forward by one year, i.e. to 2001; the basic and top tax rates were cut to 19.9 and 48.5 per cent, respectively, and the basic allowance increased to DM 14,000. Second, as of 2001 the corporate tax rate was to be cut to 25 per cent and unincorporated businesses were to be relieved by the measures explained above. Part of this reform was financed by scrapping the special top tax rate for personal business income and by broadening the tax base. Third, the reform plan included tax cuts across the entire progressive tax schedule. The basic tax rate was to be lowered to 17 per cent by 2003 and 15 per cent by 2005, the top rate to 47 per cent by 2003 and 45 per cent by 2005; the basic allowance was to be increased to DM 14,500 by 2003 and DM 15,000 by 2005. Fourth, capital gains taxes on *corporations'* sale of shares were to be abolished. While the initial stimulus for this radical proposal was the equal treatment of foreign and domestic shares (Ganghof 2004: 110–11), the coalition also emphasised the goal of unblocking the restructuring of the German economy (Höpner 2003). Finally, the decision added to the attractiveness of the reform proposal, thus making it more difficult for the

Bundesrat majority to veto the reform. In fact, Hans Eichel explicitly argued that because businesses were in favour of the reform, the Bundesrat would not dare to block it (*Frankfurter Allgemeine Zeitung* 22.12.1999). The Finance Minister also emphasised that the government would stay on its consolidation course but did not specify all the budgetary adjustments required by the expanded reform plans.

As hoped by the government, business representatives' views on the tax reform plans became much more favourable. The tax exemption of corporations' capital gains from shares was of course emphatically embraced by the leaders of big financial corporations like Allianz or Deutsche Bank, but the leaders of the peak business associations also acknowledged the government's increasing spiritedness with respect to tax reform and announced 'massive attacks' on the opposition if it blocked tax reform in the Bundesrat—an announcement that provoked indignation on the side of the opposition parties (*Frankfurter Allgemeine Zeitung* 17.2.2000).

In May the coalition majority in the Bundestag's Finance Committee accepted a modified reform bill. The modifications made reflected criticism within the coalition but certainly also the veto position of the Bundesrat. They included, for instance, the increase of a tax allowance for the sales of unincorporated businesses. The modifications were estimated to jointly increase the annual net reduction (by 2005) by DM 5 billion to DM 45 billion (*Frankfurter Allgemeine Zeitung* 19.5.2000).

But the final hurdle was still to come. The government lacked a majority (of congruent state governments) in the Bundesrat, and it also had to get congruent (SPD or SPD-Green) state governments' consent on a tax bill that would lead to significant revenue losses for the states. The latter task was less of a problem. The planned net reduction was a bitter pill to swallow, to be sure, especially since the states believed (based on estimates of the Finance Ministry in North Rhine-Westphalia) that the final net reduction would be DM 60 billion rather than DM 45 billion (*Financial Times Deutschland, Online Edition* 1.6.2000). Nevertheless, it was clear that congruent states wanted to do their best to accommodate the government's plans. Moreover, the states' hesitance to shoulder a large net reduction of the tax burden was a welcome counterweight to the opposition's demands for even larger net reductions. But congruent states did not only worry about the revenue losses, they also wanted to fine-tune the tax reform bill. Most notably, state politicians of the SPD were quite sceptical on the 'option model' for unincorporated businesses. Already in March 2000, congruent governments' criticism of this model had given rise to speculation that the scheme would eventually be scrapped in return for a lower top personal income tax (*Frankfurter Allgemeine Zeitung* 17.3.2000).

Getting the consent of additional oppositional or mixed state government was more difficult. The opposition parties' stated policy positions had become somewhat more radical compared to their reform bill in 1998. The FDP (1999) wanted to abolish the distinction between corporate and personal income and reduce the top personal tax rate to 35 per cent (income threshold: DM 60,000). The local business tax was to be abolished. The FDP proposal would have led to massive revenue losses, the financing of which was not specified.

In response to the government's new reform concept with a net reduction of over DM 40 billion, the CDU and the CSU agreed on a reform proposal that was designed to outnumber the net reduction of the government. To avoid any rises in effective tax rate and to make the proposal politically more attractive, the two parties even abandoned—at least officially—their earlier commitment to the scrapping of tax relief for extra payments for Sunday-, holiday- and night time-work. The top personal income tax rate was to fall to 35 per cent (threshold: DM 110 106), the corporate tax rate on retained corporate profits to 30 per cent. The local business tax was to be reduced. The Christian Democrats were also decidedly opposed to the half-income system. They wanted to retain the imputation system in order to achieve a truly uniform income tax. Their proposal implied a net reduction of DM 50 billion by 2003 according to their own estimates and DM 77 billion according the Ministry of Finance.

This sketch of policy preferences shows that the government's proposal posed a strategic challenge for the opposition. An FDP-type tax reform was out of the question in the short run, as was a reform of the local business tax. Everyone knew that even the DM 45 billion net reduction planned by the government was very difficult for public budgets to accommodate. Especially the CDU prime ministers of the small and poor states, such as Saarland's Peter Müller, made it clear that the planned net reduction of the government was the maximum of what state budgets could bear (*Frankfurter Allgemeine Zeitung* 12.2.2000). It was thus rather obvious that agreement about the overall net reduction would be possible.

The main dimension of conflict was thus income tax *structure*. The government wanted a differentiated income tax, while the opposition parties wanted to move toward a flat income tax. The conflict was thus serious, especially since structure and level are likely to be related in the long run (Chapters three and four). Deadlock was nevertheless highly unlikely. Business wanted the reform to be blocked under no circumstances and the general public did not understand very well or care much about the technical issues of tax structure. Therefore, the strategy of the Christian Democrats was to stand firm in the negotiations and extract as many concessions from the government as possible. After a first round of negotiations in the Mediation Committee in June and July 2000 had failed, the CDU's floor leader Friedrich Merz accepted the government's claim that the states could not bear a net reduction of more than DM 50 billion. He wanted to use a new round of negotiations to 'talk about how this sum can be distributed more equally' and suggested to cut the corporate tax rate only to 30 per cent and find an agreement that would guarantee the 'equal taxation of all types of income' (*Handelsblatt* 13.7.2000).

However, Merz and the rest of the Christian Democratic leadership were too confident that it would actually come to a second round of negotiations. Because the government had a majority in the Mediation Committee, it passed a 'false mediation result', based on its last offer to the opposition: the 'option model' was scrapped in return for a further reduction of the top personal income tax rate from 45 to 43 per cent, the threshold for the tax rate was increased from DM 98,000 to DM 102,000 and a special tax depreciation for small businesses was retained; the tax exemption for corporations' capital gains from shares was postponed by one year. The overall net reduction increased by DM 5 billion to DM 50 billion. Given this further improvement of the proposal, it became quite attractive for mixed state governments to enter into deals with the federal government. After all, it was rather clear that an agreement would eventually be reached and that the net reduction would not be larger than what had already been offered by the government. So the real choice for mixed state governments was between further improvements for their parties (with respect to more-or-less technical issues of tax structure) or further improvements for their states. In the end, they opted for the latter. On the 14th July the Bundesrat passed a modified version of Tax Reform 2000 with a large majority of 41 to 28. The votes of all mixed state governments were 'bought off' by the Red-Green coalition.

The details, of course, are somewhat complicated. A number of state governments (e.g. Berlin and Mecklenburg-Western Pomerania) received financial help from the federal government in specified areas. Some governments received the federal government's support in other policy areas. Most notably, Bremen (as well as Berlin) gained the government's support with respect to the general reform of the federal fiscal equalisation system (*Länderfinanzausgleich*). Mecklenburg-Western Pomerania was granted the right to participate in consensus talks on pension reform. Finally, in the night before the final vote, the federal government offered to further reduce the top personal income tax rate to 42 per cent and to accept a provision making it easier for medium-sized companies to sell holdings—a provision that the Red-Green government had abolished. As a result of these last-minute changes the total annual net reduction increased to around DM 60 billion (EUR 32 billion) by 2005.[9] These changes were sufficient (and necessary) for winning the support of the Liberals in Rhineland-Palatinate.

What started out as a plan for a structural business tax reform thus evolved into a comprehensive income tax reform with overall income tax reductions of about 1.5 per cent of GDP (in 2005). Because these reductions contributed to a rise in the structural budget deficit (almost 3 per cent of GDP in 2001 and 2002), the government subsequently tried to bring in more revenues (OECD 2004a: 43–9). The 2003 step of the tax reform was postponed one year as a financing measure of damages arising from a widespread flooding in 2002. In addition, the corporate tax rate was temporarily increased slightly (to 26.5 per cent) in 2003 (Figure 7.1). In 2003, after the Red-Green coalition had been re-elected (Table 7.2), the government tabled legislation that brought forward into 2004 the income tax reductions that were originally scheduled for 2005 (to increase the fiscal stimulus in the *short-term*) and introduced new revenue-raising measures and cuts in tax expenditures and direct subsidies (as long-term budgetary consolidation measures). However, as a result of another mediation process between the Bundestag and the Bundesrat, legislation was not only delayed but also diluted. While there was substantial agreement, in principle, on reducing or scrapping certain tax expenditures and direct subsidies such as home ownership subsidies, the opposition certainly had to 'conserve' these subsidies in order to use them as financing measures for their own plan of further flattening the personal income tax. In contrast, the government wanted to continue the clean-up of the income tax base on the basis of the *existing tax rate structure* in personal income taxation. A compromise on the reduction of (tax) subsidies was reached and some parts of the tax reductions were brought forward into 2004 (Figure 7.1). However, due to the deadlock between different models of income tax reform the Bundesrat significantly 'reduced the volume of consolidation that would have been possible under the government's original proposal' (OECD 2004a: 43).[10]

In March 2005 the government and the Christian Democrats achieved agreement that the corporate tax rate of 25 per cent was still not competitive—given the local business tax burden—and wanted to reduce it to 19 per cent in a revenue-neutral manner. The financing measures discussed, which initially included higher dividend taxes for shareholders, were once more controversial. This tax cut did not materialise, however. In June 2005 the Social Democrats suffered a serious election defeat in North Rhine-Westphalia—the last of a series of defeats at the state level, which made the seat share of congruent state governments in the Bundesrat drop to zero (Table 7.3). As a response, Gerhard Schröder used the vote of confidence procedure to call early elections at the federal level, which were held in September.

In the run-up to the election income tax reform was again a—if not *the*—crucial issue, and the tax policy differences between the two camps became clearer than ever. On the one hand, the Social Democrats and the Greens had become increasingly sympathetic to something like a dual income tax as a systematic alternative to a flat tax. This partly reflected a change in the debate among economic policy advisors. Most notably, the Council of Economic Advisors, which had traditionally defended the idea of uniform income taxation, embraced the dual income tax in its 2003–4 report (Sachverständigenrat 2003), as did other prominent economists (Sinn 2003; Spengel 2003). On the other hand, it became more transparent that the natural endpoint of the reform ideas of the opposition parties was a full-fledged flat income tax. This transparency resulted from the fact that Paul Kirchhof—former judge at the Federal Constitutional Court (1987–99) and the main protagonist of the Court's activism in tax policy—joined the campaign of the Christian Democrats as a Shadow Finance Minister. After he had left the bench, Kirchhof had worked out a model of a flat income tax with a top tax rate of 25 per cent. While the CDU emphasised that a flat tax would not be enacted in the first legislative term of a new centre-right government, this tax nevertheless played a central role in the election campaigns. While the opposition parties embraced Kirchhof's long-term 'vision' for the German income tax, the governing parties emphasised its 'injustice'.

CONCLUSION

The German case study supports the explanation advanced in Chapters three and four. First, corporate tax competition was clearly of major importance. It increasingly became the main driving force of income tax reform in Germany. Second, tax policy choices were influenced by the interaction of party ideology, economic constraints, and veto power in a rather straightforward manner. The competitive imperative of corporate tax cuts was so strong that the respective policy preferences of the relevant parties converged rather quickly. However, adjusting corporate taxation to competition was nevertheless difficult, because the German Bundesrat and the Federal Constitutional Courts were powerful veto players in tax policy and because parties' disagreed about what lower corporate tax rates implied for the personal income tax. One side aimed at a differentiated or dual income tax, the other side wanted to move toward a flat income tax. The result of this constellation was first relatively small corporate tax cuts (until 1996), later policy deadlock (until 1998), and still later a form of 'neoliberalism by default' (tax reform 2000). That is, in order to achieve urgently needed cuts in the corporate tax rates, the Social Democrats eventually had to enact comprehensive income tax cuts, including an eleven percentage point cut in the top personal income tax rate. While both the Social Democrats and the Greens had emphasised revenue-neutrality of tax reform upon entering the government, the total net reduction of the tax burden resulting from the government's tax reforms after 1998 is put at around EUR 60 billion, roughly 3 per cent of GDP (BMF 2004: 45).

In Germany, then, income tax reform and adjustment to corporate tax competition implied a significant reduction of income tax revenue and higher budget deficits. This shows how corporate tax competition can spill over into personal income taxation. While the *extent* of this spill-over effect in Germany was influenced by the complex interaction of actors in German politics, the underlying mechanisms are essentially the same as in the countries covered in Chapters five and six. The next chapter summarise the case evidence for the seven countries and complements it with quantitative evidence on the effect of party ideology and veto institutions on the setting of income tax rates.

NOTES

1   The reform maintained a lower rate (36 per cent) for distributed profits. However, for German shareholders the tax on distributed profits was only a pre-payment on their personal income tax.

2   Before 1998, there was also a local business tax on capital (*Gewerbekapitalsteuer*). In what follows, I neglect this tax for the sake of simplicity.

3   Local governments are allowed to increase the local tax within limits, leading to significant variation in tax rates. While the resulting local tax rate could become as high as around 20 per cent, the effective increase of the (combined federal-local) headline corporate tax rate

was smaller. The reason is that the local business tax was deductible from its own base and from the base for personal and corporate income taxes.

4   For the period before the introduction of the Euro, I present the DM figures.

5   This proposal was actually developed by a tax policy expert of the Federation of German Industries. See Ganghof (2004: 75–7).

6   The Bundestag and the Bundesrat had agreed on this reinstatement already in May 1993, as part of a comprehensive post-unification reform of intergovernmental fiscal relations (Altemeier 1999: 226).

7   Note, however, that in 1997 an agreement was reached on the scrapping of the local business tax on capital. See Ganghof (2004: 84–5) for more detail.

8   Recall that under the post-1977 tax system, there was a lower rate on distributed profits, which was a pre-payment on domestic investors' final income tax burden. This split-rate system was to be abolished.

9   Legally, of course, these changes could not be passed by the Bundesrat because they had not been adopted by the Mediation Committee. They were the subject of a separate bill that was subsequently approved.

10 It also proved once more impossible to achieve a comprehensive reform of the local business tax, despite the fact that the government had appointed a tax reform committee to prepare such a reform. The Bundestag and the Bundesrat could only agree on incremental reforms to increase the tax revenues of local jurisdictions (Döring and Feld 2005).

chapter eight | party ideology, veto points and the setting of top marginal tax rates

The seven case studies on income tax reform in Australia, Denmark, Finland, Germany, Sweden, New Zealand and Norway provided many insights in the factors that shape the making of income tax policy in advanced OECD countries. The case studies were to a large extent descriptive and explorative. My goal was to summarise important historical facts relating to tax policy adjustment in the seven countries as well as to provide a better understanding of the way policymakers framed the relevant choices and trade-offs. However, the case studies were also explanatory. The goal was to present evidence supporting the explanation developed in Chapters three and four. The case evidence shows that tax competition was indeed an important driving force behind corporate tax cuts (the *tax competition argument*), that low corporate tax rates create downward pressure on top personal income tax rates (the *spill-over argument*) and that domestic constraints counteract these downward pressures (the *domestic constraints argument*). Moreover, the case studies corroborate my claim that the effects of party ideology and veto institutions depend on the tightness of constraints (the *conditional importance of politics argument*). Because tax competition led to a strong convergence of policy preferences, partisan-institutional configurations did not matter much in the setting of corporate income tax rates. In contrast, because the domestic 'constraints' are more amenable to change by governments, at least in the medium term, partisan-institutional configurations did matter more in the setting of *top personal income tax rates*.

In this chapter I want to summarise the case evidence and complement it with quantitative evidence for 21 OECD countries. The next section discusses the setting of corporate tax rates, the subsequent section the setting of top personal income tax rates. In both sections I shall first discuss socio-economic constraints and then analyse the role of party ideology and veto institutions.

CORPORATE TAX RATES

The importance of international constraints
The case studies presented above clearly show that tax competition has been a major driving force behind corporate tax cuts. Policymakers regarded low

corporate tax rates as an important signal to international investors, but they also understood the more subtle mechanisms of tax competition explained in Chapter three. Therefore, a 'competitive' corporate tax rate was increasingly seen as a necessity.

Of course, the causal importance of tax competition also depends on policymakers' general policy preferences in income taxation. Right-wing policymakers that prefer a flat income tax with a low tax rate in any case—like New Zealand's former Finance Minister Roger Douglas—are not much constrained by tax competition. However, we have seen that this case was the exception rather than the rule. Policymakers often preferred relatively high corporate tax rates, either because they wanted to maintain certain investment incentives (most notably accelerated depreciation of business assets) or because they wanted to align the corporate tax rate with the top tax rate on personal capital income. Prime examples are Australia, Denmark and Germany, where both reasons were important, especially for centre-left governments. Given competitive pressure, however, corporate tax rates had to be cut nevertheless and the resulting cuts in investment incentives as well as the increasing tax rate gap between corporate and personal capital income taxation had to be accepted.

The tax reform experiences of other countries are in line with this conclusion. First, there are other countries, e.g. Canada, where corporate base-broadening was partly driven by the need to bring down the corporate tax rate to a 'competitive' level (Bossons 1987; Daly 1993: 125-6; Bird et al. 1998: 65, 87). Second, there are countries where the move toward full-fledged Expenditure Taxes was discussed and where one main argument against such taxes was that the narrowing of the tax base would imply an unacceptable increase of the tax rate. In the UK, for instance, it was argued that the complete tax exemption of normal capital income would require an increase of the corporate tax rate to 45 per cent or higher—compared to a current rate of 30 per cent—and that this would be unacceptable (Isaac 1997: 313). Finally, Croatia did introduce a full-fledged Expenditure Tax system in 1994 but tax competition seems to have contributed to the recent abolition of this system. The choice of the corporate tax rate was controversial from the start. The Ministry of Finance had proposed a corporate rate of 35 per cent to align it with the top personal income tax rate but, due to competitiveness considerations, the Croatian parliament ended up setting the corporate rate at 25 per cent (Rose and Wiswesser 1998: 272). Since the tax rate gap between corporate and top personal taxation led to tax arbitrage the corporate tax rate was later raised to 35 per cent. However, in 2001 the government decided to abandon the Expenditure Tax and lower the corporate rate from 35 to 20 per cent (Keen and King 2003).

There is also robust quantitative evidence that the strong downward trend in corporate tax rates since the mid-1980s has been driven to a large extent by tax competition (Griffith and Klemm 2004). The most straightforward evidence concerns the relationship between tax rates and country size (population). The economic theory of tax competition predicts that if two countries of unequal size compete with each other for mobile tax bases (capital), the smaller country will in

Figure 8.1: Corporate tax rates and their correlation with country size, 1980–2005

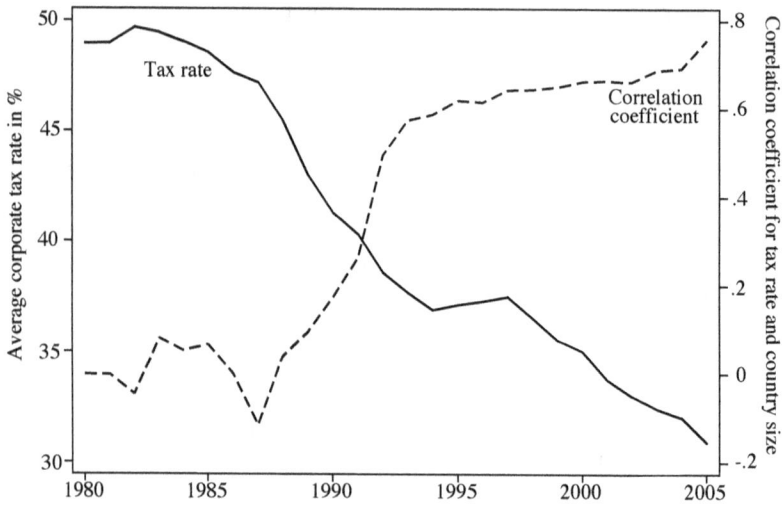

Notes: Unweighted average of 21 OECD countries, correlation coefficient = Pearson's *r*.
Sources: See appendix.

equilibrium have a lower tax rate (Bucovetsky 1991; Dehejia and Genschel 1999). In a small country with a small existing capital stock, a tax cut does not lead to large revenue losses. At the same time, relatively high revenue can be expected due to the inflow of foreign capital. Hence, if tax competition has played a role in the setting of corporate tax rates, we would expect an increasingly strong positive correlation between corporate tax rates and country size.

The data pattern displayed in Figure 8.1 is in line with this prediction. The figure shows that the downward trend in corporate tax rates of OECD countries (solid curve, left-hand scale) is associated with an increasing correlation (Pearson's *r*) between corporate tax rates and country size, measured as the natural logarithm (ln) of population (dashed curve, right-hand scale).[1] In the early 1980s there was virtually no correlation between tax rates and country size. As a result of the famous tax reforms in the UK (1984) and the US (1986) a moderate negative correlation emerged, but only for a few years. As the downward spiral of competitive tax cuts progressed, small countries made deeper cuts than large ones and the correlation coefficient increased to .76 in 2005.[2] It is not surprising, therefore, that the standard deviation of corporate tax rates only decreased from 8.0 to 6.6 between 1980 and 2005. For what we see is less a pattern of *absolute* convergence than a pattern of *conditional convergence* (*cf.* Sala-i-Martin 1996; Ganghof 2005c). The distribution of tax rates did not shrink (much) but was increasingly shaped by countries' structural position in the 'race toward the bottom'.

Figure 8.2 provides a snapshot of the situation in 2005. We see that the variation around the regression line is indeed rather small. Only Ireland is an outlier, with a corporate tax rate of only 12.5 per cent. The variation is significantly larger

Figure 8.2: Corporate tax rates and country size, 2005

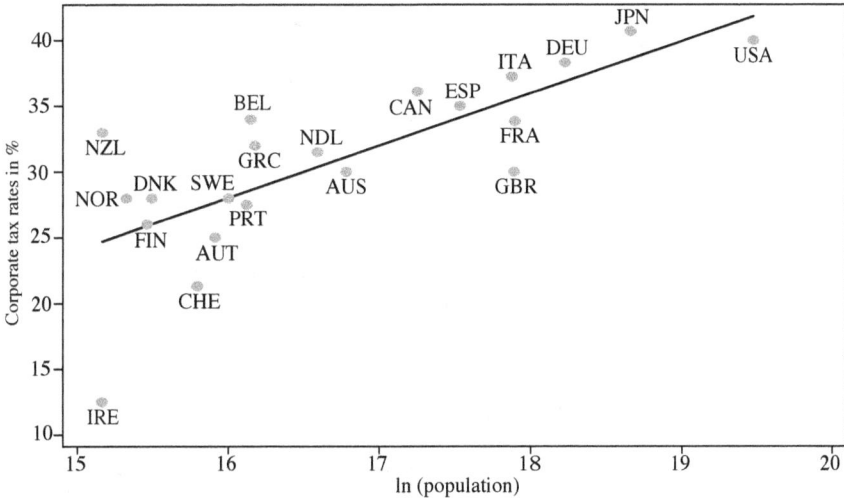

Notes: Population data is for the year 2002.
Sources: See appendix.

when we extend the sample beyond the OECD world, but the sizeable positive association between country size and corporate tax rates continues to exist (Ganghof 2005a). In combination, then, qualitative and quantitative evidence provide strong support for the tax competition argument advanced in Chapter three.

The role of party ideology and veto institutions
I have argued in Chapters two and three that—*contra* Hallerberg and Basinger (1998)—strong tax competition should *not* lead us to expect that party ideology and veto institutions play an important role in the setting of corporate tax rates. For if socio-economic constraints are tight, parties' policy preferences are likely to converge. By extension, left and right governments will implement similar policies and left and right veto players will not have much difficulty agreeing on policy change (Ganghof 2003).

The case evidence presented in Chapters five through seven supports this view. Parties' policy preferences generally converged rather quickly and the remaining policy differences between left and right were minor. Moreover, left parties or governments did sometimes prefer *lower* corporate tax rates than their counterparts on the right. Part of the reason is that left parties are more likely to prefer differentiated or dual income taxes, which, by 'decoupling' the corporate tax rate from the top tax rate on personal income, facilitate corporate tax cuts. This helps to explain why, in the 1990s, a right-leaning government in New Zealand maintained a higher corporate tax rate than left-leaning governments in Sweden or Norway, and why Germany's Social Democrats recently proposed deeper cuts in the federal corporate tax rate than the opposition parties on the right.

The only partial exception to the general irrelevance of parties and veto players for the level of corporate tax rates is the German case. In this case the veto power of the Bundesrat *contributed* to the *retardation* of corporate tax cuts in 1997–8. However, this exception is to a large extent explained by the exceptional power of the Federal Constitutional Court and the resulting 'constitutionalisation' of German taxation policy. As argued in Chapter seven, partisan conflict in Germany did not concern corporate tax cuts but their implications for personal income taxation; and the severity of this conflict is partly explained by the Court's veto power.

Now, the question is how the case study results can be reconciled with the regression results presented by Hallerberg and Basinger (1998). These authors analyse the magnitude of corporate tax cuts (in *per cent*) between 1986—i.e. after the 'shock' of the US tax reform—and 1990/91. They find that left-leaning governments made *deeper* cuts in corporate tax rates than their right-leaning counterparts and that countries with more than one veto player achieved much smaller corporate tax cuts than those with only one player—regardless of additional veto players' ideology. Similar results were presented by Wagschal (1999a; 1999b), who used veto point indices such as those developed by Lijphart (1999), Huber, Ragin and Stephens (1993) and Schmidt (1996). On closer inspection, however, these studies do not challenge the conclusions of the case studies presented here. To the contrary, the theoretical framework developed above helps to explain why their results are misleading. I shall focus on the study by Hallerberg and Basinger (1998) because it predated Wagschal's and is published in English. However, some of the following discussion also applies to Wagschal's analysis (*cf.* Ganghof 1999).

First of all, the results of Hallerberg and Basinger (1998) are due to measurement errors and inconsistent coding decisions. While the authors generally look at central government tax rates, they include the *general* government tax rate for Switzerland (Hallerberg and Basinger 1998: 328). In addition, their data on corporate tax rates in Finland, Ireland and New Zealand is erroneous.[3] Finally, and most importantly, the authors generally opt for letting the adjustment period end in 1990 but include the 1991-rate for Sweden. Obviously, consistency demands that the analysis should determine *all* countries' tax cuts either in 1990 or in 1991. If either of these two options is chosen, the results for parties and veto players break down.

Table 8.1 shows the results for the latter option.[4] I used Hallerberg and Basinger's (1998: 341) original data and included those independent variables that they report to be significant. The only change is to include all countries' tax cuts until 1991 and to correct errors in the tax rate data. For Switzerland I continue to use the *general* government tax rate because this case would otherwise become a large outlier (a central government tax rate of below 10 per cent in 1986). As the results for model 1 show, there is no evidence for an effect of the partisan composition of government or the number of veto players. Except for the starting tax rate in 1986, coefficients are small and do not get near the conventional standards

Table 8.1: Re-analysis of Hallerberg and Basinger (1998)

Independent variable	Dependent variable: *Percentage* change of top corporate tax rates, 1986 to 1991	
	Model 1	Model 2
Veto dummy	-2.63 (7.56)	-1.12 (5.20)
Partisanship	-2.57 (2.20)	-2.29 (1.72)
Inflation	-.77 (2.02)	
Real growth	-3.10 (3.04)	
Corporate tax rate in 1986	.92** (.34)	0.97*** (.32)
Constant	6.86 (33.80)	-10.11 (18.02)
N	19	19
Adjusted R-squared	.33	.37

Notes: Ordinary Least Squares estimation; standard errors in parentheses, * p < .1, ** p < .05, *** p < .01. For variable definitions and sources, see Hallerberg and Basinger (1998).

of statistical significance. This picture remains unchanged when the two economic control variables, inflation and growth, are dropped (model 2).

While this analysis refutes the conclusions of Hallerberg and Basinger (1998) with respect to corporate tax rates, it points towards two important conceptual issues: how are corporate tax rates to be measured (*central* versus *general* government tax rates), and when did the period of adjustment to the US tax reform of 1986 end? I believe that adequate answers to both questions contradict those given by Hallerberg and Basinger.

As to the measurement of corporate tax rates, *general government* tax rates have to be chosen because it is the overall level of the statutory tax rate that matters in corporate tax competition. Hallerberg and Basinger (1999: 622) do not take issue with this argument but wonder whether large tax rate differences across US states can usefully be fitted under one average. The United States, however, are the exception rather than the rule. In virtually all of the countries that operated sub-national profit taxes in the mid-1980s, policymakers clearly included these taxes in their competitiveness considerations. The case studies presented above provide examples, but there are many others (e.g. Guger 1998; Bordignon *et al.* 2001; Masui 2001). In fact, in Switzerland sub-national tax rates are so much more important than the central government rate of below 10 per cent that corporations would not even consider focusing on this rate alone; and as we have seen above, Hallerberg and Basinger (1998) did also include cantonal and local taxes in their analysis. To be sure, if sub-national rates are taken into account, sub-national governments and/or second chambers have to be included as additional veto players in some countries. This is suggested by Hallerberg and Basinger (1999: 622) and practised in Ganghof (1999: 466).

Determining the end of the adjustment period is a more difficult issue. If we understand 'adjustment' in a broad sense of 'playing the tax competition game', the adjustment process is still ongoing (Figure 1.1). Hence any choice of an adjustment period would be a pragmatic matter. If we understand 'adjustment' in the more narrow sense of countries' *first response* to the US tax reform of 1986, the problem is how to determine this response. While there is no need to discuss this problem in much detail here (Ganghof 1999: 463–4), the case study evidence and the data pattern in Figure 1.1 suggest that the best choice of an adjustment period is 1986–94. For this figure shows that the downward trend in corporate tax rate came to a temporary halt in 1994, before it continued with an almost unchanged slope from 1997. In addition, the case studies of Finland and Norway show that letting the adjustment period end before 1994 distorts the regression results (Chapter six). In Norway, policymakers' first response in corporate taxation was started to be prepared by a tax reform committee already in 1988 but only implemented in 1992. The time lag is not explained by conflicts between veto players but by the government's intention to develop a systematic reform approach. Similarly, the Finnish response to the US tax reform was only fully implemented by 1993 — not because of conflicts between veto players but because policymakers searched for a systematic reform approach and were uncertain about the depth of adjustment in neighbouring countries.

In Ganghof (1999) I show that if we focus on general government tax rates and extend the adjustment period to 1994, there is no evidence for an effect of political parties or veto players on the size of corporate tax rate cuts. Instead, the most important predictor of tax rate cuts between 1986 and 1994 is the tax rate level in 1986 — as is true for central government tax rates and shorter adjustment periods (see Table 8.1). As argued in Chapters two and four, this is what we should expect if adjustment pressure (tax competition) is strong: parties' policy preferences converge, so that the sizes of tax cuts reflect countries' structural adjustment requirements (i.e. the existing tax rate level) much more than partisan-institutional configurations.

However, we have also seen above that countries' position in the tax competition game was determined not only by their starting tax rate in 1986 but also by their size. The expected size of tax cuts depends not only on where countries start, i.e. the existing tax rate level, but also on where they can be expected to end, i.e. the 'equilibrium' tax rate level, which is influenced by country size. However, neither Hallerberg and Basinger (1998) nor Wagschal (1999a) nor Ganghof (1999) controlled for country size. The final task of this section is therefore to remedy this omission.

Table 8.2 presents the results of three cross-section regressions. The dependent variable is the *percentage point* change of the corporate tax rate between 1983 and 2003; large tax cuts imply high *negative* values. The period 1983–2003 is chosen because the focus is now on corporate tax competition more generally rather than adjustment to the US reform of 1986. The starting year 1983 is chosen because the first significant corporate tax cut of the 1980s was implemented in the United Kingdom in 1984. The end year 2003 is chosen because I intend to *compare* the regression results for corporate and personal tax rate cuts, and because

Table 8.2: Explaining corporate tax rate cuts between 1983 and 2003

Independent variables	Dependent variable: Percentage *point* change in corporate tax rate between 1983 and 2003			
	Model 1	Model 2	Model 3	Model 4
Corporate tax rate in 1983	-.88*** (.18)	-.92*** (.14)	-.92*** (.14)	-.91*** (.09)
Population (ln) in 2001		3.44*** (.86)	3.54*** (1.02)	2.68*** (.70)
Veto points (Lijphart 1999)			-.21 (1.05)	-.13 (.70)
Constant	-26.54***(9.24)	-28.81* (15.48)	-30.52 (17.79)	-16.04 (12.13)
N	21	21	21	20
Excluded case	None	None	None	Ireland
Adj. R-squared	.52	.73	.72	.84

Notes: Ordinary Least Squares estimation; standard errors in parentheses, * p < .1, ** p < .05, *** p < .01. Variable definitions and data sources: See appendix.

the relevant data (on tax revenues) for the personal tax rate regressions is only available until 2003. But the choice of the period under consideration is not critical to the regression results.

The independent variables are the tax rate in 1983, country size (population in 2001) and a veto point index (for data sources see the appendix). The index chosen is the 'federal-unitary dimension' of Lijphart (1999), which is perhaps the best-known of a group of highly correlated veto point indices (e.g. Huber *et al.* 1993; Schmidt 1996; Kaiser 1997). The choice of the veto point indicator is not critical for the results. However, I think that Lijphart's veto point index has important advantages over the kind of veto player variable used by Hallerberg and Basinger (1998). For one thing, it de-emphasises the coalition type and focuses more on underlying institutional structures, e.g. the difference between unicameralism and bicameralism (see Chapter two). For another, it captures, albeit roughly, the complications arising from federal and/or decentralised state structures. This is important because we focus on *general government* tax rates.

Model 1 presents the results for a bivariate regression that only includes the tax rate in 1983 as a predictor. As in the results reported in Table 8.1, the effect of this variable is sizeable and highly significant. It explains roughly 50 per cent of the variance in tax cuts. When we add country size to the equation (model 2) its effect is also sizeable and highly significant, the coefficient for the starting tax rate *increases* slightly and the explained variance increases to almost three-fourths. In contrast, the veto point index has no explanatory power whatsoever (model 3). Its regression coefficient is very small, statistically insignificant, has the wrong sign (more veto points are associated with greater tax cuts) and *reduces* the explanatory power of the model in terms of the adjusted R-squared. Model 4 shows that this result for the veto point variable remains unchanged when the Irish case with its very low corporate tax rate is excluded. The main effect of this exclusion is to reduce the coefficient for country size and *increase* the explained variance to 85 per cent.

In sum, then, the quantitative evidence supports and complements the case study evidence. Party ideology and veto institutions were rather unimportant in the setting of corporate tax rates because tight international economic constraints led to a convergence of parties' policy preferences.

TOP PERSONAL INCOME TAX RATES

The importance of domestic constraints

The seven case studies presented in Chapters five through seven reveal the importance of domestic constraints. Policymakers aimed at 'neutral' or 'market-conforming' taxation and knew that equal top tax rates on corporate and personal incomes would be a powerful instrument for pursuing this goal. Nevertheless, tax rate equality was not achieved or maintained in any of the seven countries. Top personal tax rates are invariably above corporate rates, with the tax rate gaps ranging from 6 percentage points in New Zealand to more than 30 percentage points in Denmark (all values for 2005). The resulting lack of tax neutrality is explained by socio-economic constraints at the domestic level. Large cuts in top personal tax rates tend to be associated with significant revenue losses and/or a significant reduction of (labour) income tax progressivity. As we have seen, these 'costs' of tax cuts have also kept centre-right governments from cutting top personal income tax rates as much as corporate tax rates.

However, the comparative case studies cannot conclusively answer the question discussed in Chapter four: is the relevant constraint best captured by the *level of income taxation* (as per cent of GDP) or the *level of total taxation* (as per cent of GDP)? In other words: how important is what I have called the 'progressivity adjustment' function of the income tax? The comparative case evidence on this question is mixed. On the one hand, the spill-over effect of corporate tax competition was indeed most obvious in the two countries with the lowest income tax ratios, Norway and Germany, and in these countries even centrist parties have increasingly discussed the option of a pure flat tax as a realistic policy option. On the other hand, discussions are just that. Although it would be relatively easy for a country like Germany to move to a pure, indirectly progressive flat tax in a revenue-neutral manner, this move has not yet taken place and is unlikely to take place in the near future.

Given the limitations of qualitative case comparisons, it is useful to investigate how different tax revenue levels are correlated with top personal rates in advanced OECD countries. Table 8.3 shows the correlation coefficients for the year 2003 (the last year for which revenue data was available, see appendix). The table distinguishes between *personal income* tax revenue, *personal plus corporate income* tax revenue and *total tax* revenue. In addition, the last row of the table presents the coefficients that result from the exclusion of the Japanese case. The results are straightforward: the best predictor of top personal income tax rates is the total tax ratio. This suggests that the progressivity adjustment function plays an important

Table 8.3: Correlation of Tax Revenue Indicators with top personal income tax rates, 2003

	Personal income tax revenue	Corporate and personal income tax revenue	Total income tax revenue
Correlations with Japan	.56	.55	.75
Correlations without Japan	.51	.50	.84

Notes: Pearson's *r*. All revenue data is expressed in per cent of GDP. Sources: See appendix.

role and that a focus on income taxation alone can be misleading. The difference between the correlation coefficients is increased if we neglect Japan, an outlier with a very low total tax ratio (26–27 per cent) and a rather high personal income tax rate (50 per cent).

Table 8.3 only presents a snapshot for the year 2003. It is again interesting to investigate how the relationship between total taxation and top personal income tax rates has developed over time (Figure 8.3). The set-up of Figure 8.3 is identical to that in Figure 8.1. That is, the solid curve gives the OECD-21 average of top personal rates, the dashed curve the correlation coefficient between top tax rates and total tax ratios. The Japanese outlier is omitted in order to make the pattern clearer.

Figure 8.3: Top personal income tax rates and their correlation with total taxation, 1980–2005

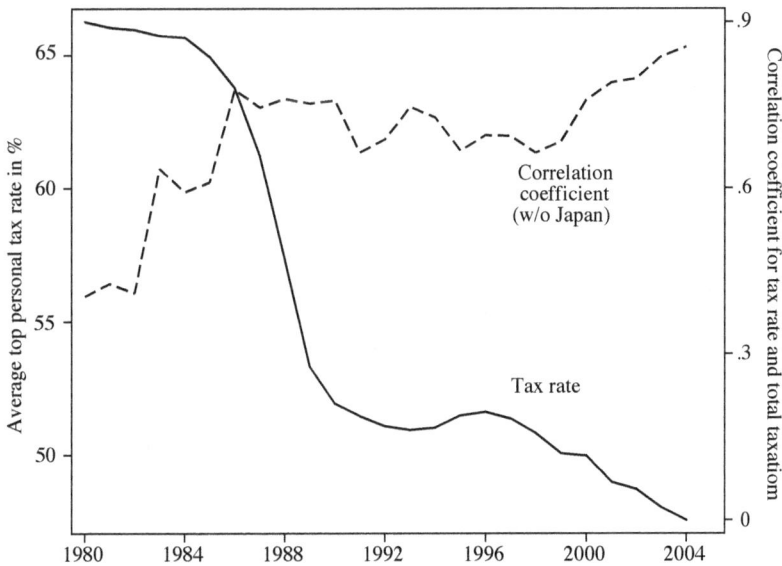

Notes: Unweighted average for 20 OECD countries, correlation coefficient = Pearson's *r*. Sources: See appendix.

The interesting findings are that the correlation between top personal tax rates and total tax ratios *had already been established before* the US tax reform in 1985–6 and that the correlation *remained robust* to the downward trend in tax rates. In fact, the bivariate regression coefficients for the total tax ratio suggests that we see a downward shift but more-or-less unchanged slope of the regression line: the coefficient was .84 in 1983, .95 in 1993 and .89 in 2003 (all significant at the 1 per cent-level). In sum, then, the combination of qualitative and quantitative evidence provides significant support for the domestic constraints argument advanced in Chapter four.

The role of party ideology and veto institutions
As argued in Chapters three and four, the domestic constraints resulting from high total tax ratios are less tight or less 'exogenous' than the international constraints resulting from tax competition. That is, parties can choose to reduce taxation levels and/or the degree of income tax progressivity. As a result, the argument that party ideology and veto institutions matter in the setting of top tax rates (Hallerberg and Basinger 1998; Wagschal 1999a) is much more plausible with respect to the personal income taxation *of wages*. The case evidence presented in Chapters five through seven supports this view. While left-right differences in *policy* preferences were reduced by short-term constraints, the seven case studies nevertheless show that partisan-institutional configurations affect legislative outcomes in ways that are in line with common sense: left parties tend to prefer higher and more progressive taxes on labour income, the opposite is true for right parties. Let us briefly review the case evidence with respect to the setting of top personal income tax rates.

In *New Zealand* a Labour majority government with *a rightist ideology* used its power under the 'Westminster' system to cut the top personal income tax rate in half. The subsequent majority government of the other right-leaning party, the Liberals, maintained the 'neo-liberal' status quo created by its predecessor. Finally, after the introduction of a proportional representation system, a minority coalition led by a remodelled Labour Party could rely on the support of a left majority in parliament to increase the top personal tax rate again. *Australia* differed from New Zealand in that its Labor government had a less rightist ideology. In addition, both Labor and Liberal-National governments lacked a majority in the Senate, in which the more leftist Democrats had a powerful position. As a result, cuts in the top tax rate were less pronounced than in New Zealand in the 1980s and completely absent thereafter. When the Liberal-National government gained a majority in the Senate in June 2005, it decided to maintain the given top personal income tax rate but to greatly increase its income threshold. Moreover, cuts in the top rate remain on the policy agenda.

In *Denmark* both centre-right and centre-left governments implemented fairly moderate cuts of the top personal income tax rate, and when the Social Democrats needed the support of more leftist veto players, wage tax progressivity increased slightly. Afterwards, a centre-right minority government with a right majority in parliament decreased taxes but left the top personal tax rate unchanged. In *Sweden*, the Liberals used their power as a support party of a Social Democratic minority government to increase the reduction of the top personal income tax rate. The subsequent centre-right minority government, checked by the Social Democrats, maintained the status quo. Finally, the Social Democrats relied on left opposition parties to increase and maintain a higher top personal tax rate. In *Norway* a Labour government, supported by the Centre Party, reduced the top personal income tax rate. Later the Labour Party used its power vis-à-vis a very small centrist minority government to increase the top personal rate again. Finally, a centre-right minority government relied on a right-wing support in parliament to reduce the top personal rate, with further reductions already planned. Finally, in *Finland* a centre-right coalition reduced the top personal income tax rate moderately. Subsequent governments, all of which included the Social Democrats, focused labour tax cuts onto lower and medium wages and achieved only moderate cuts in the top personal income tax rate.

The *German case* is most complex, partly due to the role of the Federal Constitutional Court as a 'hidden' veto player whose policy preferences have to be anticipated and taken into account by the partisan actors. The most important effect of the Court's power was probably to stack the decks in favour of the flatter income taxes. For it was widely believed in Germany that a large tax rate gap between corporate and personal taxation would turn out to be unconstitutional. As a result, especially the Christian Democrats developed more rightist policy preferences than their centre-right counterparts in other countries. This is true not only with respect to the Oceanian and Nordic countries discussed above but also with respect to European welfare states that combine rather low income taxes with high social security contributions. As Table 8.4 shows, countries like Austria, Belgium, France or the Netherlands implemented tax reforms that maintained higher top personal income tax rates than in Germany; and these reforms were often passed by centre-right coalitions or with the consent of centre-right parties (e.g. Cnossen and Bovenberg 2001; OECD 2005).[5] Because centre-right parties in these countries accepted differentiated income taxes and because the 'constitutionality' of such taxes was no issue, there was less partisan conflict about the basic model of income tax reform than in Germany.

Despite the complexities of the German case, however, it fits the basic pattern visible in the other countries: a centre-right government first achieved a very moderate cut in the top personal rate, partly due to the influence of more left-leaning party factions and state governments. By the time the centre-right government was willing to implement deeper cuts in the top personal tax rate the Social Democrats had assumed veto power in the Bundesrat and used it to block tax reform. Finally, when the Social Democrats, together with the Greens, were in government and urgently needed to cut the corporate tax rate to a 'competitive' level, the right-wing players in the Bundesrat used their power to extract significant concessions from the government, including more significant cuts in the top personal income tax rates.

Table 8.4: Top personal income tax rates, 1983 and 2003

	Central government			General government				
	Levels (%)		Change (p.points)	Levels (%)		Change (p.points)	Tax increases	
	1983	2003		1983	2003		Amount	Year
AUS	60.0	47.0	-13.0	60.0	48.5	-11.5		
AUT	62.0	50.0	-12.0	62.0	50.0	-12.0		
BEL	60.0	52.0	-8.0	71.6	56.4	-15.1		
CAN	34.0	29.0	-5.0	50.3	45.6	-4.7		
CHE	11.5	11.5	0.0	44.2	38.9	-5.3		
DEU	56.0	48.5	-7.5	56.0	51.2	-4.8		
DNK	39.6	26.5	-13.1	73.0	62.7	-10.3		
ESP	65.0	45.0	-20.0	65.0	45.0	-20.0		
FIN	51.0	35.0	-16.0	67.0	53.0	-13.9		
FRA	65.0	49.6	-15.4	65.0	57.6	-7.4	6.1	1997–8
GBR	60.0	40.0	-20.0	60.0	40.0	-20.0		
GRE	60.0	40.0	-20.0	60.0	40.0	-20.0	5.0	1995
IRL	65.0	42.0	-23.0	65.0	42.0	-23.0		
ITA	65.0	45.0	-20.0	70.7	46.2	-24.5		
JPN	75.0	37.0	-38.0	93.0	50.0	-43.0		
NLD	72.0	52.0	-20.0	72.0	52.0	-20.0		
NOR	41.0	19.5	-21.5	68.4	55.3	-13.1	6.0	2000
NZL	66.0	39.0	-27.0	66.0	39.0	-27.0	6.0	2000
PRT	70.0	40.0	-30.0	70.0	40.0	-30.0		
SWE	58.0	25.0	-33.0	88.2	57.0	-31.2	5.2	1996
USA	50.0	35.0	-15.0	53.1	38.6	-14.6	8.2	1993

Notes: Rounded to nearest percentage point.
Sources, definitions and country labels: See appendix.

Hence we see that the common sense view of partisan tax policymaking is quite adequate with respect to the setting of top personal income tax rates and that the effect of 'veto players' is therefore dependent on these players' partisan identity. A first, simple step to extend this finding to the broader group of advanced OECD countries is to check whether there are more countries—like New Zealand, Norway, and Sweden—in which the top personal income tax rates were increased against the general downward trend and, if so, which majority was responsible for this increase. As Table 8.4 shows in the last two columns, there are three further cases with 'substantial', i.e. greater than 4 percentage points, increase of the central government tax rate between 1983 and 2003. The first case is *Greece,* where a left one-party majority government (PASOK) increased the top personal rate from 40 to 45 per cent in

1995. This tax increase partly reversed a ten percentage point cut implemented in 1993 by the previous government. It was part of a more general effort to significantly increase tax revenue (*Athens News Agency Bulletin* 1.12.1994).

Similarly, in *France* a right-leaning government planned to reduce the top personal rate from 56.8 per cent to 52 per cent in 1997. However, the Socialist government elected in June 1997 set the top rate to 54 per cent in 1997 and one year later increased the proportional income tax earmarked for social security (called CSG) from 3.4 to 7.5 per cent (Blotnicki and Heckly 1998: 127). The overall top rate on personal income thus increased to 61.5 in 1998, as part of a more general effort to increase the progressivity of the tax system (Levy 1999). When the Socialist government was replaced by a right-wing majority in 2002, tax rates for the highest (labour) incomes were cut again and in autumn 2005 the government announced significant cuts in the top marginal tax rate (Ysmal 2003: 956; Leibfritz and O'Brien 2005).

Finally, the tax rate increase in the *United States* is also fully consistent with the common sense view of partisan tax policy—despite the fact that US parties are less disciplined than parties in most parliamentary systems. Under the Republican President Ronald Reagan the US strongly reduced the *federal* top rate from 50 per cent in 1986 to 28 per cent in 1988, which made for an average *general government* tax rate of around 32 per cent. When the Republican President George Bush Sen. three years later urgently needed the Democrats' agreement on the budget bill, the Democrats used their veto power to push through a slight increase in the federal top rate from 28 to 31 per cent (Quirk and Nesmith 2000: 587–8). When the Democrat Bill Clinton won the White House in 1992, he used the short period of 'unified' government until 1994—the first after 12 years of divided government—to increase the federal top rate more, from 31 to 39.6 per cent, and created a new 36 per cent bracket (Steuerle 2002: 148). Similarly, when George W. Bush became president in 2000 he also used a short period of unified government to reduce the federal top rate to 35 per cent (from 2006) (Krugman 2001).

Of course, the focus on tax rate *increases* is rather narrow. We have seen that left parties have also used their power to reduce the magnitude of tax *cuts*. For this reason, it is quite useful to adopt the set-up of Hallerberg and Basinger (1998) and analyse whether the *number* of veto points or veto players had a negative effect on the size of tax cuts. The results reported by these authors support this hypothesis but unfortunately lack validity. The main reason is that local income taxes are ignored. This is most obvious in Hallerberg and Basinger's analysis. The two cases that most strongly drive their regression results are Norway and Sweden, which allegedly achieved the largest tax cuts between 1986 and 1990–91: 50 and 60 per cent (not percentage *points!*), respectively (Hallerberg and Basinger 1998: 328). Because both countries were coded as countries with one veto player—the governments' minority status notwithstanding—they seem to strongly support the veto player argument advanced by the authors. However, the large tax cuts of Norway and Sweden are an artefact created by the neglect of local taxes. As a matter of fact, the two countries did *not* cut their top personal income tax rates by 50–60 per cent but rather transferred a larger share of income taxes to the local level. For instance, if one compares *central* government tax rates in Norway with central government tax rates in countries without local taxes, it appears as if Norway had already been one of the most 'neo-liberal' countries in 1986 and subsequently transformed itself into a tax haven with top marginal income tax rates of below 20 per cent (Table 8.4). But we know for a fact that this appearance is wrong. It is the result of comparing apples and oranges.

Therefore, we have to adapt the set-up proposed by Hallerberg and Basinger by taking *general* government tax rates as the dependent variable. In addition, we have seen above that the total tax burden has to be added to the regression equation as an important control variable. This leads us to a model very similar to that in Table 8.3 above. The two main predictor variables for changes in top personal income tax rates are the starting tax rate and a variable capturing the main socio-economic constraint, here the domestic constraint resulting from the total tax burden. In order to further increase comparability, I also use the same veto point variable (Lijphart's federal-unitary dimension) and focus on the period from 1983 to 2003. Hence the basic structure of the model is identical to that in Table 8.3 except that we now want to explain *personal* tax rates and therefore control for *domestic* constraints.

Table 8.5 presents the results.[6] The overall pattern is rather similar to the results for corporate tax rates (Table 8.3): the two economic variables jointly explain almost 80 per cent of the variance in tax cuts. However, in sharp contrast to the corporate tax rate regressions the veto point variable has a sizeable and statistically significant coefficient and adds around 10 per cent to the explained variance. According to model 3, the difference in institutional structures between New Zealand (Lijphart score: -1.77) and Germany (2.53) accounts for a difference in tax rate cuts of more than 12 percentage points.

However, the size of coefficient is not the most important aspect and—as always with this kind of data—has to be taken with a pinch of salt (Berk 2004). More important than the exact size of putative causal effects is that the regression results *contribute* to making inferences about underlying causal processes and capacities. It is noteworthy, therefore, that we used the very same veto point index in both regressions. For while there can always be debate about the adequacy of a particular veto point or veto player indicator, the *difference* in the sizes of the coefficients and standard errors for the veto point variable between the corporate and personal tax regressions certainly supports the arguments developed in Chapters two through four.[7] The domestic constraints resulting from large overall tax burdens (on labour income) are less tight and exogenous than the international constraints resulting from corporate tax competition. As a result, differences in *party ideology* should translate to a greater extent into differences in *policy preferences*, and, by extensions, the number of veto points should play a greater role. For if the number of veto points increases, so does the likelihood that left-leaning actors have the institutional power to reduce the magnitude of tax cuts.

Note that what makes the regression analysis work as intended is the downward trend in tax rates. If there was no downward trend, the effect of veto points

Table 8.5: Explaining top personal income tax rate cuts between 1983 and 2003

Independent variables	Dependent variable: Percentage *point* change in top personal income tax rate between 1983 and 2003		
	Model 1	Model 2	Model 3
Top tax rate in 1983	-.69*** (.13)	-.84*** (.10)	-.71*** (.09)
Tax revenue/GDP ratio in 2003		.66*** (.15)	.78*** (.12)
Veto points (Lijphart 1999)			2.95*** (.81)
Constant	27.76*** (8.64)	13.26* (7.14)	-1.04 (6.72)
N	21	21	21
Adj. R-squared	.58	.78	.87

Notes: Ordinary Least Squares estimation; standard errors in parentheses;
* $p < .1$, ** $p < .05$, *** $p < .01$. Variable definitions and data sources: See appendix.

would have to be modelled as being dependent on veto player partisan identity. Whether or not an agenda-setter proposes tax cuts would depend on this setter's ideology, and whether a veto player vetoes the proposal would likewise depend on this players' ideology. Hence the *number* of veto points might not, on average, have an effect on changes in top personal tax rates because these points might be as likely to allow rightist veto players to block tax increases as they are to allow leftist players to block tax cuts. In contrast, if *all* agenda-setters propose tax cuts but right-leaning parties propose *deeper* ones, a higher number of veto points will tend to favour the left. For if a left government proposes a moderate tax cut, a right-leaning veto player will have little reason to block this policy change. But if a right government proposes a large tax cut, a left-leaning veto player will have a credible threat to block policy change unless the size of the tax cut is reduced.

This discussion also highlights the limits of the regression analysis. One theoretical assumption underlying these results is that the partisan actors treat the setting of corporate and personal tax rates as separable dimensions, at least within certain limits. The case studies have shown that this is *generally* an adequate assumption. In almost all OECD countries corporate tax competition quickly led to a broad agreement on the fact that income taxes have to be differentiated or dual taxes. As a result, right-leaning parties were willing to fight their fight for lower corporate and personal taxes separately. As the German case study shows, however, this must not always be the case. Hence the relationship between veto points and tax cuts can be quite different from what is assumed in the regression analysis. More specifically, right-leaning players can make their agreement to corporate tax cuts dependent on cuts in top personal rates; and if a left-leaning government values the corporate tax cut very highly for economic reasons it may prefer across-the-board-cuts in income tax rates to the status quo even thought its first preference would have been targeted tax rate cuts for businesses. Hence rightist veto players can force leftwing governments to make deeper cuts in top personal income tax rates. This is part of the German story, and this story is *not* well represented in the regression analysis.[8]

As explained in Chapter one, however, I consider it useful more useful to combine case studies with focused and simple regression analyses on the aggregate outcomes of complex causal processes rather than to overburden regression analyses by trying to actually *model* these complex causal processes. For if we tried such modelling, the required interaction effects would quickly exhaust the few degrees of freedom we have in a comparison of advanced OECD countries. In fact, due to the exceptional power of the German Constitutional Court in taxation policy, any effort to model the complexities of the German case in regression analyses would be equivalent to representing this case with a simple dummy variable—hardly a satisfactory solution. Hence the results in Tables 8.3 and 8.5 should be taken for what they are: not causal inferences about the size of assumed causal effects, but part of the broader set of *observations* that help us to distinguish between better and worse causal explanations.

CONCLUSION

This chapter has presented quantitative evidence that supports the explanation advanced in Chapters three and four and complements the findings of the case studies. The evidence suggests that party ideology and veto institutions are important in shaping income taxation, but how important they are depends on which parts of income tax systems one looks at. Because the setting of corporate tax rates is strongly constrained by international competition, party ideology and veto institutions are less important. Because the setting of top tax rates on personal (labour) income is less constrained domestically, party ideology and veto institutions are more important. It is worth emphasising, however, that the differences between countries are generally not very large. This should not be surprising given the countervailing pressures policymakers face. The next and last chapter summarises these pressures and discusses policy options.

NOTES

1 Due to lack of data for recent years, and because population only changes slowly, the population values of 2001 or 2002 are used for the years 2002 through 2005.

2 In 1980 the beta coefficient of a bivariate regression was -.01 (R-squared = 0.00), in 1995 it was 4.07 (R-squared = 0.38) and in 2005 3.98 (R-squared = 0.57).

3 Hallerberg and Basinger also mistakenly treat Australia as a unicameral system (see Chapters 2 and 5).

4 I am grateful to Mark Hallerberg for providing the data for this replication analysis.

5 Note that the last step of the German income tax reform, which reduced the top personal rate to 44 per cent, is not yet reflected in the Table.

6 The regression analyses are based on the general government tax rates shown in Table 8.4.

Analyses for general government tax rates that exclude all 'social security contributions', even those that clearly are income taxes in an economic sense, lead to very similar results (Ganghof 2005c).

7 Very similar differences exist for other veto player/point variables.

8 There are several reasons why Germany is not an outlier in the regression analysis. One is that—due to data limitations—the last step of the tax reform in 2005 is not taken into account. Another is that Germany's total tax revenue (as per cent of GDP) is underestimated relative to most other countries in the OECD Revenue Statistics. One reason for this is that subsidies that are classified as transfers in other countries are classified as tax reductions in Germany. In 2001, for instance, the OECD (2004c: 68) put Germany's total tax ratio at 36.8 per cent (almost identical to the value for Greece), while the estimate based on national accounts data was 42.1 per cent.

conclusion | income tax policy in open economies

The previous chapter has summarised my main arguments about the interaction of party ideology, socio-economic constraints and veto institutions as well as the evidence supporting them. In this short and final chapter the focus is shifted from explaining international policy differences to discussing the trade-offs and challenges faced by the 'typical' advanced OECD country. I shall discuss how the trade-offs have changed due to increasing tax competition and what policy options governments have today, both at the national and the international level.

Policymakers face trade-offs between different notions of tax efficiency and equity. The central problem is to strike an adequate balance between the *equal treatment* of different types of incomes and activities and the right type of *differentiation* of tax burdens. I have shown that the history of post-war income taxation can to a large extent be understood as a search for this balance. In the absence of corporate tax competition, a likely result of the historical learning process would have been a tax that I have called 'Italian-style' dual income tax (Bordignon *et al.* 2001). In its pure form, this tax subjects all types of *normal* capital income to a uniform, moderate and proportional tax rate. This makes it 'market-conforming' in two ways: the uniform tax rate creates a *level playing field* between different types of savings and investments ('intersectoral neutrality') and the moderate tax rate helps to increase the overall *level of savings and investment* ('intertemporal neutrality'). On the other hand, the Italian-style dual income tax subjects *above-normal* business profits, as well as labour incomes, to a progressive tax rate schedule with top marginal tax rate above the tax rate on normal capital income. The higher and more progressive taxation of labour incomes allows governments to raise more revenue through income taxation, to strengthen the redistributive profile of the tax system and to alleviate the tax burden of low-income workers. The higher taxation of above-normal profits serves the same goals and in addition fulfils a *safeguarding function* for the progressive income tax on wages. The incentive of proprietors or managers of closely-held companies in the top income tax bracket to transform wage income into capital income is reduced because above-normal capital income is taxed at the same marginal tax rate as wages.

Corporate tax competition undermined the viability of the Italian-style dual income tax. Because high corporate tax rates tend to deter direct investment and stimulate international tax avoidance, they cannot be sustained even if they only apply to above-normal profits. As a result, policymakers' ability to differentiate the tax burdens on normal and above-normal profits and to use the corporation tax as a safeguard of a progressive wage tax is reduced. The latter fact implies that corporate tax competition tends to spill over into personal taxation, creating downward pressure on the top tax rate on wages. I have argued that the downward trend in top personal income tax rates is to some extent the result of this spill-over effect.

However, the force of this effect is moderated by the domestic costs of drastic cuts in top marginal tax rates on wages. Because high-tax countries rely mainly on the taxation of labour incomes to finance their spending commitments, such cuts imply substantial revenue losses or a significant reduction of wage tax progressivity or both. Therefore, flat income taxes have not yet been implemented in advanced OECD countries. Virtually all of these countries operate differentiated or (Nordic-style) dual income taxes, whose top tax rate on personal (labour) income is well above the corporate tax rate. Because policymakers cannot increase the corporate tax rate on above-normal profits, one central problem of these taxes is the tax avoidance incentives of high-income taxpayers and hence the preservation of the income tax system's integrity.

The most systematic way to reduce these tax-avoidance incentives in a systematic way — and despite corporate tax competition — is perhaps to follow the general logic of the Italian-style dual income tax but transfer the taxation of above-normal profits *to the level of the shareholder*, i.e. to the taxation of dividends (and capital gains). As discussed in Chapter six, this kind of shareholder taxation, elaborated in Sørensen (forthcoming-b), was recently introduced for all corporations in Norway. The problem, however, is that transferring the taxation of above-normal profits to the level of the shareholder seems to be associated with a significant increase of administrative complexity. In Norway a centralised, computerised register of all resident Norwegian personal shareholders was created to keep track of the (adequately adjusted) values of shares and of the utilisation of tax allowances for normal profits. To avoid the resulting administrative burden, Sørensen (forthcoming-a) has pragmatically proposed to tax only the above-normal dividends of corporations not listed on the stock exchange and exempt the dividends of listed companies. While this would abandon the idea of finding a systematic compromise between Income and Expenditure Taxation, it would greatly reduce administrative complexity. Only the above-normal profits of unlisted corporations would be taxed more highly than normal profits. The main rationale of this differentiation would be to prevent owners of small companies from transforming heavily taxed management salaries into lightly-taxed capital income.

The discussion highlights two important lessons of this study. The first lesson is that there *are* viable and attractive alternatives to a continuous lowering and flattening of income taxes. Hence if a government chooses to implement a flat income tax, this is not because there are no efficient and equitable alternatives but because policymakers lack the will or skill to act otherwise. The second lesson, however, is that the downward pressure on corporate tax rates has nevertheless made it more difficult and costly for national governments to balance the goals of equity and efficiency (including administrative efficiency) in income taxation.

The second lesson is important for the debate about *international* tax policy, especially in the European Union. This debate, much like the theoretical debate in political science, has focused mainly on the *direct* effects of corporate tax competition on corporate tax revenue. Because such effects are apparently lacking, the conclusion drawn by the European Commission and many others has been that a minimum company tax rate—proposed by a tax reform committee in 1992 (Ruding Report 1992)—would violate the principle of subsidiarity, i.e. *unnecessarily* limit the freedom of national governments to set their own tax rates. In the light of the findings presented here, however, this argument is questionable (Ganghof and Genschel 2006). For example, if a minimum corporate tax rate at the EU level only applied to above-normal profits, policymakers at the national level would remain free to set the corporate tax rate on *normal* profits well below the EU minimum tax rate, thus stimulating domestic investment and attracting foreign capital. At the same time, the ability of national governments to maintain progressive income taxation of *personal* income, especially wages, would *increase*. Governments preferring dual or differentiated income taxes would not have to reduce top marginal tax rates on individuals in order to respond to the downward spiral in corporate tax rates. They would still be free to cut these tax rates, of course. But they would not have to pursue such cuts *only to keep the tax rate gap between corporations and individuals within certain limits*. Moreover, governments preferring flat income taxes could also benefit—especially if the downward trend in corporate tax rates continues unabated. For while a flat tax of, say, 25 per cent might be acceptable to the electorate, a flat tax of 15 or 10 per cent might not. Achieving political agreement on a minimum corporate tax rate is of course difficult but not impossible.

The first insight—on the viability of dual or differentiated income taxation even in the presence of tax competition—is important for debates about *national* tax policy. In some countries, for example in Germany, public debates have increasingly created the impression that the continuous flattening of the income tax is the only path to efficiency and equity and that a dual income tax with a significant tax rate gap between capital and labour taxation would create an administrative nightmare. However, this impression is wrong, and the German case is itself the best example for the costs of the flat tax model. The Nordic countries have used their dual (or differentiated) income taxes to make capital income taxation more neutral, consolidate their budgets and target tax cuts to low labour incomes. In the same way, Germany could have used the dual income tax model to achieve urgently needed budget consolidation, reduce the very high *social security contributions* for low-wage earners and invest in better schools, universities and day-care. Instead, the normative fixation on the ideal of uniform income taxation with equal (top) tax rates on corporate and personal income contributed significantly to large tax cuts for the well-off and the persistence of high budget deficits.

To be sure, this outcome owes much to the many peculiarities of the German case, including the existence of a powerful Constitutional Court that has achieved a far-reaching 'constitutionalisation' of tax policy. However, given the recent political success of the flat tax model in Eastern Europe, it seems clear that we will see similar debates in many other advanced OECD countries—especially those that have low income tax burdens because they rely heavily on social security contributions and value-added taxes.

Of course, national policy choices and debates about international tax policy are connected in complex ways. If the ideal of dual income taxation outrivals the ideal of flat income taxation at the national level, a minimum corporate tax rate on above-normal profits may seem more important. Conversely, if agreement on such a minimum rate seems infeasible at the European level, this may reduce the attractiveness of dual income taxation at the national level. But these types of interactions are the topic for another book. The goal of the present one was to contribute to a more balanced discussion of tax policy goals and options at both the national and international levels.

appendix | country abbreviations, sources and definitions

COUNTRIES AND ABBREVIATIONS

The reference group of 21 OECD countries includes the following cases (abbreviations in parentheses):

Australia (AUS)	Japan (JPN)
Austria (AUT)	Netherlands (NLD)
Belgium (BEL)	New Zealand (NZL)
Canada (CAN)	Norway (NOR)
Denmark (DNK)	Portugal (PRT)
Finland (FIN)	Spain (ESP)
France (FRA)	Sweden (SWE)
Germany (DEU)	Switzerland (CHE)
Greece (GRC)	United Kingdom (GBR)
Ireland (IRE)	United States (USA)
Italy (ITA)	

VARIABLE DEFINITIONS AND DATA SOURCES

Top personal income tax rates
This data is generally available for the period from 1975 to 2004. For the seven countries covered by the comparative case studies, the data for 2005 was also collected. The data set is based on information from the following sources: OECD (1986), BMF (various years), Coopers&Lybrand (various years), the World Tax Data Base (http://www.bus.umich.edu/OTPR/otpr/introduction.htm) and national sources. In what follows, I shall provide some information on the taxing powers of sub-national governments in income personal taxation in the 21 OECD countries as well as the inclusion of certain 'social security contributions'.

In the following countries only income taxes at the central government level are reflected in the data: Austria, France, Greece, Ireland, the Netherlands, New Zealand, Portugal, Spain and the United Kingdom.

In the following countries, the data on top personal income tax rates reflects levies other than income taxes at the central government level. The rules for distinguishing income taxes from social security contributions are those of the OECD (2004c). For *Australia* a Medicare levy, introduced in 1986, is taken into account. For *Belgium* local income taxes and surcharges are included. Between 1978 and 1988 there was a ceiling for the overall statutory income tax burden, which is reflected in the data. For *Canada* the provincial taxes of Ontario are taken into account. Until 2000 provincial taxes took the form of surcharges. Provincial tax rate data for recent years comes from www.taxpayer.com. For *Denmark* local income taxes and proportional income taxes earmarked for social security are included. The top tax rate of the progressive income tax is defined by a ceiling for the overall income tax burden. For *Finland* (missing values: 1975–8) local income taxes and a social security contribution for health care are included. The average for local income tax rates was provided by the Finnish Ministry of Finance. For *Germany* the solidarity surcharge is included. For *Italy* the local income tax is included. It was abolished in 1998. From 2000 there were regionally varying surcharges. For *Japan* prefectural and local income taxes are included. In *Norway* (missing values: 1975–8) local taxes and an employee social insurance contribution is included. The data was partly provided by Statistics Norway. For *Sweden* the average of local income tax rates is included, based on information provided by the Swedish Ministry of Finance. For *Switzerland* (missing values: 1975–8) cantonal and local income tax rates are included. The latter refer to the situation in Zurich. Missing values for the years 1982–3, 1987 and 1992–5 are interpolated. For the *USA* an unweighted average of local state income tax rates is taken into account.

Corporate tax rates
This data is generally available for the period from 1975 to 2005. The data set is based on information from the following sources: BMF (various years), Coopers&Lybrand (various years), the World Tax Data Base (http://www.bus.umich.edu/OTPR/otpr/introduction.htm), the Institute for Fiscal Studies (Chennells and Griffith 1997; Devereux et al. 2002), the KPMG Corporate Tax Rate Survey (http://www.us.kpmg.com/microsite/global_tax/ctr_survey/) and national sources. In what follows, I shall provide some information on the taxing powers of sub-national governments in business taxation in the 21 OECD countries.

In the following countries only profit taxes at the central government level are taken into account: Australia (missing values: 1976–79), Denmark, Greece, Ireland, Netherlands, New Zealand, Spain and the United Kingdom.

In the following countries the data on corporate tax rates includes local taxes and/or surcharges. The coding rules are identical to those of the KMPG Corporate Tax Surveys (http://www.us.kpmg.com/microsite/global_tax/ctr_survey/). *Austria* had a progressive corporate income tax until 1988. Hence the data for Austria for the period 1975–88 reflects the top rate. Until 1993 a local business tax existed, the average of which is included. For *Belgium* a surcharge of 3 per cent (from 1994) is included. For *Canada* (missing value: 1975) the provincial tax rates for Ontario are taken into account. Missing values for 1982–3 are interpolated. For *Finland* (missing values: 1975–9) local corporation taxes, abolished in 1993, are included. The *French* tax rate is the one applicable to retained corporate profits. Surcharges, introduced in 1995, are included. The *German* tax rate is also the one applicable to retained corporate profits. Also included are the 'solidarity' surcharge and the average local business tax rate. In *Italy* a local corporation tax existed until 1998, which was partly deductible against the central government corporation tax. In 1998 the corporation tax was replaced by a business tax with a much broader tax base. For *Japan* (missing values: 1975–8) prefectural and local business taxes are included. The prefectural tax is deductible against the central government tax (in the following year). For *Norway* local taxes, abolished in 1998, are included. For *Portugal* (missing values: 1975–81) local taxes and surcharges are included. For *Sweden* (missing values: 1975–9) local taxes, abolished in 1985, are included. In *Switzerland* (missing values: 1975–82) there are progressive corporate income taxes at federal, cantonal and local levels. The sub-national data refers to Zurich. Missing values for 1983, 1985, 1987 and 1990 are interpolated. For the *USA* an unweighted average of local corporation tax rates is taken into account.

Other data

Data on population comes from World Bank (2003), revenue data from OECD (2004c). For the data used in the replication in Table 8.2 see Hallerberg and Basinger (1998).

bibliography

Aaberge, R., Colombino, U. and Strøm, S. (2000) 'Labor supply responses and welfare effects from replacing current tax rules by a flat tax: empirical evidence from Italy, Norway and Sweden', *Journal of Population Economics*, 13: 595–621.

Aalberg, T. (1999) 'Reaction against public policies or adjusting preferences? Egalitarian values in comparative perspective', in H. M. Narud and T. Aalberg (eds) *Challenges to Representative Democracy: Parties, Voters, and Public Opinion*, Oslo: Fagbokforlaget.

Aaron, H. J., Galper, H. and Pechman, J. A. (eds) (1988) *Uneasy Compromise. Problems of a Hybrid Income-Consumption Tax*, Washington, DC: Brookings.

Abel, A. B. (1992) 'Equipment investment and economic growth: how strong is the nexus? Comments and discussion', *Brookings Papers on Economic Activity:* 200–11.

Achen, C. H. (forthcoming) 'Let's put garbage-can regressions and garbage-can probits where they belong', *Conflict Management and Peace Science*.

Agell, J., Englund, P. and Södersten, J. (1998) *Incentives and Redistribution in the Welfare State*, Houndmills: Macmillan.

Agell, J., Persson, M. and Sacklén, H. (1994) 'The effects of tax reform on labor supply, tax revenue and welfare when tax avoidance matters', *European Journal of Political Economy*, 20/4: 963–982 (2004)

Alexy, R. (2003) 'Constitutional rights, balancing, and rationality', *Ratio Juris*, 16: 131–40.

Alivizatos, N. (1995) 'Judges as veto players', in H. Döring (ed.) *Parliaments and majority rule in Western Europe*, Frankfurt am Main: Campus.

Altemeier, J. (1999) *Föderale Finanzbeziehungen unter Anpassungsdruck. Verteilungskonflikte in der Verhandlungsdemokratie*, Köln: Campus.

Andersen, P.S. (1998) 'Denmark: tax changes enacted', *European Taxation*, 38: 347–54.

Andersen, T.M., Jensen, S.E.H. and Risager, O. (1999) 'Macroeconomic perspectives on the Danish economy: problems, policies and prospects', in T.M. Andersen and S.E.H. Jensen (eds) *Macroeconomic Perspectives on the*

Danish Economy, London: Macmillan.

Andersson, E. (1993) 'The Finnish business income tax reform of 1992', in Nordic Council for Tax Research (ed.) *Tax Reform in the Nordic Countries*, Uppsala: Iustus.

Andersson, K. *et al.* (1998) 'Corporate tax policy in the Nordic countries', in P. B. Sorensen (ed.) *Tax Policy in the Nordic Countries*, Houndmills: MacMillan.

Andersson, K. and Mutén, L. (1998) 'Sweden', in K. Messere (ed.) *The Tax Systems of Industrialized Countries*, Oxford: Oxford University Press.

Arnold, B.J., Li, J. and Sandler, D. (1996) *Comparison and Assessment of the Tax Treatment of Foreign-Source Income in Canada, Australia, France, Germany and the United States*, Working Paper no. 96–1 prepared for the Technical Committee on Business Taxation, Ottawa.

Arter, D. (1987) *Politics and Policy-Making in Finland*, Wheatsheaf: Brighton.

_____ (1994) '"The war of the roses": conflict and cohesion in the Swedish Social Democratic Party', in D. S. Bell and E. Shaw (eds) *Conflict and Cohesion in the West European Social Democratic Parties*, London: Pinter.

_____ (1999) *Scandinavian Politics Today*, Manchester: Manchester University Press.

Atkinson, A. B. (2004) 'The Luxembourg Income Study (LIS): past, present and future', *Socio-Economic Review*, 2: 165–90.

Auerbach, A.J. (1989) 'The deadweight loss from "nonneutral" capital income taxation', *Journal of Public Economics*, 40: 1–36.

_____ (1997) 'The future of fundamental tax reform', *American Economic Review*, 87: 143–6.

Auerbach, A. J., Hassett, K. and Oliner, S. (1994) 'Reassessing the social returns to equipment investment', *Quarterly Journal of Economics*, 109: 789–802.

Avi-Yonah, R.S. (2004) 'Risk, rents, and regressivity: why the United States need both an Income Tax and a VAT', *Tax Notes: 1651–66*.

Bale, T. and Bergman, T. (forthcoming) 'Captives no longer, but servants still? Contract Parliamentarism and the new minority governance in Sweden and New Zealand', *Government and Opposition*.

Bareis, P. (2000) 'Die Steuerreform 2000 – ein Jahrhundertwert?', *Wirtschaftsstudium*, 29: 602–09.

Bartelborth, T. and Scholz, O.R. (2002) 'Understanding utterances and other actions', in G. Grewendorf and G. Meggle (eds) *Speech Acts, Mind, and Social Reality. Discussions with John Searle*, London: Kluwer.

Basinger, S. and Hallerberg, M. (2004) 'Remodeling the competition for capital: how domestic politics erases the race-to-the-bottom', *American Political Science Review*, 98: 261–76.

Bates, R.H. *et al.* (1998) *Analytical Narratives*, Princeton: Princeton University Press.

_____ (2000) 'The analytic narrative project', *American Political Science Review*, 94: 696–702.

Becker, G.S. and Mulligan, C.B. (1998) 'Let's revamp the tax code – but how?, *Wall Street Journal*: A22.

_____ (2003) 'Deadweight costs and the size of government', *Journal of Law and Economics*, 46: 293–340.

Benoit, K. and Laver, M. (2006) *Party Policy in Modern Democracies*, London: Routledge.

Bergman, T. (2000) 'Sweden. When minority cabinets are the rule and majority coalitions the exception', in W.C. Müller and K. Strøm (eds) *Coalition Governments in Western Europe*, Oxford: Oxford University Press.

Berk, R.A. (2004) *Regression Analysis: A Constructive Critique*, London: Sage.

Bille, L. (2002) 'Denmark', *European Journal of Political Research*, 41: 941–6.

_____ (2004) 'Denmark', *European Journal of Political Research*, 43: 989–92.

Bird, A. (1998) *Philosophy of Science*, Montreal: McGill/Queen's University Press.

Bird, R. A., Perry, D. B. and Wilson, T. A. (1998) 'Canada', in K. Messere (ed.) *The Tax System of Industrialized Countries*, Oxford: Oxford University Press.

Blom-Hansen, J. (1999) 'Avoiding the "joint-decision trap": lessons from inter-governmental relations in Scandinavia', *European Journal of Political Research*, 35: 35–67.

Blotnicki, L. and Heckly, C. (1998) 'France', in K. Messere (ed.) *The Tax System in Industrialized Countries*, Oxford: Oxford University Press.

BMF [German Ministry of Finance] (ed.) (1995) *Thesen der Einkommensteuer-Kommission zur Steuerfreistellung des Existenzminimums ab 1996 und zur Reform der Einkommensteuer*, Heft 55 der Schriftenreihe des BMF, Bonn: BMF.

_____(ed.) (1997) *Reform der Einkommensbesteuerung - Vorschläge der Steuerreformkommission – vom 22. Januar 1997 "Petersberger Steuervorschläge"*, Heft 61 der Schriftenreihe des BMF, Bonn: BMF.

_____(1999a) *Brühler Empfehlungen zur Reform der Unternehmensbest-euerung*, Heft 66 der Schriftenreihe des BMF, Bonn: BMF.

_____ (ed.) (1999b) *Gutachten und Stellungnahmen 1988–1998*, Bonn: BMF.

_____ (1999c) *Reform der Kapitaleinkommensbesteuerung. Gutachten erstattet vom Wissenschaftlichen Beirat beim Bundesministerium der Finanzen*, Heft 65 der Schriftenreihe des BMF, Bonn: Stollfuß.

_____ (1999d) *Tax Reform 2000. Cutting Taxes – Strengthening Growth – Tackling Unemployment.*, Statement by Hans Eichel, Federal Minister of Finance, during the presentation of the federal government's plans for the tax reform at the *Bundespressekonferenz* in Berlin, 21 December 1999, Berlin.

_____ (2000a) *Administrierbarkeit der Modelle zur Unternehmensteuerreform bei Finanzverwaltung, Steuerpflichtigen und Steuerberatern. Ergebnisse der Planspiele und des Modellvergleichs. Abschlussbericht*, Heft 67 der Schriftenreihe des BMF, Bonn: BMF.

_____(2000b) *Finanzbericht 2001*, Bonn: BMF.

_____(2002) *Steuerpolitik der Bundesregierung. Eine Politik im Interesse der Arbeitnehmer und Familien*, Bonn: BMF.

_____(2004) *Monatsbericht des BMF. Dezember 2004*, Berlin: BMF.

_____(various years) *Die wichtigsten Steuern im internationalen Vergleich*, Bonn: BMF.

BMWi [German Ministry of Economics] (1996) *Anstehende große Steuerreform. Gutachten des Wissenschaftlichen Beirates beim Bundesministerium der Wirtschaft*, Heft 94 der Schriftenreihe des BMWi, Bonn.

Boadway, R. and Bruce, N. (1984) 'A general proposition on the design of a neutral business tax', *Journal of Public Economics*, 24: 231–9.

Bond, S. R. (2000) 'Levelling up or levelling down? Some reflections on the ACE and CBIT proposals, and the future of the corporate tax base', in S. Cnossen (ed.) *Taxing Capital Income in the European Union*, Oxford: Oxford University Press.

Bordignon, M., Giannini, S. and Panteghini, P. (2001) 'Reforming business taxation: lessons from Italy?', *International Tax and Public Finance*, 8: 191–210.

Bork, C. and Mueller, K. (1998) 'Effekte der Verrechnungsmöglichkeit negativer Einkünfte im deutschen Einkommensteuerrecht', *Konjunkturpolitik*, 44: 353–66.

Bossons, J. (1987) 'The impact of the 1986 tax reform act on tax reform in Canada', *National Tax Journal*, 40: 331–8.

_____(1988) 'International tax competition: the foreign government response in Canada and other countries', *National Tax Journal*, 41: 347–55.

Boston, J. (1998) *Governing under Proportional Representation: Lessons from Europe*, Wellington: Institute of Policy Studies.

_____(1999) 'New Zealand's welfare state in transition', in J. Boston, P. Dalziel and S. Saint John (eds) *Redesigning the Welfare State in New Zealand: Problems, Policies, Prospects*, Oxford: Oxford University Press.

Boston, J., Dalziel, P. and Saint John, S. (1999) 'Rebuilding an effective welfare state', in J. Boston, P. Dalziel and S. Saint John (eds) *Redesigning the Welfare State in New Zealand: Problems, Policies, Prospects*, Oxford: Oxford University Press.

Boston, J. *et al.* (1996) *New Zealand under MMP: A New Politics?* Auckland: Auckland University Press.

Bradford, D.F. (1986) *Untangling the Income Tax*, Cambridge, MA: Harvard University Press.

_____(1991) 'The politics of tax reform in the 1980s: comment', in A. Alesina and G. Carliner (eds) *Politics and Economics in the Eighties*, Chicago: University of Chicago Press.

Bräuninger, T. and Ganghof, S. (2005) 'Parteienwettbewerb im Zweikammersystem', in S. Ganghof and P. Manow (eds) *Mechanismen der Politik. Strategische Interaktion im deutschen Regierungssystem*, Frankfurt: Campus.

Bucovetsky, S. (1991) 'Asymmetric tax competition', *Journal of Urban Economics*, 30: 167–81.

Burger, C. (1996) *Die Gewerbesteuer in Deutschland. Eine fehltentwickelte und überholte Steuer*, PhD dissertation, University of Fribourg, Switzerland.

Bye, B. and Åvitsland, T. (2003) 'The welfare effects of housing taxation in a distorted economy: a general equilibrium approach', *Economic Modelling*, 20: 895–921.

Campbell, J. L. (2004) *Institutional Change and Globalization*, Princeton: Princeton University Press.

Carey, J.M. (2002) *Getting Their Way, or Getting in the Way? Presidents and Party Unity in Legislative Voting*, Paper prepared for delivery at the 2002 Annual Meeting of the American Political Science Association, Boston, August 29–September 1, 2002.

Chapman, R. (1992) 'A political culture under pressure: the struggle to preserve a progressive tax base for welfare and the positive state', *Political Science*, 44: 1–27.

Chennells, L. and Griffith, R. (1997) *Taxing Profits in a Changing World*, London: Institute for Fiscal Studies.

Clarke, K.A. (forthcoming) 'The phantom menace: omitted variable bias in econometric research', *Conflict Management and Peace Science*.

Cnossen, S. (1999) 'Taxing capital income in the Nordic countries: a model for the European Union?', *Finanzarchiv*, 56: 18–50.

Cnossen, S. and Bovenberg, L. (2001) 'Fundamental tax reform in the Netherlands', *International Tax and Public Finance*, 8: 467–80.

Conlan, T. J., Wrightson, M. T. and Beam, D. R. (1990) *Taxing Choices. The Politics of Tax Reform*, Washington, D.C.: CQ Press.

Coopers&Lybrand (various years) *International Tax Summaries. A Guide for Planning and Decisions*, New York: John Wiley&Sons.

Daly, M. J. (1993) 'Canada', in D. Jorgenson and R. Landau (eds) *Tax Reform and the Cost of Capital*, Washington DC: Brookings.

Damgaard, E. (2000) 'Denmark: The life and death of government coalitions', in W.C. Müller and K. Strøm (eds) *Coalition Governments in Western Europe*, Oxford: Oxford University Press.

Damgaard, E. and Svensson, P. (1989) 'Who governs – parties and policies in Denmark', *European Journal of Political Research*, 17: 731–45.

De Long, J.B. and Summers, L.H. (1991) 'Equipment investment and economic growth', *Quarterly Journal of Economics*, 106: 445–502.

Deaton, A. (1987) 'Econometric issues for tax design in developing countries', in D.M. Newbery and N.H. Stern (eds) *The Theory of Taxation for Developing Countries*, New York: Oxford University Press.

Dehejia, V.H. and Genschel, P. (1999) 'Tax competition in the European Union', *Politics and Society*, 27: 304–30.

Denmark, D. (2001) 'Choosing MMP in New Zealand: explaining the 1993 electoral reform', in M. S. Shugart and M.P. Wattenberg (eds) *Mixed-Member*

Electoral Systems, Oxford: Oxford University Press.

Dengel, A. (1987) 'Germany', in J. A. Pechman (ed.) *Comparative Tax Systems: Europe, Canada, and Japan*, Arlington: Tax Analysts.

Devereux, M. P. and Griffith, R. (1998) 'Taxes and the location of production: evidence from a panel of us multinationals', *Journal of Public Economics*, 68: 335–67.

Devereux, M. P., Griffith, R. and Klemm, A. (2002) 'Corporate income tax reforms and international tax competition', *Economic Policy*, 17: 451–95.

Diamond, P. A. and Mirrlees, J. A. (1971) 'Optimal taxation and public production, part I: production efficiency and part II: tax rules', *American Economic Review*, 61: 8–27 and 261–78.

Döring, T. and Feld, L.P. (2005) 'Reform der Gewerbesteuer: Wie es Euch gefällt? Eine Nachlese', *Perspektiven der Wirtschaftspolitik*, 6: 207–32.

Dowding, K. (forthcoming) 'A defence of revealed preference analysis', *Economics and Philosophy*.

Drejer, J. (1988) 'Denmark', in J.A. Pechman (ed.) *World Tax Reform. A Progress Report*, Washington, D.C.: Brookings.

Eccleston, R. (2004) *The Thirty Year Problem: The Politics of Australian Tax Reform*, Sydney: The Australian Tax Research Foundation.

Edlund, J. (2000) 'Public attitudes towards taxation: Sweden 1981–1997', *Scandinavian Political Studies*, 23: 37–65.

Eichel, H. (2000) 'Mehr Beschäftigung durch Investitionen', *Wirtschaftsdienst*, 80: 75–78.

Elster, J. (2000) 'Rational choice history: a case of excessive ambition', *American Political Science Review*, 94: 685–95.

Ervik, R. (2000) *The Hidden Welfare State in Comparative Perspective: Tax Expenditures and Social Policy an Eight Countries*, PhD Dissertation, University of Bergen, Norway.

Evans, E.A. (1988) 'Australia', in J.A. Pechman (ed.) *World Tax Reform. A Progress Report*, Washington, D.C.: Brookings.

Evans, H. (2001) *Odgers' Australian Senate Practice*, 10th edn, Canberra: Department of the Senate.

Fagerberg, J. *et al.* (1990) 'The decline of state capitalism in Norway', *New Left Review*, 181: 60–91.

Faltlhauser, K. (ed.) (1988) *Steuerstrategie*, Köln: Kölner Universitätsverlag.

FDP (1999) *Einkommensteuer aus einem Guß: niedrig, einfach und gerecht*, Beschluss des 50. Ord. Bundesparteitages der FDP, Bremen 28–30. Mai 1999.

Feldstein, M. (1990) 'The second best theory of differential capital taxation', *Oxford Economic Papers – New Series*, 42: 256–67.

Feldt, K.-O. (1991) *Alla dessa dagar. I regeringen 1982–1990*, Stockholm: Norstedts.

Ferrers, T. (2000) 'The new business tax system for Australia', *Intertax*, 28: 30–35.

Findling, M. (1995) *Die Politische Ökonomie der Steuerreform – Eine*

*Untersuchung der politischen Grenzen von Steuerreformen unter beson-
derer Berücksichtigung der Steuerreform 1990*, Aachen: Shaker.

Finnish Ministry of Finance (2002) *Finland's Competitiveness and the Way
Forward*, Helsinki: Ministry of Finance.

Fitzmaurice, J. (2001) 'Divided government: the case of Denmark', in R. Elgie
(ed.) *Divided Government in Comparative Perspective*, Oxford: Oxford
University Press.

Frank, R. H. (1999) *Luxury Fever*, New York: Free Press.

_____(2000) 'Progressive taxation and the incentive problem', in J. B. Slemrod
(ed.) *Does Atlas Shrug? The Economic Consequences of Taxing the Rich*,
Cambridge: Harvard University Press.

Freedman, D. A. (1991) 'Statistical models and shoe leather', *Sociological
Methodology*, 21: 291–313.

Friedman, J. (ed.) (1996) *The rational choice controversy: economic models of
politics reconsidered*, New Haven: Yale University Press.

Fullerton, D. (1994) 'Tax policy', in M. Feldstein (ed.) *American Economic
Policy in the 1980s*, Chicago: University of Chicago Press.

Gallagher, M., Laver, M. and Mair, P. (2005) *Representative Government in
Modern Europe. Institutions, Parties, and Governments*, 4th edn, New
York: McGraw-Hill.

Ganghof, S. (1999) 'Steuerwettbewerb und Vetospieler: Stimmt die These der
blockierten Anpassung?', *Politische Vierteljahresschrift*, 40: 458–72.

_____(2000) 'Adjusting national tax policy to economic internationalization:
strategies and outcomes', in F. W. Scharpf and V. A. Schmidt (eds)
*Welfare and Work in the Open Economy. Volume II: Diverse Responses to
Common Challenges*, Oxford: Oxford University Press.

_____(2003) 'Promises and pitfalls of veto player analysis', *Swiss Political
Science Review*, 9: 1–25.

_____ (2004) *Wer regiert in der Steuerpolitik? Einkommensteuerreform zwischen
internationalem Wettbewerb und nationalen Verteilungskonflikten*,
Frankfurt/Main: Campus.

_____(2005a) 'Globalisation, tax reform ideals and social policy financing',
Global Social Policy, 5: 77–95.

_____ (2005b) *High Taxes in Hard Times. How Denmark Built and Maintained
a Huge Income Tax*, Max Planck Institute for the Study of Societies,
Discussion Paper 05/5, Cologne.

_____(2005c) 'Konditionale Konvergenz: Ideen, Institutionen und
Standortwettbewerb in der Steuerpolitik von EU- und OECD-Ländern',
Zeitschrift für internationale Beziehungen, 11: 7–40.

_____(forthcoming) 'The politics of tax structure', in I. Shapiro and P. A.
Swenson (eds) *The Politics of Distribution*, New York: Cambridge
University Press.

_____(2006)'Tax Mixes and the Size of the Welfare State. Causal Mechanisms
and Policy Implications', *Journal of European Social Policy*, 16: 360–373

Ganghof, S. and Bräuninger, T. (2006) 'Government status and legislative behavior. Partisan veto players in Australia, Denmark, Finland and Germany', *Party Politics,* 12: 521–539.

Ganghof, S. and Eccleston, R. (2004) 'Globalisation and the dilemmas of income taxation in Australia', *Australian Journal of Political Science*, 39: 519–34.

Ganghof, S. and Genschel, P. (2006) 'How much corporate tax competition in the single market?', unpublished work, Max Planck Institut Cologne/ International University Bremen.

Garfinkel, A. (1981) *Forms of Explanation. Rethinking the Questions in Social Theory*, New Haven: Yale University Press.

Garrett, G. (1998a) *Partisan Politics in the Global Economy*, Cambridge: Cambridge University Press.

_____(1998b) 'Shrinking states? Globalization and national autonomy in the OECD', *Oxford Development Studies*, 26: 71–97.

Garrett, G. and Lange, P. (1991) 'Political responses to interdependence: what's left for the left?', *International Organization*, 45: 539–64.

Gaube, T. and Schwager, R. (2004) 'Does old capital matter', *Public Finance Review*, 32: 220–31.

Genschel, P. (2002) 'Globalization, tax competition, and the welfare state', Politics & Society, 30: 245–75.

_____ (2005) 'Globalization and the transformation of the tax state', *European Review*, 13: 53–71.

Gjelsvik, E. (1998) 'Recent tax reforms in Norway: what have we learned?', in D. Foden and P. Morris (eds) *The Search for Equity*, London: Lawrence&Wishart.

Gjems-Onstad, O. (1993) 'Beyond progression – taxation of the very rich', in Nordic Council for Tax Research (ed.) *Tax Reform in the Nordic Countries*, Uppsala: Iustus.

_____ (2005) 'Norway's tax reform 2004–2006', *Bulletin for International Fiscal Documentation*, 59: 141–45.

Goode, R. (1976) *The Individual Income Tax*, Washington, D.C.: Brookings.

Goolsbee, A. (1998) 'Taxes, organizational form, and the deadweight loss of the Corporate Income Tax', *Journal of Public Economics*, 69: 143–52.

Gordon, R. H. and Slemrod, J. B. (2000) 'Are "real" responses to taxes simply income shifting between corporate and personal tax bases?', in J. B. Slemrod (ed.) *Does Atlas Shrug? The Economics Consequences of Taxing the Rich*, New York: Russell Sage/Harvard University Press.

Gordon, R. K. and MacKie-Mason, J. K. (1994) 'Tax distortions to the choice of organizational form', *Journal of Public Economics*, 55: 279–306.

Government Institute for Economic Research (1995) *Finnish Corporate Tax Reforms*, Helsinki: VATT.

Gravelle, J. G. (1994) *The Economic Effects of Taxing Capital Income*, Cambridge: MIT Press.

Green-Pedersen, C. (1999) 'The Danish welfare state under bourgeois reign. The dilemma of popular entrenchment and economic constraints', *Scandinavian Political Studies*, 22: 243–60.

Griffith, R. and Klemm, A. (2004) *What Has Been the Tax Competition Experience of the Last 20 Years?* Institute for Fiscal Studies, WP 04/05, London.

Guger, A. (1998) 'Economic policy and social democracy: the Austrian experience', *Oxford Review of Economic Policy*, 14: 40–58.

Gustafsson, S. (1996) 'Tax regimes and labour market performance', in G. Schmid, J. O'Reilly and K. Schömann (eds) *International Handbook of Labour Market Policy and Evaluation*, Cheltenham: Edward Elgar.

Hagen, K.P. and Sørensen, P. B. (1998) 'Taxation of income from small businesses: taxation principles and tax reforms in the Nordic countries', in P. B. Sørensen (ed.) *Tax Policy in the Nordic Countries*, Houndmills: Macmillan.

Hall, P. A. (1993) 'Policy paradigms, social learning, and the state. The case of economic policymaking in Britain', *Comparative Politics*, 25: 275–96.

Hallerberg, M. and Basinger, S. (1998) 'Internationalization and changes in tax policy in OECD countries: the importance of domestic veto players', *Comparative Political Studies*, 31: 321–52.

_____ (1999) 'Globalization and tax reform: an updated case for the importance of veto players', *Politische Vierteljahresschrift*, 40: 618–27.

Harris, P. (1999) 'Australia: corporate tax reform down-under: maybe not the full Monty but', *Bulletin for International Fiscal Documentation*, 53: 249–66.

Haufler, A. and Schjelderup, G. (2000) 'Corporate tax systems and cross country profit shifting', *Oxford Economic Letters*, 52: 306–25.

Hausman, D. (2000) 'Revealed preference, belief, and game theory', *Economics and Philosophy*, 16: 99–115.

Hausman, D. M. (2001) 'Explanation and diagnosis in economics', *Revue Internationale De Philosophie*, 55: 311–26.

Head, J. G. (1989) 'Australian tax reform: an overview', in J. G. Head (ed.) *Australian Tax Reform in Retrospect and Prospect*, Sydney: Australian Tax Research Foundation.

_____ (1997) 'Company tax structure and company tax incidence', *International Tax and Public Finance*, 4: 61–100.

Head, J. G. and Krever, R. (1997) 'Introduction and summary', in J. G. Head and R. Krever (eds) *Taxation Towards 2000*, Melbourne: Australian Tax Research Foundation.

Head, M. (1999) Consumption tax will hurt workers, students, pensioners and the poor. Online. Available HTTP: <www.wsws.org> (accessed 3 June 1999).

Heidar, K. (1993) 'The Norwegian Labour Party: "En Attendant l'Europe"', in R. Gillespie and W. E. Paterson (eds) *Rethinking Social Democracy in Western Europe*, London: Frank Cass.

_____ (2001) *Norway: Elites on Trial*, Colorado: Westview Press.

Helminen, M. (2001) 'Finland's imputation system under the pressure of globalization', *Bulletin for International Fiscal Documentation*, 55: 17–21.

Hines Jr., J. R. (1999) 'Lessons from behavioral responses to international taxation', *National Tax Journal*, 52: 305–22.

Hobson, J. M. (2003) 'Disappearing taxes or the "race to the middle"? Fiscal policy in the OECD', in L. Weiss (ed.) *States in the Global Economy*, Sydney: Cambridge University Press.

Hoover, K. D. (1994) 'Econometrics as observation: the Lucas critique and the nature of econometric inference', *Journal of Economic Methodology*, 1: 65–80.

_____(2002) 'Econometrics and reality', in U. Mäki (ed.) *Fact and Fiction in Economics. Models, Realism, and Social Construction*, Cambridge: Cambridge University Press.

Höpner, M. (2003) *European Corporate Governance Reform and the German Party Paradox*, MPIfG Discussion Paper 03/4, Cologne.

Huber, E., Ragin, C. and Stephens, J. D. (1993) 'Social Democracy, Christian Democracy, constitutional structure and the welfare state', *American Journal of Sociology*, 99: 711–49.

Huber, E. and Stephens, J. D. (1998) 'Internationalization and the Social Democratic model: crisis and future prospects', *Comparative Political Studies*, 31: 353–97.

Immergut, E. (1992) *Health Politics: Interests and Institutions in Western Europe*, Cambridge: Cambridge University Press.

Institute for Fiscal Studies (1978) 'The structure and reform of direct taxation', London: Institute for Fiscal Studies.

Isaac, J. (1997) 'A comment on the viability of the allowance for corporate equity', *Fiscal Studies*, 18: 303–18.

Johnson, J. D. (1991) 'Rational choice as a reconstructive theory', in K. R. Monroe (ed.) *The Economic Approach to Politics: A Critical Reassessment of the Theory of Rational Action*, New York: HarperCollins.

Jones, R. (1993) 'Australia', in D.W. Jorgenson and R. Landau (eds) *Tax Reform and the Cost of Capital*, Washington, D.C.: The Brookings Institution.

Joumard, I. and Suyker, W. (2002) *Options for Reforming the Finnish Tax System*, Economics Department Working Papers No. 319, Paris.

Jungar, A.-C. (2000) *Surplus Majority Government. A Comparative Study of Italy and Finland*, Uppsala: Acta Universitatis Upsaliensis.

_____(2002) 'A case of a surplus majority government: the Finnish rainbow coalition', *Scandinavian Political Studies*, 25: 57–82.

Kaiser, A. (1997) 'Types of democracy. From classical to new institutionalism', *Journal of Theoretical Politics*, 9: 419–44.

_____(2002) *Mehrheitsdemokratie und Institutionenreform. Verfassungspolitischer Wandel in Australien, Großbritannien, Kanada und Neuseeland im Vergleich*, Frankfurt: Campus.

Kaltenborn, B. (1999) *Streit um die Einkommensteuer: Die Reformvorschläge der*

Parteien im Vergleich, Baden-Baden: Nomos.

Keating, M. S. and Dixon, G. (1989) *Making Economic Policy in Australia*, Sydney: Longman Cheshire.

Keen, M. and King, J. (2003) 'The Croatian profit tax: an ACE in practice', in M. Rose (ed.) *Integriertes Steuer- und Sozialsystem*, Heidelberg: Manfred Rose.

Kemmerling, A. (2005) 'Tax mixes, welfare states and employment: tracking diverging vulnerabilities', *Journal of European Public Policy*, 12: 1–22.

King, G., Keohane, R.O. and Verba, S. (1994) *Designing Social Inquiry*, Princeton: Princeton University Press.

Kirchhof, P. (2003) 'Der Grundrechtsschutz des Steuerpflichtigen. Zur Rechtsprechung des Bundesverfassungsgerichts im vergangenen Jahrzehnt', *Archiv des öffentlichen Rechts*, 128: 1–51.

Kobetsky, M. (2000) 'Tax reform in Australia – the new tax system', *Bulletin for International Fiscal Documentation*, 54: 67–79.

Koch-Nielsen, R. (1988) 'Denmark: comment', in J.A. Pechman (ed.) *World Tax Reform. A Progress Report*, Washington, D.C.: Brookings.

Kommers, D. P. (1994) 'The Federal Constitutional Court in the German political system', *Comparative Political Studies*, 26: 470–91.

Koren, C. (1993) 'Taxation of wage earner households in Norway 1980–1992', in Nordic Council for Tax Research (ed.) *Tax Reform in the Nordic Countries*, Uppsala: Iustus.

Koskenkyla, H. (1992) 'Paaomatulojen verouudistus jatkuu: Ehdotettu rakenne oikeansuuntainen, mutta taso vaara (Capital Income Tax Reform. With English Summary)', *The Finnish Journal of Business Economics*, 41: 130–42.

Kraeusel, J. (1997) *Die Große Steuerreform. Stand der Diskussion*, Bonn: Stollfuß.

Krause-Junk, G. (1993) 'Tax policies in the 1980s and 1990s: the case of Germany', in A. Knoester (ed.) *Taxation in the United States and Europe. Theory and Practice*, Houndmills: Macmillan.

Krüer-Buchholz, W. (1982) *Steuerpolitik und Steuerreformen in der Bundesrepublik Deutschland unter besonderer Berücksichtigung der "Großen Steuerreform" 1975*, München: Minerva.

Krugman, P. (2001) *Fuzzy Math. The Essential Guide to the Bush Tax Plan*, New York: W.W.Norton.

Krusell, P., Quadrini, V. and Ríos-Rull, J.-V. (1996) 'Are consumption taxes really better than income taxes?', *Journal of Monetary Economics*, 37: 475–503.

Kuhn, T. (1962) *The Structure of Scientific Revolutions*, Chicago: University of Chicago Press.

Laine, V. (2002) *Evaluating Tax and Benefit Reforms in 1996–2001*, VATT Discussion Papers No. 280, Helsinki.

Lang, J. (2000) *Europa- und verfassungsrechtliche Maßstäbe für eine Besteuerung der Unternehmen*, unpublished manuscript, Cologne.

_____(2001) 'Prinzipien und Systeme der Besteuerung von Einkommen', in I. Ebling (ed.) *Besteuerung von Einkommen*, Köln: Otto Schmidt.

Laver, M. and Hunt, W.B. (1992) *Policy and Party Competition*, New York: Routledge.

Layard, R. (2005) *Happiness. Lessons from a New Science*, New York.

Leibfritz, W., Büttner, W. and van Essen, U. (1998) 'Germany', in K. Messere (ed.) *The Tax System in Industrialized Countries*, Oxford: University Press.

Leibfritz, W. and O'Brien, P. (2005) *The French Tax System: Main Characteristics, Recent Developments and Some Considerations for Reform*, Economics Department working papers No. 439.

Leunig, S. (2005) Die Entwicklung der parteipolitischen Mehrheitsverhältnisse in Bundestag und Bundesrat seit 1949. Online. Available HTTP: http://de.geocities.com/svenleunig/MehrheitsverhaeltnisseBRat.doc (accessed 4.8.2005).

Levi, M. (1988) *Of Rule and Revenue*, Berkeley: University of California Press.

Levy, J. D. (1999) 'Vice into virtue? Progressive politics and welfare reform in Continental Europe', *Politics and Society*, 27: 239–73.

Lijphart, A. (1994) *Electoral Systems and Party Systems. A Study of Twenty-seven Democracies, 1945–1990*, Oxford: Oxford University Press.

_____(1999) *Patterns of Democracy*, New Haven: Yale University Press.

Lindencrona, G. (1992) 'Taxation of capital in Sweden and international tax competition', in P. Timonen (ed.) *Nordic Perspectives on European Financial Integration*, Helsinki: University of Helsinki.

_____(1993) 'The taxation of financial capital and the prevention of tax avoidance', in Nordic Council for Tax Research (ed.) *Tax Reform in the Nordic Countries*, Iustus: Uppsala.

Lindert, P. H. (2004) *Growing Public: Social Spending and Economic Growth Since The Eighteenth Century. Volume One: The Story*, Cambridge: Cambridge University Press.

Lipton, P. (2004) *Inference to the Best Explanation*, 2nd edn, London: Routledge.

Ljungh, C. (1988) 'Sweden', in J. A. Pechman (ed.) *World Tax Reform. A Progress Report*, Washington D.C.: The Brookings Institution.

Lotz, K. (1993) 'The Danish tax reform 1987', in Nordic Council for Tax Research (ed.) *Tax Reform in the Nordic Countries*, Uppsala: Iustus.

Lyon, A. B. (1996) *International Implications of U.S. Business Tax Reform*, Working Paper no. 96–6 prepared for the Technical Committee on Business Taxation, Ottawa.

McCaw, P. (1982) *Report of the Task Force on Tax Reform*, Wellington: Government Printer.

McDonald, M. D., Mendes, S.M. and Budge, I. (2004) 'What are elections for? Conferring the median mandate', *British Journal of Political Science*, 34: 1–26.

McGann, A. J. (2005) *The Calculus of Consensual Democracy*, unpublished manuscript.

Mackerras, M. (2002) 'Australia', *European Journal of Political Research*, 41: 897–905.

Mackerras, M. and McAllister, I. (1999) 'Australia', *European Journal of Political Research*, 36: 317–25.

Mackie, G. (2003) *Democracy Defended*, Cambridge: Cambridge University Press.

MacKie-Mason, J.K. and Gordon, R.K. (1997) 'How much do taxes discourage incorporation?', *Journal of Finance*, 52: 477–505.

McLure, C. E. *et al.* (eds) (1990) *Influence of Tax Differentials on International Competitiveness*, Deventer: Kluwer.

McLure, C.E. and Zodrow, G.R. (1994) 'The study and practice of income tax policy', in J. M. Quigley and E. Smolensky (eds) *Modern Public Finance*, Cambridge: Harvard University Press.

Mann, S. (1994) *Macht und Ohnmacht der Verbände*, Baden-Baden: Nomos.

Masui, Y. (2001) 'Transformation of Japan's Corporation Tax: 1988 to 2000', *Bulletin for International Fiscal Documentation*, 55: 100–106.

Messere, K. (1993) *Tax Policy Choices in OECD Countries*, Amsterdam: IBFD Publications BV.

Messere, K., de Kam, F. and Heady, C. (2003) *Tax Policy: Theory and Practice in OECD Countries*, Oxford: Oxford University Press.

Miller, R. (2005) *Party Politics in New Zealand*, Oxford: Oxford University Press.

Mintz, J. M. (1995) 'Corporation tax: a survey', *Fiscal Studies*, 16: 23–68.

Moses, J. W. (2000) *Open States in the Global Economy: the Political Economy of Small-State Macroeconomic Management*, New York: St. Martin's.

Murphy, L. and Nagel, T. (2002) *The Myth of Ownership. Taxes and Justice*, Oxford: Oxford University Press.

Muscheid, J. (1986) *Die Steuerpolitik der Bundesrepublik Deutschland 1949–1982*, Berlin: Duncker und Humblot.

Mutén, L. (1988) 'Comment', in J.A. Pechman (ed.) *World Tax Reform. A Progress Report*, Washington, D.C.: The Brookings Institution.

_____(1996) 'Dual income taxation: Swedish experience', in L. Mutén *et al.* (eds) *Towards a Dual Income Tax?* London: Kluwer Law International.

Nannestad, P. and Green-Pedersen, C. (Forthcoming) 'Keeping the bumblebee flying: economic policy in the welfare state of Denmark, 1973–99', in E. Albäk, L. Eliason and A.S. Norgaard (eds) *Managing the Danish Welfare State under Pressure: Towards a Theory of the Dilemmas of the Welfare State*, Aarhus: Aarhus University Press.

Narud, H.M. and Strøm, K. (2000) 'Norway. A fragile coalitional order', in W. C. Müller and K. Strøm (eds) *Coalition Governments in Western Europe*, Oxford: Oxford University Press.

Narud, H. M. and Valen, H. (2000) 'Norway', *European Journal of Political Research*, 38: 481–87.

New Zealand Planning Council (1981) *An Agenda for Tax Reform*, Wellington: NZPC.

Nielsen, H.J. (1999) 'The Danish Election 1998', *Scandinavian Political Studies*, 22: 67–81.

Nielsen, S. B. and Sørensen, P. B. (1997) 'On the optimality of the Nordic system of dual income taxation', *Journal of Public Economics*, 63: 311–29.

Norges Bank (1999) *Norges Bank recommends lower tax on income from employment*, Press Release, June 1st 1999, Oslo.

NOU [Norges Offentlige Utredninger] (1984) *Personbeskatning. Skattekommisjonens vurderinger av og forslag til system for personbeskatning*, Oslo.

_____(1989) *Bedrifts –og kapitalbeskatningen – an skisse til reform*, Oslo.

_____(1999) *Flatere skatt*, Oslo.

Norrman, E. and McLure, C.E. (1997) 'Tax policy in Sweden', in R. B. Freeman, R. Topel and B. Swedenborg (eds) *The Welfare State in Transition*, Chicago: University of Chicago Press.

Norwegian Ministry of Finance (2000) *The National Budget 2001. A Summary*, Oslo.

Nousiainen, J. (2000) 'Finland. The consolidation of parliamentary governance', in W.C. Müller and K. Strøm (eds) *Coalition Governments in Western Europe*, Oxford: Oxford University Press.

OECD [Organisation for Economic Co-operation and Development] (1986) *Personal Income Tax Systems under Changing Economic Conditions*, Paris: OECD.

_____(1994a) *Economic Surveys: Denmark 1993–1994*, Paris: OECD.

_____(1994b) *Taxation and Small Businesses*, Paris: OECD.

_____(1996a) *Economic Surveys: Denmark 1995–1996*, Paris: OECD.

_____(1996b) *Model Tax Convention on Income and on Capital. September 1996. Condensed Version*, Paris: OECD.

_____(1999) *Taxing Powers of State and Local Government*, Paris: OECD.

_____(2000a) *Economic Surveys: Denmark 1999–2000*, Paris: OECD.

_____(2000b) *OECD Economic Surveys: Australia 1999–2000*, Paris: OECD.

_____(2000c) *OECD Economic Surveys: Finland*, Paris: OECD.

_____(2000d) *OECD Economic Surveys: New Zealand*, Paris: OECD.

_____(2001a) *Economic Outlook*, Paris: OECD.

_____(2001b) *OECD Economic Surveys: Australia*, Paris: OECD.

_____(2001c) *OECD Economic Surveys: Finland*, Paris: OECD.

_____(2001d) *Tax and the Economy. A Comparative Assessment of OECD Countries*, Paris: OECD.

_____(2004a) *Economic Surveys: Germany. Volume 2004/12 – September 2004*, Paris: OECD.

_____(2004b) *Economic Surveys: Norway,* Paris: OECD.

_____(2004c) *Revenue Statistics 1965–2003*, Paris: OECD.

_____(2005) *Economic Surveys: Austria*, Paris: OECD.

Ottaviani, M. (2002) 'Comment', *Economic Policy,* 17: 490–92.

Pedersen, J. (1992) 'Taxation of capital income in Denmark – survey on the actual situation and development trends', in P. Timonen (ed.) *Nordic Perspectives On European Financial Integration*, Helsinki: University of Helsinki.

Poguntke, T. (2003) 'Germany', *European Journal of Political Research*, 42: 957–63.

Porter, M.G. and Trengove, C. (1990) 'Tax reform in Australia', in M. J. Boskin and C. J. McLure (eds) *World Tax Reform. Case Studies of Developed and Developing Countries*, San Fransisco, CA: ICS Press.

Poß, J. (1992) 'Aufkommensneutrale Reform der Unternehmensbesteuerung für mehr Invesition und Arbeitsplätze', *Wirtschaftsdienst*, 72: 449–52.

_____(1996) 'Grundsätze und Perspektiven einer sozialdemokratischen Steuerreformpolitik', in S. Baron and K. Handschuch (eds) *Wege aus dem Steuerchaos*, Stuttgart: Schäffer-Poeschel Verlag.

Powell, G. B. (2000) *Elections as Instruments of Democracy: Majoritarian and Proportional Visions*, New Haven: Yale University Press.

Przeworski, A. and Meseguer Yebra, C. (2005) 'Globalization and democracy', in P. Bardhan, S. Bowles and M. Wallerstein (eds) *Globalization and Egalitarian Redistribution*, Princeton: Princeton University Press.

Przeworski, A. and Wallerstein, M. (1986) 'Popular sovereignty, state autonomy, and private property', *Archives européennes de sociologie*, 27: 215–19.

_____(1988) 'The structural dependence of the state on capital', *American Political Science Review*, 82: 11–29.

Quiggin, J. (1992) 'Fightback and one nation: a comparative analysis', *Australian Tax Forum*, 9: 127–54.

_____(1998a) 'Social democracy and market reform in Australia and New Zealand', *Oxford Review of Economic Policy*, 14: 76–95.

_____(1998b) *Taxing Times. A Guide to Australia's Tax Debate*, Sydney: UNSW Press.

_____(1999) 'Forget the GST and focus on the real issues' in: Australian Financial Review, 20 May 1999.

Quirk, P. J. and Nesmith, B. (2000) 'Divided government and policy making: negotiating the laws', in M. Nelson (ed.) *The Presidency and the Political System*, 6th edn, Washington, D.C.: CQ Press.

Qvortrup, M. (2000) 'Checks and balances in a unicameral parliament: the case of the Danish minority referendum', *Journal of Legislative Studies*, 6: 15–28.

_____(2002) *A Comparative Study of Referendums: Government by the People*, Manchester: Manchester University Press.

Rasch, B.E. (2005) *Do Parliamentary Governments Control the Legislative Agenda? The Case of Norway*, Oslo.

Review of Business Taxation (1999) *A Platform of Consultation: Discussion Paper 2. Building on a Strong Foundation*, Canberra: AGPS.

Richter, W. F., Seitz, H. and Wiegard, W. (1996) 'Steuern und unternehmensbezogene Staatsausgaben als Standortfaktoren', in H. Siebert (ed.) *Steuerpolitik und Standortqualität*, Tübingen: Mohr.

Røed, K. and Strøm, S. (2002) 'Progressive taxes and the labour market – is the trade-off between equality and efficiency inevitable?', *Journal of Economic Surveys*, 16: 77–110.

Rose, M. and Wiswesser, R. (1998) 'Tax reform in transition economies: experiences from the Croatian tax reform process of the 1990s', in P.B. Sørensen (ed.) *Public Finance in a Changing World*, Houndsmills: Macmillan.

Rosenberg, A. (1995) *Philosophy of Social Science*, 2nd edn, Boulder, CO: Westview Press.

Royal Commission on Taxation (1966) *Report*, Ottawa: Queens Press.

Ruding Report (1992) *Report of the Committee of Independent Experts on Company Taxation*, Brussels: Commission of the European Communities.

Saalfeld, T. (2000) 'Germany. Stable parties, Chancellor democracy, and the art of informal settlement', in W.C. Müller and K. Strøm (eds) *Coalition Government in Western Europe*, Oxford: Oxford University Press.

Saarimaa, T. (2005) *Taxation and Debt Financing of Home Aquisition: Evidence from the Finnish 1993 Tax Reform*, VATT Discussion Papers No. 366, Helsinki.

Sachverständigenrat, z.B.d.g.E. (2003) *Jahresgutachten 2004/04: Staatsfinanzen konsolidieren – Steuersystem reformieren*, Stuttgart: Metzler-Poeschel.

Sainsbury, D. (1993) 'The Swedish Social Democrats and the legacy of continuous reform', in R. Gillespie and W.E. Paterson (eds) *Rethinking Social Democracy in Western Europe*, London: Frank Cass.

Sala-i-Martin, X. (1996) 'The classical approach to convergence analysis', *The Economic Journal*, 106: 1019–36.

Salsbäck, J. (1993) 'The tax reform process in Sweden', in Nordic Council for Tax Research (ed.) *Tax Reform in the Nordic Countries*, Uppsala: Iustus.

Samuelson, P. (1938) 'A note on the pure theory of consumer behavior', *Economica*, 5: 61–71.

Sandford, C. (1993) Successful Tax Reform. *Lessons from an Analysis of Tax Reform in Six Countries*, Fersfield: Fiscal Publications.

Saunders, C. (2002) 'Australian tax constitution'. E-mail (10th January 2002).

Scharpf, F.W. (1997) *Games Real Actors Play: Actor-Centered Institutionalism in Policy Research*, Boulder, CO: Westview.

_____(2000a) 'Institutions in comparative policy research', *Comparative Political Studies*, 33: 762–90.

_____(2000b) 'The viability of advanced welfare states in the international economy: vulnerabilities and options', *Journal of European Public Policy*, 7: 190–228.

Schaumburg, H. and Rödder, T. (2000) *Unternehmenssteuerreform 2001*, München: C. H. Beck.

Schmidt, M.G. (1996) 'When parties matter: a review of the possibilities and limits of partisan influence on public policy', *European Journal of Political Research*, 30: 155–83.

_____(2003) *Political Institutions in the Federal Republic of Germany*, Oxford: Oxford University Press.

Schnapp, K.-U. (2004) *Ministerialbürokratien in westlichen Demokratien*, Opladen: Leske+Budrich.

Schwartz, H. (2000) 'Internationalization and two liberal welfare states. Australia and New Zealand', in F. W. Scharpf and V. A. Schmidt (eds) *Welfare and Work in the Open Economy. Diverse Responses to Common Challenges*, Oxford: Oxford University Press.

Scriven, M. (1966) 'Causes, connections and conditions in history', in W. H. Dray (ed.) *Philosophical Analysis and History*, New York: Harper and Row.

Shonfield, A. (1965) *Modern Capitalism. The Changing Balance of Public and Private Power*, New York: Oxford University Press.

Shugart, M. S. and Carey, J. M. (1992) *Presidents and Assemblies. Constitutional Design and Electoral Dynamics*, New York: Cambridge University Press.

Simons, H. C. (1938) *Personal Income Taxation: The Definition of Income as a Problem of Fiscal Policy*, Chicago: Chicago University Press.

Singleton, G. *et al.* (2000) *Australian Political Institutions*, Sydney: Longman.

Sinko, P. (2002) *Labour Tax Reforms and Labour Demand in Finland 1997–2001*, VATT Discussion Papers No. 237, Helsinki.

Sinn, H.-W. (1992) 'Doppelt gebremst', *Wirtschaftswoche*, 40: 53–6.

_____(1997) 'Deutschland im Steuerwettbewerb', *Jahrbucher für Nationalökonomie und Statistik*, 216: 672–92.

_____(2003) Ist Deutschland noch zu retten? Berlin: Ullstein.

Slemrod, J. (1990a) 'Optimal taxation and optimal tax systems', *Journal of Economic Perspectives*, 4: 157–78.

_____(1990b) 'Tax principles in an international economy', in M. J. Boskin and C. E. McLure Jr. (eds) *World Tax Reform*, San Francisco: ICS Press.

_____(1997) 'Deconstructing the income tax', *American Economic Review*, 87: 151–5.

Slemrod, J. and Bakija, J. (2004) *Taxing Ourselves. A Citizen's Guide to the Great Debate Over Tax Reform*, 3rd edn, Cambridge: MIT Press.

Södersten, J. (1993) 'The incentive effects of capital income taxation in Sweden', in Nordic Council for Tax Research (ed.) *Tax Reform in the Nordic Countries*, Iustus: Uppsala.

Sørensen, P. B. (1993) 'Recent tax reform experiments in Scandinavia', in L. Stetting, K. E. Svendsen and E. Yngaard (eds) *Global Change and Transformation*, Copenhagen: Munksgaard International Publishers.

_____(1994) 'From the global income tax to the dual income tax: recent tax reforms in the Nordic Countries', *International Tax and Public Finance*, 1: 57–79.

_____(1998) 'Recent innovations in Nordic tax policy: from the Global Income Tax to the Dual Income Tax', in P. B. Sørensen (ed.) *Tax Policy in the Nordic Countries*, London: Macmillan.

_____(ed.) (1998) *Tax Policy in the Nordic Countries*, Houndmills: Macmillan.

_____(2001) 'The Nordic Dual Income Tax – in or out?', unpublished work.

_____(Forthcoming-a) 'Dual income taxation: why and how?', *Finanzarchiv:* (page numbers in the text refer to the manuscript version).

_____(Forthcoming-b) 'Neutral taxation of shareholder income', *International Tax and Public Finance.*

SOU [Statens offentliga utredningar] (1986) 'Utgiftsskatt. Teknik och effekter', Stockholm: SOU.

SPD and Bündnis90/Die Grünen (1998) *Aufbruch und Erneuerung – Deutschlands Weg ins 21. Jahrhundert, Koalitionsvereinbarung zwischen der Sozialdemokratischen Partei Deutschlands und Bündnis 90/Die Grünen,* Bonn.

Spengel, C. (2003) *Internationale Unternehmensbesteuerung in der Europäischen Union,* Düsseldorf: IDW-Verlag.

Steinmo, S. (1993) *Taxation and Democracy,* New Haven and London: Yale University Press.

_____(2002) 'Globalization and taxation: challenges to the Swedish welfare state', *Comparative Political Studies,* 35: 839–62.

_____(2003) 'The evolution of policy ideas: tax policy in the 20th century', *British Journal of Politics and International Relations,* 5: 206–36.

Stephens, R. (1993) 'Radical tax reform in New Zealand', *Fiscal Studies,* 14: 45–63.

Steuerle, E. (2002) 'Tax policy from 1990 to 2001', in J. Frankel and P. Orszag (eds) *American Economic Policy in the 1990s,* Cambridge, MA: MIT Press.

Stewart III, C.H. (1991) 'The politics of tax reform in the 1980s', in A. Alesina and G. Carliner (eds) *Politics and Economics in the Eighties,* Chicago: University of Chicago Press.

Stoltenberg, G. (1997) *Wendepunkte. Stationen deutscher Politik 1947–1990,* Berlin: Siedler.

Stotsky, J. (1995) 'Summary of IMF policy advice', in P. Shome (ed.) *Tax Policy Handbook,* Washington, DC: International Monetary Fund.

Strand, H. (1999) *Some Issues Related to the Equity-Efficiency Trade-Off in the Swedish Tax and Transfer System,* Economics Department Working Papers No. 225, Paris.

Strøm, K. (2000) 'Delegation and accountability in parliamentary democracies', *European Journal of Political Research,* 37: 261–89.

Strøm, K. and Narud, H.M. (2003) 'Norway: virtual parliamentarism', in K. Strøm, W. C. Müller and T. Bergman (eds) *Delegation and Accountability in Parliamentary Democracies,* Oxford: Oxford University Press.

Strøm, S. and Wiig, E. (1995) 'Attacks on the welfare state', *Nordic Journal of Political Economy,* 22: 163–72.

Summers, L. (1987) 'Should tax reform level the playing field?', *NBER Working Paper No. 2132,* Cambridge, MA.

Summers, L. H., Gruber, J. and Vergara, R. (1993) 'Taxation and the structure of labor markets: the case of corporatism', *Quarterly Journal of Economics*, 108: 385–411.

Sundberg, J. (2004) 'Finland', *European Journal of Political Research*, 43: 1000–05.

Swank, D. (1998) 'Funding the welfare state: globalization and the taxation of business in advanced market economies', *Political Studies*, 46: 671–92.

Swank, D. and Steinmo, S. (2002) 'The new political economy of taxation in advanced capitalist democracies', *American Journal of Political Science*, 46: 642–55.

Swedish Ministry of Finance (2002) 'Revised budget statement – off print to the Budget Bill for 2002', Stockholm.

_____(2005) 'Budget statement', Stockholm.

Tanzi, V. and Zee, H. (2000) 'Tax policy for emerging markets: developing countries', *National Tax Journal*, 53: 299–322.

TaxReview (2001) 'Final report. October 2001', Wellington Government Printer.

Tetlock, P. E. (2000) 'Coping with trade-offs: psychological constraints and political implications', in A. Lupia, M. D. McCubbins and S. L. Popkin (eds) *Elements of Reason: Cognition, Choice, and the Bounds of Rationality*, Cambridge: Cambridge University Press.

Thorlakson, L. (2003) 'Comparing federal institutions: power and representation in six federations', *West European Politics*, 26: 1–22.

Tikka, K. S. (1982) 'Deductibility of interest payments in Finnish income taxation', in Stockholm Institute for Scandinavian Law (ed.) *Scandinavian Studies in Law 1982*, Stockholm: Stockholm Institute for Scandinavian Law.

_____(1989) 'Business tax reform in Finland', *European Taxation*: 107–12.

_____(1993a) 'A 25 per cent flat rate on capital income: the Finnish reaction to international tax competition', in Nordic Council for Tax Research (ed.) *Tax Reform in the Nordic Countries*, Iustus: Uppsala.

_____(1993b) 'Fundamental tax reform. 25 percent rate on capital income and corporate income', *Bulletin for International Fiscal Documentation*, 47: 348–53.

_____(2001) 'Tax competition and the welfare state: time to surrender or to reconsider', in K. Andersson, P. Melz and C. Silfverberg (eds) *Liber Amicorum Sven-Olof Lodin*, Stockholm: Norstedts Juridik/Kluwer Law International.

Tipke, K. and Lang, J. (1998) *Steuerrecht*, 16th edn, Köln: Otto Schmidt.

Toder, E. and Himes, S. (1992) 'Tax reform in New Zealand', *Tax Notes International*, 56: 821–43.

Treasury [New Zealand], (1984) *Economic Management*, Wellington, NZ: Government Printer.

_____(1987) 'Budget report no. 20' (internal document released under the Official Information Act), Wellington, NZ.

Tsebelis, G. (1999) 'Veto players and law production in parliamentary democracies: an empirical analysis', *American Political Science Review*, 93: 591–608.

_____(2002) *Veto Players. How Political Institutions Work*, Princeton, NJ: Princeton University Press.

Tsebelis, G. and Money, J. (1997) *Bicameralism*, Cambridge: Cambridge University Press.

Tucker, A. (2004) 'Holistic explanations of events', *Philosophy*, 79: 573–89.

van den Noord, P. (2000) *The Tax System in Norway: Past Reforms and Future Challenges*, OECD Economics Department Working Papers No. 244, Paris: OECD.

Van Fraasen, B. (1980) *The Scientific Image*, Oxford: Claredon Press.

Vann, R. (1997) 'General description: Australia', in Ault (ed.) *Comparative Income Taxation.*

Vowles, J. (1995) 'The politics of electoral reform in New Zealand', *International Political Science Review*, 16: 95–115.

_____(1999) 'New Zealand', *European Journal of Political Research*, 36: 473–81.

_____(2002) 'The general election in New Zealand, November 1999', *Electoral Studies*, 21: 151–4.

_____(2003) 'New Zealand', *European Journal of Political Research*, 42: 1037–47.

Wagschal, U. (1999a) 'Blockieren Vetospieler Steuerreformen?', *Politische Vierteljahresschrift*, 40: 628–40.

_____(1999b) 'Schranken staatlicher Steuerungspolitik: Warum Steuerreformen scheitern können', in A. Busch and T. Plümper (eds) *Nationaler Staat und internationale Wirtschaft*, Baden-Baden: Nomos.

_____(2001) 'Deutschlands Steuerstaat und die vier Welten der Besteuerung', in M. G. Schmidt (ed.) *Wohlfahrtsstaatliche Politik: Institutionen – Prozesse – Leistungsprofil*, Opladen: Westdeutscher Verlag.

Walker, C. E. (1994) 'Comment', in M. Feldstein (ed.) *American Economic Policy in the 1980s*, Chicago: University of Chicago Press.

Wallerstein, M. and Przeworski, A. (1995) 'Capital taxation with open borders', *Review of International Political Economy*, 2: 425–45.

Wallis, J. (1997) 'Conspiracy and the policy process: a case study of the New Zealand Experiment', *Journal of Public Policy*, 17: 1–29.

Weichenrieder, A. (1996) 'Fighting international tax avoidance: the case of Germany', *Fiscal Studies*, 17: 37–58.

Weisbach, D. A. and Bankman, J. (2005) *The Superiority of a Consumption Tax over an Income Tax*, University of Chicago Law School/Stanford Law School.

Weiss, R. D. (1996) 'The Tax Reform Act of 1986: did Congress love it or leave it?', *National Tax Journal*, 49: 447–59.

Wendt, R. (1993) 'Steuerreform durch Tarifbegrenzung für gewerbliche Einkünfte', *Finanz-Rundschau*: 1–8.

_____(1996) 'Spreizung von Körperschaftsteuersatz und Einkommensteuer-spitzensatz als Verfassungsproblem', in R. Wendt *et al.* (eds) *Staat-Wirtschaft-Steuern: Festschrift für Karl Heinrich Friauf*, Heidelberg.

Whitehead, J. and Oliver, R. (1999) 'Memorandum for Cabinet: implementing a 39% top personal income tax rate', Wellington New Zealand Treasury.

Widfeldt, A. (2003) 'Sweden', *European Journal of Political Research*, 42: 1091–1101.

Willemsen, A. (1991) 'Die Steuerreformvorstellungen der Arbeitgeber-Verbände', in D. Döring and P.B. Spahn (eds) *Steuerreform als gesellschaftspolitische Aufgabe der neunziger Jahre*, Berlin: Duncker und Humblot.

Willoch, K. (1995) 'What can other countries learn from the Scandinavian experience? II', *Nordic Journal of Political Economy*, 22: 177–82.

Woldendorp, J., Keman, H. and Budge, I. (2000) *Party Government in 48 Democracies (1945–1998). Composition – Duration – Personnel*, Dordrecht: Kluwer.

World Bank (2003) *World Development Indicators*, CD ROM, Washington, D.C.: The World Bank.

Young, L. (1999) 'Minor parties and the legislative process in the Australian Senate: a study of the 1993 budget', *Australian Journal of Political Science*, 34: 7–27.

Ysmal, C. (2003) 'France', *European Journal of Political Research*, 42: 943–56.

Zimmer, F. (1992) 'Taxation of capital in the Nordic countries and international tax competition – Norway', in P. Timonen (ed.) *Nordic Perspectives on European Financial Integration*, Helsinki: University of Helsinki.

_____(1993) 'Capital income and earned income following the Norwegian income tax reform: is the dual income tax fair?', in Nordic Council for Tax Research (ed.) *Tax Reform in the Nordic Countries*, Uppsala: Iustus.

Zohlnhöfer, R. (2001) *Die Wirtschaftspolitik der Ära Kohl*, Opladen: Leske+Budrich.

_____(2003) 'Partisan politics, party competition and veto players: German economic policy in the Kohl Era', *Journal of Public Policy*, 23: 123–56.

index

www.ingramcontent.com/pod-product-compliance
Lightning Source LLC
Chambersburg PA
CBHW050441280326
41932CB00013BA/2200